FIRMNESS OF MIND

Avery,

Thanks for the support!

FIRMNESS OF MIND

A COLLECTION OF EXPERT
ADVICE ON BECOMING HAPPIER
THROUGH MENTAL CONDITIONING

IAN KAHNG

NEW DEGREE PRESS

COPYRIGHT © 2021 IAN KAHNG

All rights reserved.

FIRMNESS OF MIND
A collection of expert advice on becoming happier through mental conditioning

ISBN 978-1-63676-561-7 *Paperback*
      978-1-63676-144-2 *Kindle Ebook*
      978-1-63676-145-9 *Ebook*

"Look unto God with **firmness of mind**, and pray unto him with exceeding faith, and he will console you in your afflictions, and he will plead your cause"

— JACOB 3:1

This book is dedicated to all the young people in the world who have the desire to improve their mental well-being and live happier lives. A special prayer goes out to those facing debilitating mental and emotional trials, and to those who have lost loved ones as a result of these challenges.

Thanks to your support, 100 percent of the profits of this book have gone to nonprofit organizations including the National Alliance on Mental Ilness, the American Foundation for Suicide Prevention, and Latter-day Saint Charities.

CONTENTS

SECTION 1: FIRMNESS OF MIND — **33**

CHAPTER 1A: WHAT IS FIRMNESS OF MIND? — 35

CHAPTER 1B: INTRODUCTION TO LIFESTYLE ROUTINES — 47

CHAPTER 1C: SETTING UP LIFESTYLE ROUTINES — 63

CHAPTER 1D: INTRODUCTION TO THE EXERCISES SECTION — 103

SECTION 2: EXERCISES FOR THE MIND — **109**

CHAPTER 2A: OUR BIASED BRAINS — 113

CHAPTER 2B: REWIRING OUR BRAINS AGAINST BIAS — 127

CHAPTER 2C: MANAGING CHALLENGES TO THE HAPPINESS BALANCE — 183

CHAPTER 2D: SPIRITUALITY AND THE MIND — 205

SECTION 3: EXERCISES FOR THE BODY — **213**

CHAPTER 3A: PHYSICAL EXERCISE — 219

CHAPTER 3B: SLEEP — 235

CHAPTER 3C: NUTRITION — 251

SECTION 4: EXERCISES IN OUR IMMEDIATE RELATIONSHIPS — **271**

CHAPTER 4A: BENEFITS FROM OUR RELATIONSHIPS — 273

CHAPTER 4B: PRIORITIZING OUR RELATIONSHIPS — 283

CHAPTER 4C: DEEPENING OUR RELATIONSHIPS — 289

SECTION 5: EXERCISES WITHIN OUR COMMUNITIES   **307**

CHAPTER 5A: BENEFITS OF BEING ACTIVE
            IN OUR COMMUNITIES   309

CHAPTER 5B: CHALLENGES WITHIN
            OUR COMMUNITIES   321

CHAPTER 5C: OUTWARD MINDSET
            AND COMMON HUMANITY   331

APPENDIX   **357**

APPENDIX 1: CHAPTER TAKEAWAYS   359

APPENDIX 2: LIFESTYLE ROUTINES WORKSHEET   375

APPENDIX 3: FULL ACTIVITIES LIST   381

APPENDIX 4: ADDITIONAL RESOURCES   385

HOW TO USE THIS BOOK

―

This book was written to help young members of the Church of Jesus Christ of Latter-day Saints improve their happiness and well-being through the application of research-backed activities. While this book was written with this specific audience in mind, the science of positivity shared in this book can be applicable to anyone, as it addresses the universal topic of human happiness.

Also, important to note: This book (and investing in mental wellness in general) is not written just for those struggling with serious mental challenges but is meant for those at all levels of well-being. In the same way that nutrition and exercise are critically important for people of all physical health levels, improving your mental well-being is important for people at all levels of mental health. A regular person who is at an average level of happiness can benefit just as much as people who are flourishing or struggling.

Remember, this book is not designed to be a replacement for therapy or support from a mental health professional for those with serious mental challenges. In the event that you or a loved one are facing serious mental or emotional challenges, please seek out the help of a mental health professional.

That being said, here are four main ways you can use this book:

1. **A quick summary on good life tips**
You can go to the appendix at the end and see an overview of all the chapter takeaways in the entire book. I think it's a very good summary, and honestly, if you're like me, you might not get to reading this whole book anytime in the near future or at all. At the very least, whether you bought this book yourself or got it as a gift from someone else, promise me that you will read this summary. It should only take you ten or so minutes, and you will learn a lot.

2. **An introduction to the field of positive psychology**
You can treat this as any other book. You can pick it up, read it cover to cover in a few hours, enjoy the messages and interesting facts, and then move on with life. You will have a basic understanding of the science of positive psychology and well-being, but you may choose not to incorporate the principles or activities in your day-to-day life.

3. **A regularly referenced supplement to self-improvement routines and/or therapy**
You can take your time, working through the sections slowly, to see what activities fit in your life and see how your well-being improves. You can also use it to supplement counseling and therapy. As behavioral changes and improvement of your well-being are slow processes that require consistent progress, implementing this book as a regular reference will be more helpful than simply reading the book once.

4. **A collaborative guide to be used with friends, family, or community members**
The most effective way to get the most out of this book is to incorporate it as a part of your relationships in addition to embracing it as part of your regular routine. You can study it with family or friends, or you can use it to help those in groups you are part of (such as extracurricular groups, sports teams, or church classes) throughout your life. Learning in a group setting is one of the best ways to internalize these principles, and you can also help many people in your circles by sharing important information for their mental well-being. A book study group can also be a fun way to spend more time with people that are important in your life.

I personally believe this book can greatly improve the quality of your life—not because I'm an amazing author, but because there is a lot of good content in this book from professionals that are committed to improving your life and mental well-being of you. However, it's up to you to take the time to read it and act on what you learn to see positive effects in your life.

Also, I have done my best to be up to date with the research and to give as comprehensive of a guide as possible, but this book is not the end-all-be-all for your happiness and mental well-being. Read lots of books and articles and talk to as many experts as you can. The field of positive psychology is constantly changing, and new discoveries are being made daily, so it's on you to be up to date with the most relevant and accurate information.

With that, I hope you enjoy the book and that it changes your life!

For updates on events and opportunities to participate in free virtual book groups and well-being discussions, email info@firmnessofmind.com or visit www.firmnessofmind.com.

Spheres of Influence

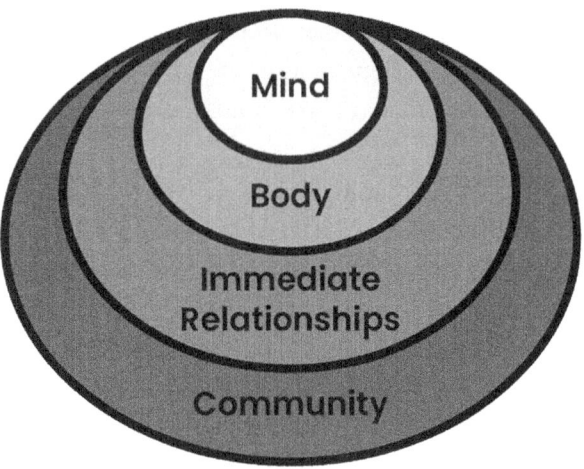

INTRODUCTION

Maria is a happy and smiley young woman from Florida, currently living with her husband and love of her life in Utah. She went on a full-time mission for the Church of Jesus Christ of Latter-day Saints and afterward studied at a four-year university. At first glance, Maria may seem like any other woman in her twenties. She enjoys spending time with friends and family, and in her spare time she likes to rock climb, do yoga, and listen to Juice WRLD. However, one thing that makes her extraordinary is her commitment and desire to improve her mental well-being. Here is her story:

"Throughout my life, I have experienced varying levels of stress and anxiety, whether that was growing up, during my mission, and since coming home. I have definitely had several moments in my life where I felt like my anxiety and depression were unmanageable. For example, when I first returned from my mission, I began experiencing a variety of digestive issues and stomach trouble. My first thought was that I needed to change my diet, so I went to see a nutritionist. The nutritionist, upon discovering my stress levels, suggested that before making a food plan, I should go see a therapist, as what goes on in your head is closely related to what goes on with your digestion. So, I decided to go and see a therapist.

"My therapist helped me with a lot of things. The first thing that we worked on was changing my brain. We began by practicing how to recognize unhelpful, anxious thoughts. He helped me discover many instances throughout the day when my thoughts were telling me things that were untrue, biased, and unhelpful, and he helped squeeze these thinking patterns out of me. He asked me to do things like asking myself, 'If you could approach your anxious self and sit on a bench next to her and talk to her, what would you say,' and helped me to talk to myself as if I was talking to a friend. He helped me realize that I was in control of a lot more things in my life than I realized, and that it was okay to not be okay.

"He also recommended several ways to improve my mental well-being through taking care of my physical body through adequate exercise, sleep, and nutrition. I started going to the gym more regularly and made it fun through listening to my favorite rap music and tracking improvements in lifting weights. I also put sleep as a priority. Nothing gets in the way of my sleep! I make sure that I don't feel guilty about getting all the sleep my body needs. I also gradually improved my diet. I slowly incorporated more fruits and vegetables into my diet, and I also made sure to take in some protein and Omega-3s regularly.

"Lastly, I made sure to surround myself with social support, and also to support those around me. I told my friends and my mom about what I was working on and what my goals were, and every Sunday, I made sure to go over my goals and my plans. Some weeks I met my goals, and some weeks I didn't. When I didn't meet my goals, I made sure to adjust my goals to make them easier to meet. My friends and mom were always encouraging me during this process. I also found ways to be a support to others by teaching free yoga lessons and by teaching at the MTC (Missionary Training Center).

"After doing these things, I definitely saw a change in my life. Obviously, it didn't happen overnight. It took me a long time to get to the point that I am today, and I am still working on things, but overall, my happiness has definitely improved."

By exercising her mind, taking care of her body, investing in her close relationships, and being positively involved in her community, Maria shows us how anyone can improve their happiness baseline through making their mental well-being a priority. In this book, you will read advice on how you, like Maria, can use techniques that mental health professionals recommend on changing your life for the better. By applying small principles on a regular basis in life, you can improve your happiness and mental condition. Let's start on this by talking about what happiness is.

HAPPINESS: OUR ULTIMATE GOAL

All people have the natural desire to be happy. Happiness is the ultimate goal. If someone were to ask you why you do something and you say it is because it makes you happy, your answer can't be challenged, because happiness is the last answer to all of life's pursuits. This is in contrast to other pursuits such as wanting to go to college or getting married, which have a variety of underlying reasons.

Take going to college as an example. If someone asks you why you want to go to college, you could say that you want to gain an education. If someone asks you why you want to gain an education, you could say that it is because you want a job. If someone were to ask you about why you want a job, and all the other following questions, eventually you would get to the final answer, which is that you do these things to be happy. Although the term "happiness" can be interpreted in many different ways, the fact of the matter is that happiness is everyone's ultimate goal.

And it's no wonder. Happiness causes a multitude of benefits in almost all aspects of life. Happy people have more friends, more satisfying relationships, lower likelihoods of divorce, better performance at work/school, and more creativity. In terms of physical and mental health, happy individuals have stronger immune systems, handle stress more effectively, and even live longer.[1]

Is your goal in life to be happy? I'm sure all of you would answer yes to this question. The next question is, do we know what makes us happy, and are we truly doing all that we can to be happy? I'm sure we all know the Sunday school answers of living the Gospel and doing what's right, but when I asked myself that question when I was eighteen years old—"Do I know what makes me happy, and am I truly doing all that I can do to be happy?"—I can tell you that while I did have a general idea of things that would probably make me happy, I

---

[1] Sonja Lyubomirsky and Jaime Kurtz, *Positively Happy: Routes to Sustainable Happiness*, 1st ed. (United Kingdom: Positive Acorn, 2008), chap. 1, Kindle.

was unsure of the specific steps and actions I needed to take in order to live a happy life.

As a scientifically minded person, I decided I needed to see what all the leading happiness researchers found truly made people happy. That's why I enrolled in six different classes at BYU on positive psychology (the study of human happiness), read dozens of books by the world's leading positive psychologists, and interviewed many experts in the field of positive psychology. I am not an expert on the science of human happiness, but I am a good collector, and this book is a collection of actionable, professional advice on how to change your brain and change your life for the better through the science of positive psychology.

Are you truly committed to being happy? If your life goal is to be truly happy, how much time are you willing to invest in improving your happiness? Are you ready to start the long journey to change your brain and achieve a higher well-being baseline? Are you willing to make this a regular part of your life and remove things in life that are distracting you from truly being happy?

If you answered yes to these questions, read on!

WHAT IS TRUE HAPPINESS, ACCORDING TO THE SCIENCE OF HAPPINESS?
In order to live happier lives, we need to understand what exactly our goal of happiness is. But first, we need to realize we are not the best judges of what we think will make us happy. Researchers Dan Gilbert and Tim Wilson describe how humans make what are called affective forecasting

errors, which basically means we are not good at predicting our feelings accurately. Part of this is because of something called the impact bias, which means that "people overemphasize the impact that a single event will have on them, and they underestimate the impact of other things that are going on in their lives."[2]

Let's take a look at some examples of how I (and several other people) inaccurately forecasted feelings and overemphasized the impact of some things on our happiness.

Let's rewind to when I was in high school. Growing up a member of the Church, I have always heard in Sunday School that focusing on certain values like service, gratitude, or spirituality would make me happier in life than focusing on things like material possessions, popularity, and physical appearance. However, I had some difficulty fully grasping this.

It was definitely more fun to choose parties over service activities. If I had a choice, I would rather be the popular guy at school with the ripped model body than the mediocre guy who was satisfied with his natural physique. The kid with the new BMW in the parking lot definitely had a bigger smile than the guy with the 1990 Honda Civic. It definitely felt more exciting when I bought a new pair of shoes with my money than if I donated it to tithing or a charity. I never quite understood why I learned that intangible values would make you happier than pursuing things that definitely made you feel good.

---

[2] Kennon M. Sheldon and Sonja Lyubomirsky, "The Challenge of Staying Happier: Testing the Hedonic Adaptation Prevention Model," *Personality and Social Psychology Bulletin* 38, no. 5 (May 1, 2012): 670–80.

In addition to that, everything I saw in the media around me told me a similar thing. Media like TV, advertisements, social media, and music taught me that it was better to be famous like Justin Bieber than be unknown like my brother Justin Kahng, better to have Thor's body than my dad Steve's body, better to shop at Nordstrom than shop at Walmart, and better to get drunk or act out to get over a breakup than to mindfully inspect your emotions. The list goes on and on of what the world tells us is better, and frankly, my brain told me that I wanted to be famous, look like Thor, wear nice clothes, and do things that make me feel good in the moment.

The truth is, psychological research tells us that while things like fame, possessions, beauty, and substances can create euphoric highs, these do not provide lasting happiness, partly due to the fact that human brains have a remarkable ability to adapt.[3] Turns out that what we may have heard growing up from parents or teachers is actually supported by research.

Even beyond research, we can see real examples of this today. In one of my positive psychology classes at BYU, our professor shared the example of the lives of lottery winners. While pretty much everyone would say yes to winning millions of dollars, surprisingly, many lottery winners have said that winning the lottery was the worst thing to ever happen to them. Many lottery winners end up in much worse life situations than before winning the lottery, with some even committing suicide shortly after their winnings. "I wish that we

---

[3] Ibid.

had torn the ticket up," said Jack Whittaker, who was already a millionaire before winning the lottery. However, the lifestyle created after his lottery winnings ended up causing him to go broke and even lose some family members from drug overdoses related to the winnings.[4]

Looking at an example closer to our age, a sixteen-year-old girl named Callie Rogers won the lottery and spent her winnings on cars, drugs, and plastic surgery. She became very popular in a short period of time, experienced exciting sensations with drugs, was able to improve her looks through surgeries, and got possessions she always wanted. However, she quickly realized those things did not raise her happiness levels for a sustained period of time, and she eventually stated that she had become miserable because of the lottery. Many of us spend a fair amount of time working toward things like popularity, temporary pleasures, and improving our looks, but Callie tells us that the pursuit of that actually made her life worse.[5]

On the flip side, we might also hear that in order to be happy, we need to denounce present pleasure and focus on the final goal. We've heard the popular scriptural phrase "endure to the end," which may conjure up images of suffering in the moment in order to achieve long-term happiness. I'm sure you've also heard references to the popular "marshmallow study" where those happiest in life were the ones able to put off gratification and suffer in the present for the larger

---

[4] Melissa Chan, "Here's How Winning the Lottery Makes You Miserable," *Time*, January 12, 2016.
[5] James Cox, "$3.5m Lotto Winner Spent Millions on Cocaine, Boob Jobs, Parties and Cars," *The Sun*, August 20, 2018.

payout in the end.[6] While it is true that happy people learn how to delay gratification, overdoing this is also a source of unhappiness.

We need to remember to treat everything in moderation. Many instances of anxiety, stress, burnout, and other psychological challenges stem from an overemphasis on present suffering for future achievement or reward.[7] Workaholism, perfectionism, unhealthy comparison, and the pressure to overachieve are real struggles that decrease the quality of our lives. The concept of delaying gratification for future reward is an important concept, but it is a fallacy (or mistaken belief) that delaying all gratification in all aspects of life will lead you to be happier. We will learn more about this, but the research shows that happiest people are the ones that find the "happy medium" between enjoying pleasure in the present and knowing when to delay gratification for a future purpose.[8]

Lastly, unhappiness can stem from illusions related to control, with people either thinking they can't control anything that happens in life, or they need to control as much as possible. While it is true that happier people are those that are able to take action and control things which are within their

---

[6] Gladys Barragan-Jason et al., "Commentary: Revisiting the Marshmallow Test: A Conceptual Replication Investigating Links Between Early Delay of Gratification and Later Outcomes," *Frontiers in Psychology* 9 (January 10, 2019).

[7] Kapo Wong, Alan H. S. Chan, and S. C. Ngan, "The Effect of Long Working Hours and Overtime on Occupational Health: A Meta-Analysis of Evidence from 1998 to 2018," *International Journal of Environmental Research and Public Health* 16, no. 12 (June 2019).

[8] Tal Ben-Shahar, *Happier* (McGraw-Hill Education (India) Pvt Limited, 2007), chap. 1, Kindle.

circles of influence, problems occur when people think that the more they change their circumstances, the happier that they will become. Similar to a workaholic mentality, having the "I will be happy when…" mentality will not lead us to happiness. Many of us think, "I will be happy when I make the basketball team, when I get in a relationship, when I get into college," but the research shows that life events and circumstances have a much smaller impact on our sustained happiness than we think, due to the nature of our brain's ability to adapt.[9]

Obviously, the situations I listed above are extreme examples; I don't expect that many of you who are reading this book are aspiring to win the lottery, be workaholics, or control all of your life circumstances. But many of us either consciously or subconsciously expend effort toward maximizing these pursuits. We might spend a few hours or a few minutes every day consuming media, improving our looks, or living life thinking, "I will be happy when." Imagine if we intentionally substituted some of that time, for as little as ten minutes a day, toward things that research shows truly does make us happier—and don't worry, I'll describe what things truly do make us happier in great detail throughout the book. I think we would see some significant changes in our lives if we reallocated our time and efforts toward things that the happiness experts say will make us happy.

So then, how do we define "real" happiness, and what should we focus our time and efforts on instead? Well, the field of

---

[9] Christina Armenta et al., "Is Lasting Change Possible? Lessons from the Hedonic Adaptation Prevention Model," in *Stability of Happiness: Theories and Evidence on Whether Happiness Can Change*, 2014, 57–74.

positive psychology, also known as the study of human happiness, tells us that happiness is comprised of two components: positive emotion and meaning.[10] I like to call the relationship between positive emotion and meaning the "happiness balance."

HAPPINESS = PLEASURE + MEANING
Positive emotion, or in other words, pleasure, is the good feeling people seek in their lives. If my previous stories throwing down on lottery winners made you think I'm completely opposed to pleasure, I'm sorry, I'm not against pleasure. Pleasure is a very necessary and important part of our lives. However, other than pursuing momentary highs from possessions or popularity, happy people strive to cultivate sustainable positive emotion, which is a key component of authentic happiness.

In order to make pleasure a sustainable positive emotion and a working component of the happiness balance, it must be paired with a future meaning. For example, if we took the drug ecstasy, it would definitely be a pleasurable experience, but it would be hard to attach to a meaningful life purpose. But also, if you suffer on a daily basis, doing something you completely hate for a future purpose, you are missing out on having present pleasure. If you achieve a good balance of both pleasure and meaning, you will have a much better happiness balance. An example could be feeling the good feelings associated with going on a jog with a friend, while keeping in mind future purposes such as investing in your

---

[10] Barbara L. Fredrickson, "The Role of Positive Emotions in Positive Psychology," *The American Psychologist* 56, no. 3 (March 2001): 218–26.

physical health and cultivating a relationship with someone you care about.

THE NATURE OF HAPPINESS

We must remember that when we think of the concept of happiness, our goal is not to be in endless pursuit of the temporary emotion of happiness, but to build a long-term and sustainable happiness baseline. This is why many positive psychologists like to refer to our happiness as "well-being," describing our goal condition as a prolonged state of being as opposed to a fleeting emotion.[11]

Dr. Tal Ben-Shahar, one of the world's leading positive psychologists and professor of Harvard's most popular course, Positive Psychology 1504, teaches us how to achieve this long-lasting well-being and find the balance between pleasure and purpose using the story of the four hamburgers.[12]

In his story, he introduced four different burgers: the junk food burger (hedonism), the veggie burger (rat race), the worst burger (nihilism), and the ideal burger (happiness).[13]

The junk food burger, representing hedonism, is what you get when you have too much present pleasure and not enough future meaning. The junk food burger may taste good while it's in your mouth, but shortly after, you feel sick, and your health suffers. Examples of hedonistic activity include uncontrolled

---

[11] Martin Seligman, "What Is Well-Being?" Authentic Happiness, accessed October 1, 2020.
[12] Tal Ben-Shahar, *Happier* (McGraw-Hill Education (India) Pvt Limited, 2007), chap. 1, Kindle.
[13] Ibid.

eating, using substances like drugs, viewing pornography, or any other activity that offers short-term, momentary highs with little or no attachment to future purpose.[14]

The veggie burger, representing the rat race, is what you get when you focus too much on future meaning and not enough on present pleasure. This burger tastes awful (personally, I am a veggie burger fan, but for the sake of this example, let's pretend it's gross), but it is good for your health in the long run. Examples of rat race behavior include workaholism, overstudying, or overtraining. The rat race cycle begins when you do something difficult that you dislike for the purpose of achieving a goal, suffer for the majority of the time you are striving toward it, eventually achieve that goal, feel the momentary relief and accomplishment from the achievement, and then plunge back into the cycle, where the majority of the time you are grinding away at something that makes you miserable.[15]

The worst burger, representing nihilism, has nothing good about it. This is when you have little to no focus on both present pleasure and future meaning. This is like eating a rat poison burger: it tastes bad and it is terrible for your health. Examples of nihilism are times when you lose the zest for life, feeling like no matter what you do, you have no control over life or happiness, and that nothing really matters. It is common to feel this way after major life crises or traumatic events, when you feel terrible in the present and have difficulty seeing purpose in the future.[16]

---

[14] Ibid.
[15] Ibid.
[16] Ibid.

The ideal burger, representing happiness, is the perfect blend of future meaning and present pleasure. It tastes good, maybe not quite as euphoric as the fast-food burger, but it is definitely good. It is also good for your health, maybe not to the extreme level of nutrition as the veggie burger, but it is definitely healthy enough. Finding a balance like this in your life is key to finding true happiness and well-being.[17]

Something to keep in mind, in case you are young person like me: Generally, young people should prioritize working on the delaying gratification part of the happiness balance (i.e., the junk food burger), as research shows that this is usually a larger priority for adolescents than an over-delay of gratification (exemplified by the veggie burger).[18] We will go into more detail as to why this is in the upcoming sections (as with many things in adolescence, our brains are fine-tuning and developing our impulse control abilities), but just keep in mind that this book will focus a little more on managing self-control than being less of a workaholic. Regardless, there are always times in your life when you can tilt too far in either direction, so it's good to learn about both.

In that same vein, with life always having ups and downs, it isn't realistic to think you will always have a perfect balance of present pleasure and future meaning. There will be times where you will have to work hard to get good results, and there will be times where you find yourself indulging

---

[17] Ibid.
[18] Daniel Romer et al., "Can Adolescents Learn Self-Control? Delay of Gratification in the Development of Control over Risk Taking," *Prevention Science: The Official Journal of the Society for Prevention Research* 11, no. 3 (September 2010): 319–30.

in temporary comforts. Also, we will all face times when we are heartbroken and downtrodden, feeling like we have no control over the direction of our lives and have no purpose in pursuing happiness. This is okay; we are all human and we all experience ups and downs in life. However, with this knowledge in mind, our goal should always be to spend as much time as possible doing things that both give us pleasure in the present and are attached to future meaning and purpose.

Let's find out how to do this in the next section, by achieving what I like to call "firmness of mind."

TAKEAWAYS FROM
THE INTRODUCTION

1. Like Maria, you can incorporate things in your life that will sustainably increase your happiness.
2. Happiness is our ultimate goal. Therefore, we should spend as much time as possible doing things that bring us closer to that goal.
3. We are poor predictors of what we think will make us happy. A lot of things that we think might make us happy (things like fame, beauty, material possessions, perfection, overachievement, or the "I will be happy when…" mentality) can be dead ends, and we should strive to be aware of when we think in these ways and try and keep these thoughts in check.
4. The true happiness we should be striving for is a sustained state, also known as well-being, that is a balance of present pleasure and future meaning. Our goal is to learn how to optimize the happiness balance in all the things we do.
5. In the next section, we will learn facts about how to unlock our brain's full potential so we can best achieve this balance and set up a plan on how to implement regular happiness-boosting activities in our lives.

SECTION 1: FIRMNESS OF MIND

From the introduction, we learned about the happiness balance between future meaning and present pleasure, and about how overemphasizing either future meaning, present pleasure, or "I will be happy when…" mindsets are distractions from true happiness. In this section, we will introduce how you can achieve this balance through building a state of mental strength, a "firmness of mind."

In the first chapter of this section, we give background on what firmness of mind looks like. We will learn about the brain's ability to change and grow with exercise, like a muscle, and how we can hardwire healthy thought patterns in our brains. We will learn a little bit more about our goal state of well-being, and how to progress toward this by capitalizing on what we have control over and accepting what we don't have control over.

In the second and third chapters of this section, we will learn how to set up routines and habits in life so we can support a new lifestyle of correctly hardwiring our brains. Learning how to set up these routines and habits in life will then be critical for the transition into the next section, where we will learn about specific activities you will choose for your own happiness plan.

In the fourth chapter of this section, we will also get a high-level preview on Sections 2, 3, 4, and 5 of this book, which will have activities to work on specific spheres in life to improve our well-being.

I hope that as you read this section, you will catch the excitement of the growing field of positive psychology and commit to take your happiness into your own hands!

(Again, this book and the lifestyle changes it suggests are not designed to be a replacement for therapy or support from a mental health professional for those facing serious mental challenges. In the event that you or a loved one are facing serious mental or emotional challenges, please seek out the help of a mental health professional.)

CHAPTER 1A:

WHAT IS FIRMNESS OF MIND?

BACKGROUND ON FIRMNESS OF MIND

While the science of happiness deals with all aspects of life, the center of happiness and well-being is in the mind. The mind (centered in the brain) is the core of everything we do. This is the seat of our thoughts, feelings, emotions, and identities. Throughout this book, we will thoroughly discuss the many aspects of our lives—bodily functions, relationships, and community roles—but at the end of the day, how we perform in all these areas is dependent on what goes on in our minds. That is why the mind is the central focus of this book's title, *Firmness of Mind*.

The inspiration for the title of the book and the term "firmness of mind" comes from Jacob 3:1 in the Book of Mormon, where Jacob teaches that if you look unto God with firmness of mind, you will have assistance with your "afflictions" and problems, and you will receive support in your "cause(s)" or endeavors. I interpret "firmness of mind" as meaning that despite the afflictions you may have, genetics you were born with, or whatever situation life has taken you to, you can make the most of your situation and achieve your goals by having a basis on a solid mental foundation.

To psychologists today, a firm mind could mean many things. Up until the late '90s, the majority of psychological research had been focused on the "negative" side of the psyche. These include disorders such as depression, anxiety, and schizophrenia. However, in the late '90s, a psychologist named Martin Seligman founded the branch of psychology known as positive psychology, which, as opposed to the study of disorders, is the study of human happiness or flourishing.[19] His studies focused on the characteristics of the positive brain in contrast to characteristics of the negative brain. I believe that firmness of mind describes the type of mind exemplified in the study of positive psychology, a mind in an improved yet steady state of well-being.

To expound what I meant by flourishing in the previous paragraph, let me illustrate what flourishing means by showing what it's not. This is important because many of you who may be reading this book might be thinking that investing in mental well-being is just for people that struggle with mental health. That's great, but one of the world's leading researchers in positive psychology, Dr. Sonja Lyubomirsky, tells us how the majority of Americans are in a stagnant, languishing state of mental well-being.[20] According to positive

---

[19] The University of Pennsylvania, "PERMA™ Theory of Well-Being and PERMA™ Workshops," Positive Psychology Center, accessed October 2, 2020

[20] Sonja Lyubomirsky and Jaime Kurtz, *Positively Happy: Routes to Sustainable Happiness*, 1st ed. (United Kingdom: Positive Acorn, 2008) chap. 1, Kindle.

psychology, flourishing is a state of mind when you are no longer languishing, but living life at your full potential.²¹

Whether the message comes from the Book of Mormon or from leading positive psychologists, the lesson is the same. If you are able to condition your mind to be a source of strength, you will be able to overcome the challenges in your life and achieve higher levels of well-being. To develop this kind of flourishing mind, doing exercises and practices to condition it is essential, in the same way that we can do exercise and conditioning for our bodies.

For that reason, you can think of this book as a workout guide for your brain. Imagine you are an elite athlete trying to achieve a high level of performance. Like an elite athlete, your goal is to reach a certain level, and once you reach this high level, it is critical to maintain it. As muscles can atrophy and athletes can get out of shape when their fitness isn't maintained, so can our well-being levels.

OUR HAPPINESS BASELINES

This mental well-being level that we can work on is called baseline well-being.²² In this book, I will also refer to baseline well-being as our "happiness baseline." Like I mentioned in the introduction, our brain has a surprising ability to go back to normal and no longer experience the same level of happiness initially felt with things like circumstantial events, new purchases, or exciting achievements. However, in the

---
[21] Ibid.
[22] Sonja Lyubomirsky et al., "Becoming Happier Takes Both a Will and a Proper Way: An Experimental Longitudinal Intervention to Boost Well-Being," *Emotion (Washington, D.C.)* 11, no. 2 (April 2011): 391–402.

same way elite athletes can sustain a high level of physical fitness, you can also achieve and sustain a higher level of mental fitness (i.e., a higher happiness baseline).

To help us achieve these higher levels of fitness, we will create a mental exercise plan. To have the best guidance in creating this plan, I have incorporated guidance from mental conditioning coaches (who have worked with professional and Olympic athletes) and professional psychologists. We'll get into their specific tips soon, but first, let's learn a little bit about how we can change the structure of our brains!

HOW DO I WORK TOWARD FIRMNESS OF MIND?
Yep, you heard me right: You can literally change the structure of your brains. When I first mentioned the concept of control in the introduction, we learned how we can have misconceptions about the degree to which we can control things. In terms of our ability to change our brains' structure, most of us greatly underestimate the amount of control we have over this.

Research in the past several decades has developed the new body of research called neuroplasticity. The term neuroplasticity refers to the ability that humans have to change the structure of our brains and, therefore, our thinking patterns. "Neuro" means nerve cell and "plasticity" means something can be molded or changed.[23] In contrast to previously held notions that the brain was a set and immovable organ, the

---

[23] Patrice Voss et al., "Dynamic Brains and the Changing Rules of Neuroplasticity: Implications for Learning and Recovery," *Frontiers in Psychology* 8 (October 4, 2017).

brain is actually very changeable.²⁴ This means that if you think you're stuck with thinking negative thoughts for the rest of your life with no ability to change them because bad things have happened to you or because you have a genetic predisposition, think again.

A fascinating real-life example of neuroplasticity was described in 2000, when the neuroscientist Eleanor Maguire ran a study taking a look at the brains of taxi drivers in London. What she found was that these taxi drivers had massive lumps in their hippocampi, a part of the brain that is responsible for memory and visual orientation. These lumps were not tumors, but in fact, overdeveloped hippocampi that formed as a result of exercising the memory and direction portions of their brains while navigating the confusing streets of London. Because these taxi drivers were exercising the memory portions of their brains so much, it ended up causing their brains to grow, much like the way our muscles grow after exercise.²⁵

Our exercises designed by psychologists and mental health professionals will help us to achieve the dramatic changes that the taxi drivers were able to experience, no matter how old we are, as the brain retains its plastic properties as we age.²⁶ Now that we know we have the ability to control the

---

[24] Ibid.
[25] Eleanor A. Maguire et al., "Navigation-Related Structural Change in the Hippocampi of Taxi Drivers," *Proceedings of the National Academy of Sciences of the United States of America* 97, no. 8 (April 11, 2000): 4398–4403.
[26] Denise C. Park and Gérard N. Bischof, "The Aging Mind: Neuroplasticity in Response to Cognitive Training," *Dialogues in Clinical Neuroscience* 15, no. 1 (March 2013): 109–19.

structures of our brains, let's talk a little more about other things we have control over.

INTENTIONAL ACTIVITIES

Have you ever heard people say, "I'll never be happy; I was just born this way," or heard people say that certain traumatic events changed their lives permanently? While it is true that past trauma and genetics have a large influence on the way that we think, research shows us that they aren't everything. In fact, Dr. Sonja Lyubomirsky has found that we can greatly influence our levels of well-being through intentional activities.[27] We can do certain activities to change the structures of our brains for the better and raise our happiness baselines. Check out this diagram that was the focus of her book, *The How of Happiness*:

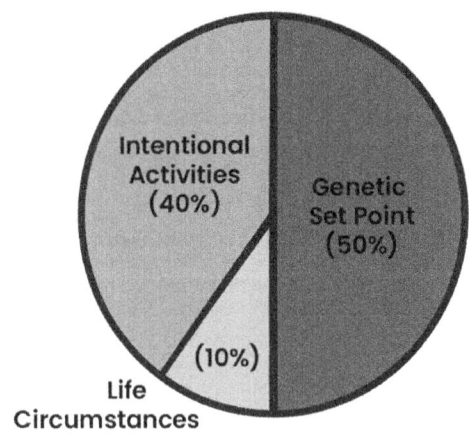

What Determines Happiness?

Intentional Activities (40%)
Genetic Set Point (50%)
(10%) Life Circumstances

---

[27] Sonja Lyubomirsky and Jaime Kurtz, *Positively Happy: Routes to Sustainable Happiness*, 1st ed. (United Kingdom: Positive Acorn, 2008) chap. 1, Kindle.

When I asked Dr. Lyubomirsky about this pie chart, she said it is essential to interpret it with nuance. These percentages are definitely not cut-and-dried and can vary greatly depending on the person or circumstance, and there are definitely areas of overlap in how certain life circumstances can open opportunities for you to increase your happiness baseline. However, the main takeaway from this is that research shows you have control over improving your long-term happiness through intentional activities.

WHAT WE CAN AND CAN'T CONTROL

On the topic of the happiness pie, let's talk more about things you can and can't control. We just learned how we can influence the structure of our brains, and we have influence over our happiness baselines. We can't control the genetic makeup that we're born with (all people are born with different levels of happiness chemicals), and for the most part, we don't have much control over things that happen to us, like unfortunate events.[28]

Surprisingly, circumstances have less to do with happiness than you think. Examples in research show how people that undergo traumatic events such as divorce or the amputation of limbs have the ability to return to (or very close to) baseline levels.[29] Socioeconomic circumstances also have remarkably little to do with happiness levels, shown by how a pushcart

---

[28] E. E. Forbes et al., "Genetic Variation in Components of Dopamine Neurotransmission Impacts Ventral Striatal Reactivity Associated with Impulsivity," *Molecular Psychiatry* 14, no. 1 (January 2009): 60–70.

[29] Christina Armenta et al., "Is Lasting Change Possible? Lessons from the Hedonic Adaptation Prevention Model," in *Stability of Happiness: Theories and Evidence on Whether Happiness Can Change*, 2014, 57–74.

driver in the slums of India can report happiness levels just as high as most Americans and how Buddhist monks with very little material wealth can report some of the highest happiness levels in the world.[30]

The truth is, it doesn't matter what you can or can't control. The secret is just being able to correctly identify what is within your ability to control and what is outside of your ability to control. Our exercises will focus on doing things within our realms of control and will also discuss tools on how to healthily identify and accept things we don't have control over. We will talk more about the concept of determining appropriate levels of control using a concept called the internal locus of control in Section 2 on the mind, but for now, just keep in mind that your perception on control is very influential on your happiness.

HOW CAN I USE FIRMNESS OF MIND TO ACHIEVE THE HAPPINESS BALANCE?

Okay, now it's time to tie everything back together. We learned from the introduction that we need to balance present pleasure with future meaning. We learned from this chapter that we can change our well-being baselines by changing our brains through intentional exercises in parts of our lives that we can control.

How do these two concepts connect? Well, we can see the physiological connection by taking another look at the structure of our brains. Our brains have two major areas that are

---

[30] KPBS Public Media, "HAPPY," KPBS Public Media, accessed October 2, 2020.

constantly playing a balancing act: the limbic system and the prefrontal cortex. Here is a simplified diagram of where in the brain they are generally located:

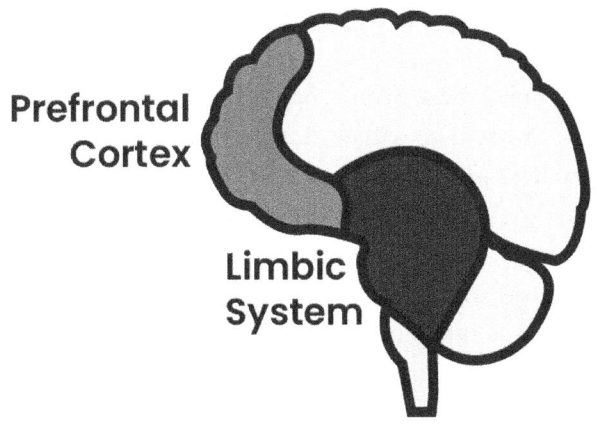

The limbic system is our primitive brain, where the pleasure and rewards center (and animalistic tendencies such as fight or flight responses) of our brain is located.[31] The prefrontal cortex is responsible for rational thought, reasoning, and making the necessary actions to progress toward a goal.[32] The prefrontal cortex acts as the higher level of thought over the quick, primal impulses created by our limbic systems.[33] You can see how these areas of the brain are related to the present pleasure and future purpose parts of the happiness balance. We will talk more about the relationship between

---

[31] V. Rajmohan and E. Mohandas, "The Limbic System," *Indian Journal of Psychiatry* 49, no. 2 (2007): 132–39.

[32] Robert Morecraft, "Prefrontal Cortex – an Overview," ScienceDirect Topics, accessed October 3, 2020.

[33] Ibid.

the prefrontal cortex and the limbic system next chapter, but one thing to keep in mind, if you are a younger reader like me, is that our brains are still developing. Our prefrontal cortices can still be "under construction," meaning that impulse control is something we are still refining. Adolescence is a critical time to refine these processes, as many of our lifelong habits are developed while we are young.[34] For now, just know the exercises we will do will be aimed at improving the quality of the relationship between these two parts of the brain, and that our youthful years are a great time to begin this.

Now let's get to the second part of this chapter, Chapter 1b. Chapter 1b will tell us about lifestyle routines, or in other words, a workout plan to condition our brains.

---

[34] Mariam Arain et al., "Maturation of the Adolescent Brain," *Neuropsychiatric Disease and Treatment* 9 (2013): 449–61.

TAKEAWAYS FROM CHAPTER 1A:

WHAT IS FIRMNESS OF MIND?

---

1. Both scripture and psychological science talk about a strong, healthy mental state (which I like to call "firmness of mind"). The new field of positive psychology focuses on the characteristics of a steadily happy brain as opposed to the defects of the brain.
2. Similar to a muscle, we can influence the physical structure of our brains through neuroplastic changes, and our happiness baseline levels can also be improved and strengthened.
3. Improving our happiness baselines has more to do with intentional activities than doing things like trying to control our circumstances. Regardless of things we have little or no control over, such as our genetic makeup, we can take action over our happiness through intentional activities we can control.
4. Many of these activities will exercise brain interactions between the higher reasoning part and the reactive impulsive parts of our brains to best achieve a balance of present pleasure and future meaning. Our youthful years are the best times to begin working on this.

CHAPTER 1B:

INTRODUCTION TO LIFESTYLE ROUTINES

Now that we've gotten to this point in the book, we know more about human happiness and the way our brain works. Now, let's put that knowledge to rest for a second and create a new priority: making sure our set of behaviors is changed for the better. The key to changing our behaviors is to set up the groundwork to ensure that our knowledge becomes implemented into our lives.

In this section, we will discuss how we can successfully apply and internalize the concepts we learn from the book through setting up lifestyle routines.

WHAT IS A LIFESTYLE ROUTINE?
A lifestyle routine can be called many things; you can also call them habits, practices, or rituals, but they are regular behaviors you do in your lives without second thought. Our goal in this section is to learn how to set up lifestyle routines to implement what we have learned about positive

psychology. It will provide a detailed explanation of how to lay out a groundwork for the other activities in future sections (Sections 2–5). When you reach the other chapters, those sections will instruct you to come back to this section to guide you in making your routine.

WHY SET UP LIFESTYLE ROUTINES?

The first thing to realize, if you are a young reader, is that adolescence and early adulthood are very important times to begin prioritizing your well-being. Like we mentioned last chapter, experts say that "adolescence is a critical developmental period with implications for the well-being of the individual," as adolescence is a time where our brains have not fully mastered our control over impulsive drives.[35] With this in mind, we need to prioritize our brain development now if possible, as a lot of the habits and routines we learn while we are in our youth can stick with us throughout our lives. An example of this is how most drug addictions develop in adolescence.[36]

Another thing to realize, regardless of our age, is that humans often do not do things that they know are good for them. Dr. Laurie Santos, the professor of the most popular class ever taught at Yale, "Psychology and the Good Life," teaches us how many people don't do what's best for them through something she calls the G.I. Joe Fallacy.[37] The G.I. Joe Fallacy

---

[35] Annamaria Di Fabio and Letizia Palazzeschi, "Hedonic and Eudaimonic Well-Being: The Role of Resilience beyond Fluid Intelligence and Personality Traits," *Frontiers in Psychology* 6 (2015).

[36] Mariam Arain et al., "Maturation of the Adolescent Brain," *Neuropsychiatric Disease and Treatment* 9 (2013): 449–61.

[37] Laurie Santos, "What Is the G.I. Joe Fallacy? – Introduction," Coursera, accessed October 4, 2020.

gets its name from a short public service announcement that aired after the '80s TV show *G.I. Joe*, where G.I. Joe would teach the audience important things like looking both ways before crossing the street or not talking to strangers. After sharing the tip, he would say, "Knowing is half the battle."[38] Santos calls this a fallacy, because for a lot of things in life, while knowing things help, it takes a lot more than just half the battle for people to do things that they know are best for them. An example is that pretty much all Americans know that regular exercise is important, yet around 80 percent of Americans do not get the optimal amount of exercise.[39] Another example of the common disconnect between what we know what is good for us and what we do follows:

"Public service announcements, educational programs, community workshops, and weight-loss programs are all geared toward improving your day-to-day habits. But are they really effective? These standard interventions are very successful at increasing motivation and desire. You will almost always leave feeling like you can change and that you want to change. The programs give you knowledge and goal-setting strategies for implementation, but these programs only address the intentional mind.

"In a study on the 'Take 5' program, 35 percent of people polled came away believing they should eat five fruits and vegetables a day. Looking at that result, it appears that the national program was effective at teaching people that it's

---

[38] Ibid.
[39] Cleveland Clinic, "80% of Americans Don't Get Enough Exercise — and Here's How Much You Actually Need," Health Essentials from Cleveland Clinic, November 20, 2018.

important to have five servings of fruits and vegetables every day. But the data changes when you ask what people are actually eating. Only 11 percent of people reported that they met this goal. The program changed people's intentions, but it did not overrule habitual behavior."[40]

This disconnect between knowledge and action could be for a variety of reasons, such as people naturally being resistant to change or people having barriers to their actions, but the important thing is to put the knowledge into action. That's why I said at the beginning that simply reading this book cover to cover likely will not improve the quality of your life over the long term. The way to overcome this disconnect is through building routines. While I have learned about many different benefits to investing in my happiness and well-being through the many books and classes I have taken, the only times that I have noticed actual changes is when I have turned my knowledge into action, which has been through developing routines. If you remember the story about Maria from the introduction, the way that she was able to reach an improved state of well-being was through her routines that she developed.

Kevin Hines, a mental health advocate and motivational speaker, tells us how critical routines are for sustaining mental well-being. Hines is diagnosed with bipolar disorder, and his struggles with this disorder once led him to attempt to take his life by taking the 220-foot jump off of the Golden Gate Bridge. After miraculously surviving the

---

[40] ScienceDaily, "How We Form Habits, Change Existing Ones," ScienceDaily, accessed October 5, 2020.

fall and recovering from his injuries, he has been able to keep a steady level of mental well-being through following a routine.[41] In fact, he goes as far to state that routine is "the common denominator for overcoming mental challenges," encouraging us to do things like training our bodies to wake up at the same time, exercise at the same times, and take medication at the same times (if you are prescribed medication for a condition).[42]

Hopefully, you will not need a life-changing event like the one Kevin went through in order to commit to a routine. In fact, it is a much better idea to invest in routines during times when you are doing well, as you will be more resilient against mental and emotional stress if you invest in building a steady foundation of good habits, as opposed to turning to routines in times of crisis.[43] During times of mental or emotional trauma, starting to develop routines and see results can be harder, as benefits from the routines take long and consistent progress in order to see significant changes.

Also, the perspective I want everyone to have when designing routines is not to focus on avoidance of the negative but instead on the approach toward the positive, an opportunity to be your best. When you look at building a routine in a positive light, you might find that just the process of developing and sticking to a routine can be rewarding in and of itself. In fact, Dr. Martin Seligman states that being

---

[41] Kevin Hines, "After My Suicide Attempt, I Made This Plan to Stay Alive and Well | HuffPost Life," *The Huffington Post*, February 26, 2016.
[42] Ibid.
[43] Mental Health America, "Creating Healthy Routines," Mental Health America, accessed November 25, 2020.

engaged in, making plans for, and achieving goals is a source of flourishing.[44]

We will get into more activities that promote flourishing in the next section, but before we even learn those, we will learn how to bridge the gap between knowledge and action through lifestyle routines to help us get to a higher sustained level of well-being. So, let's get started on making successful lifestyle routines!

ARE YOU READY FOR BEHAVIORAL CHANGE THROUGH BUILDING A LIFESTYLE ROUTINE?

The first thing that determines whether you put knowledge into action is if you decide you are ready for behavioral change or not. Psychologists James Prochaska and Carlo DiClemente described the important stages of behavioral change in their Transtheoretical Model (also called the Stages of Change Model), and looking into this can hopefully give you an insight into what factors into changing your behavior.[45] The main things to know from this, though, is that in order to change your behavior, you first have to be ready to change, and if you haven't decided this yet, you have to make the decision. Another thing to know about this is that behavioral change is rarely a singular moment; it is a process that involves continuously progressing through stages of change throughout your life. Just a note: chances are, if you've read this far in the book, you are at a stage in

---

[44] The University of Pennsylvania, "PERMA™ Theory of Well-Being and PERMA™ Workshops," Positive Psychology Center, accessed October 2, 2020.

[45] Wayne LaMorte, "The Transtheoretical Model (Stages of Change)," Behavior Change Models, accessed October 7, 2020.

the change cycle that signifies that you are ready for positive change in your life. However, you can see the stages of the cycle below and determine where you might be in terms of your progress toward improving your well-being.

Some background on this change cycle: It was developed after Prochaska and DiClemente observed reasons as to why smokers were able to quit on their own. They found out that in order to quit, the smokers first had to be ready to quit.[46] Their observations on their research subjects led them to design this model on the assumption that behavior doesn't change quickly and suddenly, but in a cycle. Like I mentioned earlier, people generally go through stages of this cycle throughout their lives. The behavioral change that we discuss in this book is not as much about completely changing the type of person you are, but it is being a person that has the desire to keep doing positive behavior and to continue to progress along the cycle. You will find that you may be in different parts of the cycle for different behaviors in your life, but the concept remains the same: Achieving a higher level of well-being is dependent on a lifetime of consistent progress in the cycle, regardless of how many times you have to restart your behaviors.

A key factor in beginning and progressing along this cycle depends on decisional balance, meaning you decide to pursue new behavior because you decide that the pros of the new behavior outweigh the cons of the old behavior. You will see that this is the first step in order to progress past the first stage of the cycle.

---

[46] Ibid.

Here is an overview of the different stages of the cycle:

1. Precontemplation: In this stage, you have not decided to change behavior, because you are either unaware of the benefits to change or may be even unaware of the undesirable behavior in general. You have not decided to weigh the pros and cons of your undesired behavior.
2. Contemplation: In this stage, your decision to change behavior hasn't happened yet, but you have begun to weigh the pros and the cons of changing your behavior.
3. Preparation: Here, you have decided to change your behavior because you believe that the pros outweigh the cons, and you have begun taking small steps in your life toward actions of behavioral change.
4. Action: Here, you have changed your behavior by either modifying problematic behavior or implementing new behaviors in your life.
5. Maintenance: In this stage, you have lived your new behavior for a substantial period of time, and you strive to maintain this behavior by trying to prevent a return to earlier stages in the cycle. This is the end goal of the cycle.

At each stage of change above, there are many strategies that professionals suggest implementing to help individuals progress along the cycle to the next stages of change. Many of these strategies work for many different people, but we will mainly discuss techniques of strengthening lifestyle routines in order to be at the maintenance phase of our well-being, or our happiness baselines.

But first, before we get into the techniques of strengthening these routines, let's start on the first action to begin the behavioral change cycle, which is the decision to change.

ACTIVITY 1.1: DECIDE TO CHANGE (DECISIONAL BALANCE SHEET)

Hopefully, by this point in the book, you should have learned enough about pros and cons of investing in your happiness and well-being. Now, in order to truly make the decision to prioritize your happiness and well-being, here you have the chance to weigh the pros and cons of living a life of well-being versus a life of languishing or unhappiness. In addition to making the decision of committing to a life of well-being, you can also refer back to this exercise in the upcoming sections for activities that you need help deciding to do.

For this exercise, we will write the pros of our new behavior (committing to making well-being a priority in life or other specific activities that you will get to choose in the next section) and then compare them to the cons of the new behavior. After weighing the pros and cons next to each other, you can write out a statement outlining your desire to change.

> **Pros:** Write out all of the benefits to committing to making happiness and well-being a priority in your life (or any other activities that support happiness and well-being).

Cons: Write out all of the downsides to committing to making happiness and well-being a priority in your life (or any other activities that support happiness and well-being).

Decision Statement: When you are ready to change your behavior, and after weighing the pros and cons above, write a short decision statement saying how you decide to invest in making happiness and well-being a priority in your life (or any other activities that support happiness and well-being).

UNDERSTANDING THE NATURE OF OUR HABITS

Now, if you've continued to this point, hopefully you have made the conscious decision that you want to invest in your happiness and well-being. In order to stay on the cycle toward achieving positive behavioral change, we need to learn how to change our habits.

First, let's learn a bit about our habits. Our habits are very influential on our behavior; in fact, around 40 percent of things we do throughout the day are due to our habits.[47] James Clear, the author of the international bestseller *Atomic Habits*, helps us outline the process, known as the habit loop, as follows:[48]

1. Cue: The cue is an external signal that influences you to start the process of performing a habit. It is something that gives you information that leads you to anticipate a reward. It can be any sight, sound, smell, or feeling that drives you to a craving. The cue of your bad breath can lead you to crave a clean mouth, the cue of your phone vibrating can lead you to desire to know what the notification is. Cues are passive external occurrences in the environment that mean nothing until they are interpreted, because cues are interpreted by subjective thoughts, feelings, and emotions of the observer. While coins jingling in a cash register may sound like background noise to you, it may trigger a gambler to crave using a slot machine.
2. Craving: This is when you desire a certain feeling from a habit. An example includes craving the feeling of a clean mouth before brushing your teeth, or the desire to know who texted you when your phone buzzes. The craving that you get is linked to something internal that your body or brain wants, which then leads you to act in response. The strength of the craving influences the level of the motivation that you will have to respond. If

---

[47] ScienceDaily, "How We Form Habits, Change Existing Ones," ScienceDaily, accessed October 5, 2020.
[48] James Clear, "The 3 R's of Habit Change: How To Start New Habits That Actually Stick," *James Clear* (blog), February 14, 2013.

you strongly crave the feeling of a clean mouth, then you will have a high motivation to brush your teeth.
3. Response: This the actual habit you perform. Brushing your teeth or picking up your phone are examples of responses to the cravings of wanting a clean mouth or wanting to know who texted you. There are two main things that determine whether or not you respond: the level of your motivation and the level of friction against performing the response. When your motivation is higher than the friction, your response will occur. Picking up a toothbrush is easy; it doesn't take too much motivation to overcome the friction from making the walk to the bathroom from your bedroom. However, if you forgot to pack a toothbrush on a remote backpacking trip, the response for you to be able to brush your teeth will be less likely because your motivation may not be high enough to overcome the friction of having to go all the way back to civilization to buy a toothbrush.
4. Reward: This is the last step of the habit loop. This is the resulting state that happens because of your action, such as the clean mouth after brushing your teeth or being up to date with the information provided in your text message. Rewards do two things that support the habit loop: They satisfy us, and they teach us. You will be satisfied (at least for the moment) and you will be rewarded with relief from your craving. The other thing that will happen is that the reward will teach you that every time that you do the habit, you will be rewarded. Your brain will remember, sometimes subconsciously, that every time that you begin the habit loop, you will receive a reward.

Obviously, many habits are in place because our brains remember that they give us helpful rewards. However, some of these habits we do may appear to be helpful in the short term (such as eating an entire tub of ice cream when we are stressed) but are not ideal in the long run. In the same way, we don't have some habits because they do not appear to have any clear reward in the short term (such as exercising regularly) but may actually be very important for us in the long term. The habits we want to focus on developing are these types of habits: the ones that may not have immediate and strong rewards (which is why we likely do not do them) but are things we know are best for us. This way, we can make sure our knowledge matches up with our actions.

Also, we can see how aspects of the habit loop can also fit into the Stages of Change Model. In order for you to progress along the Stages of Change cycle, we can strengthen habits that promote desired behavior, and weaken habits that discourage desired behavior.

We will get more specific about techniques on how to strengthen or weaken certain habits, but one thing to take note of now is that strengthening any and all portions of the habit loop will make your behavior more likely to occur, and weakening any and all portions of the habit loop will make your behavior less likely to occur. Strengthen the weakest link for habits you want to implement and weaken the weakest link for habits you want to break. To strengthen cues, make them obvious, and to weaken them, make them invisible. To strengthen cravings, make them attractive, and to weaken them, make them unattractive. To strengthen responses, make them easy, and to weaken them, make them difficult.

And finally, to strengthen rewards, make them satisfying, and to weaken rewards, make them unsatisfying.

You can see how the concept of the habit loop relates to the happiness balance between present pleasure and future purpose. As a reminder, many of the habits we will be trying to program into our lifestyle routines will be built around putting off our immediate impulses to improve our overall happiness, but sometimes we will also implement habits that make us focus on savoring what's in the present.

Now that we have this knowledge of the habit loop to help us create our lifestyle routine plans, the next time we find ourselves doing something that we know doesn't make us happy in the long run, like not getting enough sleep even though we know we should, let's resolve to bridge the gap between the knowledge and action by applying this concept to creating good habits of doing regular well-being lifestyle routines and to weakening bad habits that hurt our well-being. At the end of this section, we will have a worksheet that will instruct us on building out these lifestyle routines, and it will help guide us to build and strengthen habit loops for desirable habits and weaken and break down habit loops for undesirable habits.

Now, let's continue learning how we can build these lifestyle routines!

TAKEAWAYS FROM CHAPTER 1B:

INTRODUCTION TO LIFESTYLE ROUTINES

———

1. A lifestyle routine will be the groundwork to improving your well-being, and it is very important to learn to do this at a young age.
2. Research shows that people frequently do not do things they know are good for them. Just knowing something is good for you isn't enough to get you to do it; you need to be ready for behavioral change, and you need to build the proper routines to support it.
3. Beginning a new lifestyle routine depends on whether you are ready for behavioral change or not, and you are ready to change your behavior after you decide that the pros for changing your behavior outweigh the cons to your behavior. Chances are, if you've read this far in the book, you are at a spot in the change cycle (referred to earlier as the Transtheoretical Model of Change) that signifies that you are ready for change in your life.
4. Building a routine is critical to doing things that you know are good for you but aren't doing, and the process of building a routine and progressing toward a better life is rewarding in and of itself.

5. The behavior you do and the habits you perform are dependent on a process called the habit loop. The habit loop consists of a cue, craving, response, and reward, and changing your behavior depends on strengthening desirable habit loops and weakening undesirable habit loops.

CHAPTER 1C:

SETTING UP LIFESTYLE ROUTINES

Now that we understand a little about the importance of lifestyle routines and a little bit about the influential factors behind our habitual behavior, now let's learn how to build these routines. This chapter will cover several key components in building lifestyle routines. It starts with setting goals (higher level and lower level), plans (based around activities that will have their habit loops strengthened or weakened), and accountability (ways to make sure that you stick to your plans). You will be able to practice doing these things throughout the chapter, but at the end of the chapter and in Appendix 2, you will find a worksheet that tells you all the parts of setting up lifestyle routines, and you will be able to fill this out with exercises as you continue through the book. Just remember, lifestyle routines are meant to be refined and customized throughout your entire life, so this is a process that you will do continuously. You will also be guided to be continuously updating and refining your routines throughout the course of this book and will also be invited to check out the online resources at www.firmnessofmind.com.

I know I've said lots of things about how important it is to prioritize changing our brains while we are young and to make well-being a priority, but the truth of the matter is that change takes a lot of time and work, and the best thing is not to look for quick and easy change but begin developing routines that we will use for the rest of our lives. Charles Duhigg, the author of the New York Times best seller *The Power of Habit*, said, "If you're building a habit, you're planning for the next decade, not the next couple of months."[49]

STEP ONE: SETTING GOALS

Before we can map out our activities or apply the habit loop into our lifestyle routines, the first thing we need to do is to set goals. There are two types of goals: higher level goals and lower level goals.

> **Higher Level Goals:** Higher level goals are closely tied with the future meaning part of the happiness balance. These are what contribute to a sense of purpose in our lives and should be what dictate our actions day-to-day. Dr. Angela Duckworth, a prominent positive psychology researcher, professor at the University of Pennsylvania, and author of the New York Times bestseller *Grit*, gives us important guidance on how to set higher level goals. While interviewing her for this book, she explained to me that people are happiest

---

[49] Jen Miller, "How to Make (and Keep) a New Year's Resolution," *The New York Times*, December 18, 2017.

when they are pursuing and making progress toward goals. Research has even documented that mortality rates for men increase after they retire and receive social security benefits, as retiring from a career can greatly decrease the level of progress and achievement that people have.[50]

However, the type of goals that we progress toward is very important. When setting higher level goals, we must center them on things we can control, such as progress toward values, as opposed to outcomes that we can't control. Duckworth stated that her top-level goal, "using psychological science to help children thrive," is different from a goal like "become a NYT bestseller" or "get tenure at Penn," because it is something you can continuously pursue (you can't check off the box) and is something within your realm of control. Duckworth explained how many Olympians that she studied would struggle after receiving medals because they would lose a sense of purpose after arriving at their goals.

Tal Ben-Shahar describes this phenomenon, called arrival fallacy, by using an example from his own life. As a youth growing up in Israel, Ben-Shahar had the goal to be a national champion squash player. He trained relentlessly to achieve that goal, sticking to a strict diet and conditioning regimen. After working hard for years and competing at the

---

[50] Maria D. Fitzpatrick and Timothy J. Moore, "The Mortality Effects of Retirement: Evidence from Social Security Eligibility at Age 62," *Journal of Public Economics* 157 (January 1, 2018): 121–37.

top tournaments, he eventually achieved his dream, becoming the youngest national squash champion in Israel's history. "I thought if I win this tournament that then I'll be happy," he said. "And I won, and I was happy. And then the same stress and pressure and emptiness returned."[51] Ben-Shahar defines the arrival fallacy as "the false belief that reaching a valued destination can sustain happiness." He says, "Arrival fallacy is this illusion that once we make it, once we attain our goal or reach our destination, we will reach lasting happiness." Arrival fallacy teaches us that when aiming toward a monumental goal or accomplishment, we tend to greatly overestimate how long-lasting the resulting happiness after an achievement will make us.

While working hard and achieving our goals are important, we should not make our high-level goals dependent on short, outcome-oriented events that do not provide long-lasting happiness. Instead, we can enjoy progressing toward living true to a set of principles or values. Ben-Shahar leads a life in pursuit of his mission to "bring happiness to people's lives by creating a bridge between the Ivory Tower and Main Street," with the goal of making "research accessible to individuals, schools, organizations, and nations."

---

[51] Thomas Oppong, "The Arrival Fallacy: A Psychologist Explains Why Reaching Your Goals Won't Make You Happy," Medium, September 4, 2019.

He says the best advice that he ever has ever received was to "be true to your values."[52]

Overall, a good benchmark to assess your higher level goals is to see how well it supports your overall happiness and well-being. If it does a good job of holding up what we learned about what true happiness is (a good balance between present pleasure and future purpose), you are at a good start.

We will have a chance to practice writing out some higher level goals after this chapter, and we will also have a chance to tie these to values that you find important from a list of commonly used values. Just remember it is important to make them more like a mission/purpose statement, as opposed to making them outcome or situation-oriented goals.

Lower Level Goals: Next after making higher level goals is matching them with lower level goals. Lower level goals, unlike higher level goals, are specific, action-related goals. An example would be if a higher level goal was to be a physically healthy person, a lower level goal could be to take the stairs instead of the elevator every time you are faced with the choice.

Justin Su'a, a performance psychology and mental conditioning coach (he has coached for organizations including the Tampa Rays, Cleveland Browns, Boston

---

[52] Sumita Sehmi, "Give Yourself Permission to Be Human. An Interview with Harvard Professor and Happiness Expert Tal Ben-Shahar." LinkedIn, accessed October 12, 2020.

Red Sox, Olympics, and *Dancing with the Stars*) and former All-American BYU baseball player, gives young church members specific tips on how to create long-term habitual behaviors through setting lower level goals. When interviewing him for this book, he said, "We need to start with extremely small goals, being as detailed and as specific as we can. A lot of times we will underestimate how long our goals are going to take, and how hard it's going to be. Keep your goals as simple as possible, trying to build momentum, so you can build on automized routines to become long term habitual behaviors. So, just one at a time, build one block at a time."

Change takes time, even up to a decade, and we need to realize that the way to get to where we want to be is through little life changes, not intense short sprints. While many times we might think goals should stretch us to our very limits and transform our daily schedules, experts say we should stick to simplicity and give ourselves personal room. Tal Ben-Shahar suggests tells us that we need to simplify. He says, "We are, generally, too busy, trying to squeeze in more and more activities into less and less time. Quantity influences quality, and we compromise on our happiness by trying to do too much."[53]

So, make sure we don't try and do too much in too little time. In fact, our bodies and brains are not built

---

[53] Tal Ben-Shahar, "7 Lessons On Earning The Ultimate Currency: Happiness," *Positivity Daily* (blog), February 10, 2015.

for drastic change. You may have heard inspiring stories of people quitting smoking cold turkey or losing huge amounts of weight in short periods of time, but for most behavioral and lifestyle changes, you are setting yourself up for failure if you expect a drastic and immediate change to your life, as these are usually difficult to sustain. Our bodies are built to maintain homeostasis, or the stable equilibrium between our bodies' systems. We may find that drastic changes or rigorous exercise routines can lead to injury, which is what happened to Ben-Shahar when he set his squash training goals too high and under too short of a time constraint.

After realizing that the satisfaction of winning the Israeli national championship faded after only a couple of days, he realized he needed to become the world champion. He moved to London and quickly dove into training at the intense level that the world champion at the time was training at. While he did improve quickly, he had not gradually built up to the level of training the world champion had been training for, and he became injured on multiple occasions. Eventually, his body could not keep up, and he ended up retiring from professional competition.[54]

In the same way, lifestyle routines that improve our well-being (which can include exercise) must be gradually and realistically implemented, so we don't overexert

---

[54] Tal Ben-Shahar, "Accepting Failure – The THEORY – The Pursuit of Perfect: How to Stop Chasing Perfection and Start Living a Richer, Happier Life – Tal Ben-Shahar," Publicism, accessed October 12, 2020.

our efforts and end up becoming "injured." So, we can make small and specific goals, but it is critical that we are careful not to make too many goals and do not stretch ourselves beyond our abilities.

We can use the SMART goal framework to help us craft our lower level goals. SMART is an acronym, describing goals that are specific, measurable, achievable, relevant, and time-bound (there are some variations to the acronym, but this is the most common).[55] When we do our goal setting activity, try to make sure your lower level goals meet these criteria.

Lastly, in order to make sure our lower level goals occur, we need to pair them with proper plans. We will get into these in a second, but just know that they are coming.

OVERALL GOAL SETTING

Here are some other general tips when setting our higher or lower level goals. Make sure you frame your goals as approach goals instead of avoidance goals, as research shows that approach goals are both more motivating and sustainable.[56] Approach goals are doing more of something good, as opposed to an avoidance goal, which is doing less of something bad. An example of a higher level approach goal would be to be a friendly person, as opposed to a higher level avoidance goal, such as not being a mean person. An example for

---

[55] Mind Tools Content Team, "SMART Goals: – How to Make Your Goals Achievable," SMART Goals, accessed October 12, 2020.
[56] Timothy Pychyl, "Approaching Success, Avoiding the Undesired: Does Goal Type Matter?," Psychology Today, accessed October 12, 2020.

a lower level goal approach goal would be eating five fruits or vegetables every day, as opposed to a lower level avoidance goal, such as eating no added sugar five days a week.

The benefits of approach goals are also supported by the fact that values, like love (whether it is from your parents, friends, or romantic partners), are some of the most powerful motivators.[57] This is more applicable to making goals that involve people or relationships. Regarding goals for yourself, you can think of doing things out of the love for yourself. Dr. Jared Klundt, one of my positive psychology professors at BYU, stated that human lives are more meaningfully lived when they are driven by value-based actions rather than by fear. An example would be buying flowers for your mom on her birthday because you want her to be happy, as opposed to doing it because you could imagine how upset she would be if you didn't get her anything. Because guilt and shame can negatively impact our psychological health in the long term, our brains tend to work better when we are encouraged to do things, as opposed to being told to do things we shouldn't do.[58]

Lastly, when selecting your goals, Dr. Ben-Shahar suggests that we do three things to determine what good goals are.[59] These help us make sure our goals truly are aimed at improving our well-being, by balancing pleasure, meaning, and using your strengths. The three things are as follows:

---

[57] Meg Selig, "The LOVE Motivator," Psychology Today, accessed October 22, 2020.
[58] Lisa Rivero, "Shame and Motivation to Change," Psychology Today, accessed October 22, 2020.
[59] "Setting Meaningful Goals," *The Wellbeing Thesis* (blog), September 4, 2019.

1. Set goals that are meaningful to you. Ask yourself: What do I care about? What are my core values? What makes me excited, passionate, determined, or angry? How do I spend my time, and what do I want to change in the world?
2. Set goals to do things that bring you pleasure. Ask yourself: What do I enjoy? What is fun, interesting, exciting, or inspiring?
3. Set goals that take advantage of your strengths. Ask yourself: What am I good at? What do other people say that I am good at? What things make me feel competent and capable?

SETTING HIGHER AND LOWER LEVEL GOALS

Here we have a chance to identify personal values and principles important to your happiness. We will use these personal values and principles to make our goals at the end of the chapter. Write down some core values and principles that you think make you happy, or, if you need some help with inspiration, take a look at this list from Dr. Russ Harris as listed in his book *The Illustrated Happiness Trap*:[60]

ACTIVITY 1.2: VALUES LIST

"Read through the list below and write a letter next to each value: V = Very important, Q = Quite important, and N = Not so important—for the specific domain of life you have picked to work on.

1. Acceptance: to be open to and accepting of myself, others, life etc.

---

[60] Russ Harris, *The Illustrated Happiness Trap*, 1st ed. (United States of America: Shambhala Publications, Inc., 2013), 136-39.

2. Adventure: to be adventurous; to actively seek, create, or explore novel or stimulating experiences
3. Assertiveness: to respectfully stand up for my rights and request what I want
4. Authenticity: to be authentic, genuine, real; to be true to myself
5. Beauty: to appreciate, create, nurture or cultivate beauty in myself, others, the environment etc.
6. Caring: to be caring toward myself, others, the environment etc.
7. Challenge: to keep challenging myself to grow, learn, improve
8. Compassion: to act with kindness toward those who are suffering
9. Connection: to engage fully in whatever I am doing, and be fully present with others
10. Contribution: to contribute, help, assist, or make a positive difference to myself or others
11. Conformity: to be respectful and obedient of rules and obligations
12. Cooperation: to be cooperative and collaborative with others
13. Courage: to be courageous or brave; to persist in the face of fear, threat, or difficulty
14. Creativity: to be creative or innovative
15. Curiosity: to be curious, open-minded and interested; to explore and discover
16. Encouragement: to encourage and reward behavior that I value in myself or others
17. Equality: to treat others as equal to myself, and vice-versa
18. Excitement: to seek, create and engage in activities that are exciting, stimulating or thrilling

19. Fairness: to be fair to myself or others
20. Fitness: to maintain or improve my fitness; to look after my physical and mental health and well-being
21. Flexibility: to adjust and adapt readily to changing circumstances
22. Freedom: to live freely; to choose how I live and behave, or help others do likewise
23. Friendliness: to be friendly, companionable, or agreeable toward others
24. Forgiveness: to be forgiving toward myself or others
25. Fun: to be fun-loving; to seek, create, and engage in fun-filled activities
26. Generosity: to be generous, sharing and giving, to myself or others
27. Gratitude: to be grateful for and appreciative of the positive aspects of myself, others, and life
28. Honesty: to be honest, truthful, and sincere with myself and others
29. Humor: to see and appreciate the humorous side of life
30. Humility: to be humble or modest; to let my achievements speak for themselves
31. Industry: to be industrious, hard-working, dedicated
32. Independence: to be self-supportive, and choose my own way of doing things
33. Intimacy: to open up, reveal, and share myself—emotionally or physically—in my close personal relationships
34. Justice: to uphold justice and fairness
35. Kindness: to be kind, compassionate, considerate, nurturing or caring toward myself or others
36. Love: to act lovingly or affectionately toward myself or others

37. Mindfulness: to be conscious of, open to, and curious about my here-and-now experience
38. Order: to be orderly and organized
39. Open-mindedness: to think things through, see things from other's points of view, and weigh evidence fairly.
40. Patience: to wait calmly for what I want
41. Persistence: to continue resolutely, despite problems or difficulties.
42. Pleasure: to create and give pleasure to myself or others
43. Power: to strongly influence or wield authority over others, e.g. taking charge, leading, organizing
44. Reciprocity: to build relationships in which there is a fair balance of giving and taking
45. Respect: to be respectful toward myself or others; to be polite, considerate and show positive regard
46. Responsibility: to be responsible and accountable for my actions
47. Romance: to be romantic; to display and express love or strong affection
48. Safety: to secure, protect, or ensure safety of myself or others
49. Self-awareness: to be aware of my own thoughts, feelings and actions
50. Self-care: to look after my health and wellbeing, and get my needs met
51. Self-development: to keep growing, advancing or improving in knowledge, skills, character, or life experience.
52. Self-control: to act in accordance with my own ideals
53. Sensuality: to create, explore and enjoy experiences that stimulate the five senses
54. Spirituality: to connect with things bigger than myself

55. Skillfulness: to continually practice and improve my skills, and apply myself fully when using them
56. Supportiveness: to be supportive, helpful, encouraging, and available to myself or others
57. Trust: to be trustworthy; to be loyal, faithful, sincere, and reliable
58. Insert your own unlisted value here:

Once you've marked each value as V, Q, N (Very, Quite, or Not so important), go through all the Vs, and select out the top three that are most important to you in this domain of life, at this point in time. The next step is to start looking at ways to live these values, in this area of life; things you can say and do, guided by these values."[61]

With these values you may have selected from this activity, you can apply them to an activity to set your higher level goals at the end of the chapter.

STEP TWO: MAKING PLANS TO ACHIEVE THESE GOALS
Now we need to make sure the goals we made are now upheld by specific plans. When making lifestyle routines, we will make plans that help us stick to our routines. I will use the analogy of riding on a wagon.

When I asked Justin Su'a how he helps professional athletes stay on their routines, he told me that "to stay on the wagon, you need to make sure that you are on the best spot on the wagon." This means you want to position yourself in a way that it is hard to not do the things that you plan. The wagon

---
[61] Ibid.

is your lifestyle routine, and the plans will teach us how to have the best position on the wagon to prevent falling off. Also, things never go exactly as planned, so it is important to plan what to do if "Plan A" falls apart.

The next section on accountability will teach us how to hone and refine our goals and plans, but let's first look at some tips on making sure your plans help you stick to the goals and the routine that you made.

Su'a says to do things that strengthen the different parts of the habit loop for desired behavior such as making cues obvious, cravings attractive, responses easy, and rewards satisfying. For undesirable behaviors, you should do the reverse: make cues invisible, make cravings unattractive, make responses difficult, and make rewards unsatisfying.

STRENGTHENING GOOD CUES: MAKE IT OBVIOUS
Plan to make your goals obvious. Su'a recommends optimizing environmental design, meaning you should design your environment to always remind you of your goals. He says to write your goals down on paper, make it pretty, and put them in places where you will always see them. Whether it's your mirror, your steering wheel, your wall, your desk, or the background of your phone, make it so there is no way that you can't go through the day without seeing your goals. He says to "put it somewhere where it will serve as a trigger; what happens to a lot of people is they simply forget about their goals as the day goes on. The solution is putting it in places where it's easy for you to trip over it constantly."

For example, if you want to improve your well-being, try and leave this book out. Put it somewhere so you can regularly review it, whether it's on your desk, by your bed, on your coffee table, or in the bathroom.

The same goes for weakening bad cues: If you want to use your phone less, put it out of reach. For example, for the majority of the time when I was writing this book, I put my phone underneath the pillow of my room and set it on "Do Not Disturb" mode so I wouldn't be distracted. Another example is if you want to watch less TV, move your TV to a different room.

STRENGTHENING GOOD CRAVINGS: MAKE IT ATTRACTIVE
To strengthen good cravings, we can use a variety of methods to increase the attractiveness of our behavior. First, Su'a recommends planning your goals in ways that make you anticipate them favorably. Research on monkeys showed that anticipation of a reward can give you a larger dopamine hit (the brain chemical that is responsible for feeling pleasure) than the actual reward itself.[62] From this, we can learn that our brain's tendency to gain pleasure from anticipation can be leveraged to change our behavior. We can do this by spending time anticipating the pleasure of an activity through visualization. Su'a says to plan visualization activities to help you achieve your goals. At a set time (the start of the day is a great time), pause for a second and visualize your goals throughout the day and the pleasure they could give you. If your goal is to call your grandma that day, think about how happy it will make you feel to hear excitement

---

[62] Lisa Munoz, "From Conditioning Monkeys to Drug Addiction: Understanding Prediction and Reward," *Cognitive Neuroscience Society* (blog), June 5, 2013.

when you answer the phone, and how grateful she will be that you took the time. If your goal is to go for a jog that day, visualize the feeling of breathing fresh air, moving your legs, and the feeling of being energized after returning home.

You can also plan to make your goals more attractive through social support. According to James Clear, behaviors are attractive if they are supported by other people that are influential on your life.[63] By making plans to surround yourself with people that are likely to do the same activities that you aim to make a goal, these activities will be more attractive to you if other people are doing them. If you want to make your goal of meditation more attractive, join a meditation club or make friends with people that meditate regularly. Maria, from the introduction, said a key reason she was able to stick to her new lifestyle routines was because she had her mom and her friends help her with them. Also, try and set role models of influential people that do the things that you want to implement in your life. Looking up to people that espouse the qualities you desire to develop will help you achieve them.

STRENGTHENING GOOD RESPONSES: MAKE IT EASY

To make the action of completing your goal (the response) more likely, you need to make it easy. In the previous section on setting lower level goals, we talked about how important that it was to set very small, specific, and realistic goals. In this section, we can make plans to make goals easier to achieve. There are three main tools we can use to plan easy

---

[63] Rodion Chachura, "'Atomic Habits' by James Clear," Medium, September 10, 2020.

completion of our goals: slack, automaticity, and friction reduction.

First, slack: What I mean by this is to be easy on yourself with how you plan things. Plan things in ways so that they are really easy to do, and that it will be almost hard not to do. Don't plan too much or make things too difficult, especially at the beginning stages of change. One quick way to test how easy your lower level goals are is to use the two-minute rule, which is to see if your goal can be completed in two minutes or less. We will have two-minute versions of activities in the future sections, so they can be easy adds to your routines. Remember, it's okay to make baby steps of progress, even though it may not seem like much—it's how every change and new lifestyle routine begins. It's okay to be average, and in fact, Veronica, a college student in Utah, said that her counselor told her to "dare to be average." I know we all want to achieve great things, but start really small, because a key part of motivation is keeping promises that we make with ourselves, and a key part of keeping promises is making promises that are easy to keep. Justin Su'a tells us the more we break promises to ourselves, the easier it will be to lose motivation. On the flip side, keeping easy promises is a sure way to motivate yourself and build momentum, which takes us into the next part: automaticity.

Automaticity is planning your goals so doing them becomes automatic. Like we said previously, feeling like you're doing a good job and keeping your promises builds up momentum, and momentum is one of the best ways to get a lifestyle routine up and running to the point that it becomes automatic. When you have easy goals, it is easy to have small wins, and when you make small wins, count all of them. Su'a recommends buying a physical calendar for each little habit, putting it somewhere visible, and then crossing out a day/week/any period of time that you do your habit. Another thing you can do is have a paperclip jar, where every time that you complete your task, you can put a paperclip into the jar. When your brain sees the visual cues of progress, it releases dopamine, making us feel pleasure for doing these routines, thus making it easier and more automatic to perform them. In addition to just counting visual progress, Su'a tells us that when we build momentum, it is critical to do so with specificity. It's much easier to complete actions when they are planned specifically. You can plan them by planning a specific time, moment, and quantity of actions. An example would be flossing all of your teeth every night after brushing your teeth. Or, before you even look at your phone screen in the morning, meditate for two minutes on the floor by your bed. Lastly, a way to make your routines more automatic is by engraving them in your muscle memory. I try and schedule my activities at the same time and the same place every day, so it becomes easy to just go through the motions.

Third, you can plan to make your goals easy by reducing the friction it takes to complete them. We discussed the concept of friction earlier when we first introduced the habit loop, but as a refresher, the key determinant as to whether a response or action occurs is based on the level of motivation you have and the friction that you face. I used the example of brushing your teeth; as motivated as you are to have a clean mouth, you will face a lot more friction to brushing your teeth if you forgot your toothbrush at home on a camping trip as opposed to the friction of getting up and walking thirty feet to your bathroom. Do whatever you can to reduce friction for good habits; if you are trying to work out in the morning, get all of your gym clothes ready the night before so getting them ready in the morning is one less challenge. Or better yet, sleep in your gym clothes so when you wake up, you can just walk out the door to exercise. You can also weaken undesirable behaviors like watching excessive TV by taking the batteries out of your remote and putting them in a drawer, so every time that you want to watch TV, you have to get up, go to the drawer, and then put the batteries in your remote. Much more friction.

STRENGTHENING GOOD REWARDS: MAKE IT SATISFYING
Lastly, you can plan ways to make the completion of your goals or behaviors satisfying, to encourage you to do them again. For a lot of our current habits, we don't need to plan additional ways to make them more satisfying—that is why they are our regular habits. However, for goals we still have not completed, part of the reason that we aren't doing them now is because they are not satisfying enough for us to remember that the behavior is rewarding. We frequently choose to do alternate behavior that is more rewarding in the moment. For example, if you are dealing with discomfort of boredom or loneliness, I personally think it is a much more convenient and instant solution to mindlessly binge on Netflix or engage in excessive emotional eating than to mindfully examine my emotions or write about them in my journal. However, as the latter behaviors are healthier and better for your well-being in the long run, I try and make healthier behaviors more satisfying and the instantaneous (yet less healthy) behaviors less satisfying.

One key way is by planning to pair your behaviors with something pleasurable to make it a little more satisfying than it is. For example, if your goal is to write about your feelings every day (or times that you feel lonely or sad), you can strengthen this behavior by treating yourself every time that you complete your goal; you can allow yourself to do something pleasurable every time that you complete it, like eating your favorite snack or listening to your favorite music.

WHAT TO DO IF YOU FALL OFF THE WAGON: IF-THEN PLANNING (PLAN Bs)

Also, like I said, it is important to remember that things never go exactly as planned. That's why it is critical to incorporate If-Then plans, or Plan Bs, in our routines. These help us to be prepared for times when you fall off the wagon.

If-then planning is a way of planning the next-best thing to do if you end up breaking your lifestyle routine or missing a goal. Plan these into your routine for times when Plan A doesn't work out.

An example of if-then planning would be if there is a day that you miss your jog in the morning, you will go for a jog the evening. Or, if you miss your jog that day entirely, then make a plan to make sure that you recover the next day, as one day without a jog is much better than getting discouraged and missing a whole week of jogging. The truth is, if you are logging days you completed goals in a calendar or habit tracker, it is a big success if you have many days checked and only a few empty days, as opposed to a perfect two-week streak that ends with one day without a habit and gets extended to being many weeks without a habit.

Su'a tells us to make the next best decision after a mistake. He says, "There are a lot of people that after having one small slip up like eating one piece of pizza or missing one workout, end up thinking that now the whole day has been thrown out the window and then decide to eat the entire pizza or give up on the workout plan. Instead of giving up or feeling sorry for yourself, the best way to correct your mistake is to find the next best decision you can make."

STEP THREE: ACCOUNTABILITY FOR OUR GOALS
Accountability is the final piece to building our lifestyle routines. As I mentioned earlier, our lifestyle routines will be constantly changing throughout our lives. To make sure we continuously improve and stick to some sort of routine that is helping us improve, you can use the principle of accountability so you measure how well you are doing with your goals and how beneficial the lifestyle routine is for your life. Accountability is the way to keep track of why we are successful when we stick to our routines and stay on the wagon and find ways to get back to our routines at times that we fall off the wagon. The key parts of accountability are to identify what success means to us, how to measure it, how to keep up success, and how to reassess when we aren't successful.

WHAT IS SUCCESS?
Success is defined as meeting or progressing toward goals. Like we said in the section on goalsetting, you can progress toward living a life in line with higher level goals (that are more like values), but you can't necessarily achieve them in the same way that you can for your lower level goals.

Refer back to Step Two on setting goals to see what successful goals are, but just remember that overall, success is if you continuously, over a long period of time, are on a positive trajectory of effort and learning on how to balance well between present pleasure and future purpose.

ASSESSMENT RITUAL: HOW WE MEASURE SUCCESS
How do we measure this success? One of the best ways is to regularly have an assessment ritual. One way to do this is to have a weekly session where you go over your week (or you can do it at the end of the day) to see how you did with making your goals. If you do well, see what you did that you can repeat again or strengthen, and if you fell short, see what you can do to get back on the wagon and rolling again.

A weekly call or meeting is a great way to do this. I mentioned earlier how important social support is for making activities attractive (social support will be a recurring theme in this book), and social support is critical for successful assessment. Involve friends and family in accountability, and when you connect with them, have them go over your progress toward your goals.

While I attended BYU, one thing I did at my apartment was hold a weekly "happiness meeting," where every Sunday at 4 p.m., I would lead a meeting with a different theme from positive psychology. We would have a discussion, do an activity, plan an activity to work on for the upcoming week, and then finish with a snack. The part I felt was most important about having this weekly meeting was when we would take time for accountability to see how well we did with our activity of the week. Being able to go over our performance in this group setting was very important, as it made me feel like I was supported by others, and I was more motivated when I felt like others were cheering for me or others were invested in me doing better.

In the same way, you can incorporate accountability in your routines, whether it is with social support or on your own (but honestly, get people involved—it will be much easier and better to do it with others). During accountability, you will be able to assess what you are doing well and what you can improve on, through the metrics of achieving our goals. However, one thing to keep in mind is to assess whether your goals and expectations are healthy and realistic, so it is important to check that with other sources.

MAKING SURE OUR METRICS ARE ACCURATE

It is important to assess if the feedback you get from yourself or from others is valid. While we always have good intentions for ourselves, we sometimes might not do what's best for ourselves. For example, we can be too hard on ourselves or set too high of goals. Also, everyone has some level of bias, which gets in the way of seeing things accurately. We will get more into how we are biased (and how to overcome our biases) in the next chapter, but the first thing to keep in mind is to consult a variety of opinions when assessing feedback for yourself and your performance.

In the scientific community, researchers are able to ensure that their methods and processes are accurate by reviewing with peers. In the same way, you can check to see if your improvements or changes to your plans are sound by looking at a variety of sources. These sources include your best personal judgment (personal reflection, spiritual guidance), friends and family (or trusted leaders), and professional perspectives (direct one-on-one meeting with a counselor or therapist, or reading books or articles written by mental health professionals). By assessing your decisions with multiple viewpoints, you are more likely to have a full and unbiased perspective on your current methods and feedback on your routines.

Now that we have went over what success looks like, how to measure it, and making sure that our metrics are accurate, let's take a look at what to go over in your accountability sessions, whether you achieved your goals or whether you fell short.

IF YOU ACHIEVED YOUR GOALS: WHAT TO DO IF YOU HAVE BEEN STAYING ON THE WAGON
If you achieved your goal, the assessment you do should be straightforward. Just keep doing the things that make things work well and get rid of things that might potentially make things more challenging. Also, make sure the goals and life changes you made are sustainable. If you feel worried about being able to keep up with a difficult routine, make things simpler. Refer back to Step Two on making plans to find ways to make things sustainable and simple, or even go back to Step One on potentially reframing the goals that you have.

Again, try not to get complacent about some things like the importance of social support. Don't take it for granted, and if you find yourself lacking in that category, make sure that you reinforce anything that might change.

RESTARTING LIFESTYLE ROUTINES: GETTING BACK ON THE WAGON AFTER FALLING OFF
So, we just covered several things to evaluate during accountability if you have successfully stayed on the wagon. But as

we learned from the Stages of Change Model, it is normal and expected to have times where you fall out of the cycle, or "fall off the wagon." Falling off the wagon happens to everybody all the time. However, those who are able to make the most out of their lifestyle routines and see the most behavior change are those who can get back on the wagon the soonest.

When you fall off, it is very important that you find ways to examine these times during accountability sessions. We have four tools to use in your accountability sessions to make sure that you get back on the wagon: reassessment, if-then planning, self-compassion, and social support.

REASSESSMENT
After making a mistake, you can aim for future success by adjusting or reassessing your plans and goals. Maria, from the introduction, stated that her counselor told her that if she didn't reach her goals, she should make easier goals. If you haven't been successful at exercising every day, start by cutting down your exercise time, just doing a five-minute jog every day. It's better than nothing, and this will start building your habits. The key is to see where things went wrong and what to change. Dr. Kelly McGonigal, a psychologist and lecturer at Stanford, says that "the best way to improve your self-control is to see how and why you lose control."[64]

A lot of times, you will need to go back into your core values, the higher level goals you set, and the lower level goals. See how well-aligned your plans are to your goals, and also see

---

[64] Derek Sivers, "The Willpower Instinct – by Kelly McGonigal | Derek Sivers," Derek Sivers, accessed October 25, 2020.

how well they are planned to the parts of the habit loop they correspond to.

Also, remember that the first goals and activities that you incorporate into your lifestyle routine are a test run; throughout the course of your life, you are always learning and refining your activities, and your first goals and activities that you plan are meant to be changed. After taking a look at your test run, you can reassess your plans by looking and seeing what you can change to ensure that you have activities that are a good match for you.

Dr. Sonja Lyubomirsky, the psychologist who talked about the happiness pie chart in one of the previous chapters, tells us it is important that we plan our activities based on their natural fit, and that timing activities correctly is also critical in the amount of benefit that you can gain from them.[65]

On natural fit, Lyubomirsky suggests picking your activities based on how naturally you do them, how much you enjoy them, and how much you value them. She states that it is important not to do them just because you feel guilty if you don't do them and if you feel like you just do them for situational reasons.[66] We will have a little assessment portion at the end of each chapter that will help you determine how good of a fit the activity was for you, based on the main reasons and motivations that you did the activity. Based off those assessments, you can determine reasons as to why

---

[65] Sonja Lyubomirsky and Jaime Kurtz, *Positively Happy: Routes to Sustainable Happiness*, 1st ed. (United Kingdom: Positive Acorn, 2008), chap. 3, Kindle.
[66] Ibid.

activities may or may not have worked well for you, and you can make plans to ensure they fit you correctly.

Lyubomirsky also gives us guidance on how to time our activities effectively. She had a study that showed that the effects of doing gratitude exercises once a week compared to several times a week ended up having a deeper effect on happiness. She concluded the reason this occurred was because it is more meaningful to express gratitude genuinely once a week, and the process of doing it every day made it lose its meaning and its special effect.[67]

This is because of hedonic adaptation, which is a process where humans quickly return to a relatively stable level of happiness despite positive or negative things that happen in our lives. Basically, if our routines are getting boring or meaningless, varying their timing could help us gain more meaning from them.

This is one example she gives, but she does not claim that doing gratitude every day will lose its meaning for everyone. Personally, I do a daily gratitude journal and I feel like it has been an excellent activity. However, if you feel like you are losing meaning from your activities (especially for non-physical exercises like gratitude or intentional acts of service that could lose meaning if done too often), you may want to reassess and see how frequently you do some of these, as you may benefit more if you space out the regularity of these. Don't take this advice the wrong way, though—there are definitely some things I think are very important to do regularly, such as

---

[67] Ibid.

sleeping every day, brushing your teeth, or meditating (these are generally healthy habits that should be practiced daily), but some of these exercises can be best practiced in intervals when they are meaningful. Even exercise is something that may not be best to plan every single day; if you have a rigorous exercise regimen, it is very important to take a rest day every week or so.

I think it should be the goal of everyone to make these practices a routine. However, if it is so routine that the activities become meaningless, then you should vary them. Again, finding this as an issue amongst young people like us is very rare; the vast majority of young people are not involved in some sort of regular positive psychology regimen. However, in the rare event that after doing lots and lots of these exercises over and over and losing the meaning and efficacy of them, you can fight hedonic adaptation to these strategies by varying them and intentionally spacing them out so they hold more meaning.

Just remember, I recommend that reassessing the timing and fit of your activities is probably best to do during an accountability session after trying out activities, as often the first priority for young people like us is to build a regular routine in the first place. After falling off a routine, we can then reassess.

IF-THEN PLANNING (PLAN Bs)
As we mentioned earlier, we should already have If-Then plans incorporated into our lifestyle routine. When we have accountability after times that we didn't stick to our plans, make sure that you see whether or not you resorted to the If-Then plans.

Also, try and see if there are ways that you can improve the If-Then plans to better support your lifestyle routines.

SELF-COMPASSION

The common trait for those who are able to succeed are those who give themselves self-compassion when they are going through a hard time, as opposed to beating themselves up. Make sure that during your accountability sessions you are giving yourself plenty of self-compassion, and that your accountability partners are giving you self-compassion as well.

A lot of people think that if they mess up, being harder on yourself will motivate you to want to make the mistake less, but the research shows this is usually counterproductive—those who are able to recover the most quickly from setbacks are kinder to themselves.[68] Think about it this way: If you broke your leg, would you take a hammer and then smash your leg some more to teach yourself to remember to be more careful next time? No, that seems absurd! But in the same way, if you are tough on yourself when you make a mistake, oftentimes it will be counterproductive. Really, there are no true mistakes, only opportunities to grow.

Nelson Mandela, the anti-apartheid revolutionary and the first black president of South Africa, said, "Do not judge me by my successes, judge me by how many times I fell down and got back up again," and also said, "I never lose. I either win or learn."[69]

---

[68] Serena Chen, "Give Yourself a Break: The Power of Self-Compassion," *Harvard Business Review*, September 1, 2018.

[69] Nelson Mandela, "Nelson Mandela Quotes (Author of Long Walk to Freedom)," Goodreads, accessed November 25, 2020.

We will learn more about self-compassion techniques in the next section, but just know that falling off the wagon is just part of our process in life to learn and grow, and self-compassion is a key part of this progress toward our happiness and well-being.

SOCIAL SUPPORT

As I stated many times, definitely get other people on board with your accountability sessions. Studies show that social support from those in our circles is critical to both adhering to and getting back on your routines.[70] Social support can provide several different positive benefits at times when you fall off your routines: They can help you by being an objective perspective that provides you with compassion and helps you realize that bumps in the road are normal, and they can help you with the reassessment part on getting back on the wagon.

Make sure you plan your lifestyle routines to have many people surrounding and supporting you, so that in the event of you needing encouragement and help with reassessment, they will already be there on your side. Su'a recommends surrounding yourself with a fan base; in the same way that fans cheer on professional athletes, having friends and family around you that cheer you on during discouraging times is very important.

Also, like I mentioned in the part on staying on the wagon, social support is critical to staying on. In the event you fall off the wagon, consider slapping even more social support onto your plan than you had before.

---

[70] Laurie Weinreb-Welch, "Using Social Support to Help Our Healthy Behavior Goals," Penn State Extension, accessed October 27, 2020.

ACTIVITIES TO PRACTICE BUILDING LIFESTYLE ROUTINES

ACTIVITY 1.3: LIFESTYLE ROUTINE WORKSHEET

Follow the guidelines below, and remember, building a lifestyle routine is a dynamic process, so you will be going through this sheet and making new versions over and over. Use this as a worksheet template to design your routines for the future, and if you want updated and easy-to-read printable versions of this worksheet, visit www.firmnessofmind.com to download them for free.

SETTING HIGHER LEVEL GOALS

Tips: Make sure these are tied to your values, they are vision-based as opposed to outcome-based, they are meaningful, they are pleasurable, they focus on your strengths, and they are approach-oriented as opposed to being avoidance-oriented.

MY HIGHER LEVEL GOALS:

SETTING LOWER LEVEL GOALS

Tips: Make sure these are very specific and very small. They should be easy and manageable. To start out, don't write too many. Also, make sure they are meaningful, pleasurable, and approach-oriented as opposed to being avoidance-oriented.

MY LOWER LEVEL GOALS:

SETTING PLANS TO ACHIEVE GOALS

Tips: Plan obvious cues, attractive cravings, easy responses, and satisfying rewards to make achieving your goals a breeze. Also, incorporate If-Then plans (Plan Bs) in our routines so you can be prepared for times when things do not go exactly as planned.

MAKE CUES OBVIOUS: ENVIRONMENTAL DESIGN

Make reminders in places you frequently go by throughout the day. Put signs or reminders on places like your mirror, desk, or steering wheel. Display objects of good habits in the open; put out bowls of healthy snacks like fruits in the open, or put your water bottle out if you want to drink more water. Also, hide cues for unwanted habits; put away your TV remote or get rid of unhealthy foods. List the cues for your goals here:

MAKE CRAVINGS ATTRACTIVE: VISUALIZATION, SOCIAL SUPPORT

Imagine what it would feel like to achieve your goals through visualization and plan time to do this regularly. Also, plan ways to involve others in the completion of your goals, whether that is by finding buddies to do activities with or by finding role models of people that exemplify your goals. List the ways to make your cravings more attractive through visualization and social support here:

MAKE RESPONSES EASY:

Three ways exist to make your responses easier: slack, automaticity, and friction reduction. Give yourself plenty of slack when you plan your activities: try and keep them short, simple, and as effortless as possible. This is so you can build up momentum, which will help you develop automaticity. Try and plan your activities so they are automatic. If possible, plan them to occur at the same time and place, and use some sort visual aid to help you build momentum, like a calendar or a jar of paper clips. Also, reduce friction as much as possible, identify any potential barriers to your activities ahead of time, and plan friction reducers before you start your activities. List ways to make your responses easier here:

MAKE REWARDS SATISFYING:

Find ways to make your reward for completing a task or activity more satisfying. Create a list of things you enjoy doing or rewards you can incorporate in your routines and plan as many of them as possible to be paired with the goals that you seek to accomplish. List the rewards for your goals here:

IF-THEN PLANNING (PLAN B)

Pair an If-Then plan, or Plan B, with every action or goal that you make. In the worst-case scenario that you don't end up doing something that you planned, have a second-best option. If you miss your daily jog, then plan to do fifty jumping jacks inside as an alternative. List the If-Then for your goals here:

ACCOUNTABILITY TO MEASURE AND ASSESS SUCCESS

The last piece to your plan is to use accountability. Use the space here to list things you want to cover during your accountability meetings with your accountability partners.

1. What does success look like?
    a. Balance of pleasure and purpose?
    b. Am I achieving my goals in the right way, for the right intention that they were set?

2. How do I measure it?
    a. Personal/spiritual interpretation
    b. Friends/family/leaders
    c. Professionals/counselors/resources

3. How do I keep it up?
    a. Name of Accountability partner 1:
        i. Did I contact them? Circle Y/N
        ii. Time/date of regular meeting:
    b. Name of Accountability partner 2:
        i. Did I contact them? Circle Y/N
        ii. Time/date of regular meeting:
    c. Name of Accountability partner 3:
        i. Did I contact them? Circle Y/N
        ii. Time/date of regular meeting:

4. What should I do if I fall short of my routines?
    a. Reassessment
    b. If-Then Planning
    c. Self-compassion
    d. Social Support

TAKEAWAYS FROM CHAPTER 1C:

SETTING UP LIFESTYLE ROUTINES

---

1. A lifestyle routine is founded upon goals, plans, and accountability.
2. There are two types of goals: higher level and lower level. Higher level goals are intangible and value-based, while lower-level goals are more specific and achievable.
3. Overall, you should make sure the goals you set for yourself give you present pleasure but are also attached to future meaning.
4. Your plans are designed to ensure you achieve your goals. You will most likely achieve your goals if you plan them around parts of your habit loop. Plan obvious cues, attractive cravings, easy responses, and satisfying rewards to make achieving your goals a breeze.
5. Also, it is important to remember that things never go exactly as planned. That's why incorporating If-Then plans (Plan Bs) in our routines is critical—to be prepared for times when you fall off the wagon.
6. Accountability helps us change and refine our lifestyle routines to better fit our needs throughout our lives. A great way to incorporate accountability in our routines

is to have a weekly accountability meeting with other accountability partners.

7. The key parts of accountability are to identify what success means to us, how to measure it, how to keep up success, and how to reassess when we aren't successful.
8. If you are keeping up your routine, it is pretty straightforward: keep doing what you are doing, and if something is working well, don't get complacent with your routine.
9. If you fall short of achieving your goals or sticking to your routine, then with the help of your accountability partners, make sure that you reassess your routines and incorporate more If-Then planning, self-compassion, and social support.

MATERIALS LIST FROM CHAPTER 1C:

SETTING UP LIFESTYLE ROUTINES

- Journal or notebook to write down your goals
- Calendars you can hang on your wall or put on your desk to track your habits. Search "habit tracker" on Amazon or Etsy for some great options like a reusable acrylic habit tracker that I hang on my wall (for Plans Step 2: Make It Obvious)
- A jar and paperclips to keep track of habits
- Posters, sticky notes, or construction paper to create visual cues of your goals
- Markers or colored pencils to design these visual cues

CHAPTER 1D:

INTRODUCTION TO THE EXERCISES SECTION

―

Now that we know the basics on how to build a happiness lifestyle routine, let's now add some activities in. In Sections 2–5, we will be going into specific activities in relation to different spheres that are foundations of our mental well-being and happiness. These are all critical to achieve a life of well-being.

Each of these spheres corresponds to a critical area related to our well-being and also corresponds to a chapter of activities on it. Section 2 will be on the mind, being aware of and healthily managing our thought processes to hardwire our brains to be happy. Section 3 will be taking care of our bodies in the right way to create an optimal balance and environment for our brains to create happy chemicals. Section 4 will cover how we can enrich our immediate relationships, which are often considered the most influential factors over our happiness. Finally, Section 5 will cover how we can use our roles in the communities and groups that we are part of to find purpose and meaning and also help others to improve their well-being.

Spheres of Influence

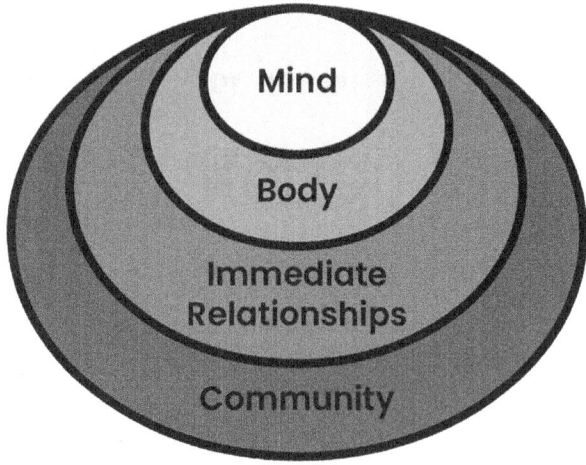

Throughout this book, we will discuss these different spheres of influence on our well-being.

Each of these sections will begin with an overview of the research associated with the activities that we list, challenges commonly confronted in these areas, then a list of activities that can help overcome these challenges. At the end of the chapter, you will have the option to select from these activities to add to your lifestyle routines based on certain criteria, which we have mentioned in Chapter 1c.

THE ACTIVITIES

The activities included in all of these sections are designed for you to take advantage of the ability for your brain to change via neuroplasticity. Like with the taxi drivers in London, we want you to exercise positive habits so you can have a healthy and firm mind.

However, in the same way that muscles become strong with exercise and also disintegrate and become weak without exercise, your brain can also lose its ability to have lasting neuroplastic change without consistent and regular exercise.

Think about it this way: If the taxi drivers weren't depending on their memory of directions and London streets as their source of living, do you think they would have gone out of their way to really build up the structural change in their hippocampi? Probably not. They had to build up these mental abilities because their lives literally depended on it. In the same way, you need to realize that your life literally depends on this as well! Your ability, your goal to live the happiest life possible, depends on the way that you can build your mind and make long lasting changes to your brain. Your standard of living depends on your ability to build up the discipline to regularly work on your mental conditioning.

Some of these activities will have simple versions that are two minutes or less to do, and some will have longer versions. You can pick whichever activities you think you will enjoy the most and be most helpful to you, and you can incorporate them into your lifestyle routines. Some of them will also have ideas on how to strengthen cues, cravings, responses, and rewards. I'm going to leave it up to you to come up with creative ways to make sure that you keep strengthen cues, cravings, responses, and rewards for your lifestyle routines.

TAKEAWAYS FROM CHAPTER 1D:

INTRODUCTION TO THE EXERCISES SECTION

---

1. The next sections, 2–5, will be where the rubber will meet the road where we can learn specific activities to do on a regular basis.
2. Section 2 is on activities for our minds, Section 3 is on activities for our bodies, Section 4 is on activities for our immediate relationships, and Section 5 is about activities for our communities.
3. It is critical we do these activities because they will help us change our brains in the same way that the London taxi drivers changed their brains.
4. You can pick and choose which activities you think will be the best for you, and you can plan simple versions of them into your lifestyle routines.

SECTION 2: EXERCISES FOR THE MIND

Like we learned about in previous chapters, this is the first section where we can learn about the activities that we can plan in our lifestyle routines to help us achieve our goals and improve our well-being levels. Our focus in this section is to build the brain to be a powerful center of our well-being and to overcome the many challenges that we face.

There are many psychological stressors young people both in and out of the church face today. Examples of stressors that many young people today face include challenges such as materialism, comparison, loneliness, instant gratification, hedonism, body shaming, bullying, and negativity. Many of these challenges are magnified by the influence of media and the digital age. More than ever before, young people today are bombarded by a wide variety of images and messages. These can take the form of advertisements, social media feeds, TV shows, movies, and music videos, to name a few.

Extensive research on the effects of these media forms has shown that that these messages subconsciously tell media consumers messages like "you aren't popular enough, beautiful enough, rich enough, smart enough, thin enough, strong enough, or cool enough." [71]

Many psychological studies have shown that repeated exposure to different messages can cause the target of these messages to actually believe these messages. The constant exposure to these messages can change the structure of your brain and literally create a new thinking pathway that defaults to these messages, telling yourself over and over again negative things like "you aren't good enough." That is one reason why in 2019, a study has shown that in the US, suicide rates among young adults and teens were the highest they have ever been.[72]

This section will be a first step of investing in mental health and well-being. Just like everyone has physical health and benefits from improvements to their physical health, everyone has levels of mental health and benefits from improving their mental health. If you are embarrassed to work on your mental health, that's okay, you're normal. I still sometimes feel embarrassed about talking about meeting a counselor or working on my mental health. Just know this stigma shouldn't exist—it is only right that people should work on

---

[71] Carol Vidal et al., "Social Media Use and Depression in Adolescents: A Scoping Review," *International Review of Psychiatry (Abingdon, England)* 32, no. 3 (May 2020): 235–53.

[72] Melissa Healy, "Suicide Rates for U.S. Teens and Young Adults Are the Highest on Record – Los Angeles Times," *The Los Angeles Times*, accessed November 9, 2020.

their happiness, and we can all help get rid of this stigma against working on your mental health in this section on the mind.

This section begins on the "Mind" sphere, which is the first sphere of influence in our well-being. Here is a picture of the diagram, showing that this section is going to focus on exercises for the mind and also showing how the mind is the center of all of the spheres that are influential to our happiness. The internal sphere is step one to mastering the different spheres of influence. We first need to master our thoughts and our minds before we can move on to working on other areas of our lives. Once you "cleanse the inner vessel," you will find it much easier to move on to work on the next spheres in our lives.

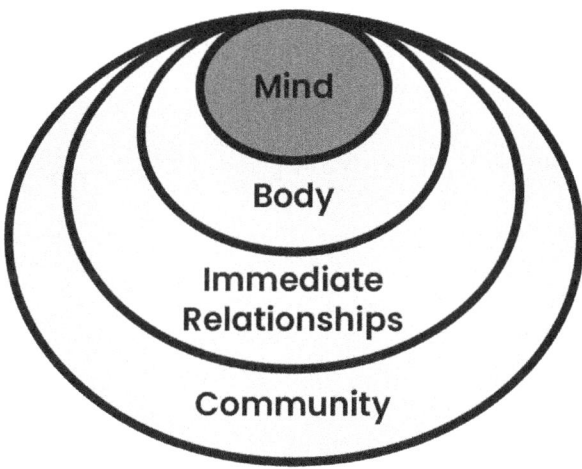

The first chapter of this section, Chapter 2a, will tell us more about the internal challenges all of our brains face, called biases, and will lead us into activities on fighting against these biases through rewiring our brains to think clearly and accurately in Chapter 2b. The third chapter, 2c, is going to tell us about the variety of challenges to our happiness balance and will tell us how to reach a good balance of pleasure and meaning. Chapter 2d will be a special chapter on spirituality, where we will learn about the crossover between what we learn in Gospel study and positive psychology, and how to use spiritual strength to improve our well-being.

CHAPTER 2A:

OUR BIASED BRAINS

In Disney's animated film *Meet the Robinsons*, the viewer is taken on a flashback to the childhood of Michael Yagoobian, the main villain of the film.

The scene shows the young villain, nicknamed "Goob," walking down the hall with a sullen expression as he is enthusiastically greeted by his classmates, with one complimenting his binder and another inviting him to come over to his house after school. Goob ignores his classmates and continues walking down the hall. The adult Michael Yagoobian narrates the flashback scene, saying the other kids at school "all hated me."

This scene has a somewhat comic effect on the viewer, as they see that it is clear his classmates did not hate him, and it was a total misconception by the young villain.

However, this scene holds a lot of shocking truth. In the same way Goob was very far off in his perception that others had of him, people (and young people especially) are naturally off in the ways they view their thoughts, themselves, circumstances, people, or life events. These errors in our ways of thinking are known as biases. The particular bias that Goob had when he thought his relationships were far worse than they actually were is an example of negativity bias. We'll get more into the types of biases that are interfering with your well-being, but negativity bias is one of the big challenges we will be working against.

The moral of the story is that our brains are biased, which means we can often convince ourselves that something is true, even though it may not be. This ability of our brains to be biased can be dangerous, especially if you are telling yourself things that can be limiting your happiness. We are often our worst critics, which is a strong reason why negative thinking can lead to diminished feelings of self-worth and other psychological challenges like depression. Like Goob, we might think that everyone hates us much more or loves us much less than they actually do, and what seems like the truth to us can be very far off from what the truth actually is. We will go into these topics in more depth in this chapter, but just know these are areas everyone struggles with.

Our goal in this chapter is to learn about areas where we are often off in our thoughts and perceptions of ourselves and find ways to healthily resolve them. Like I mentioned in the introduction, the goal is to identify healthy thinking patterns and reinforce them and identify not-so-healthy thinking patterns and weaken them.

THE NEGATIVITY BIAS
Often, our brains can be overly negative toward ourselves in a misperception known as the negativity bias. While I think the negativity bias is probably the top priority to work on for

young people, you should be aware of many other biases as well. There are problems with being extreme in any direction; for example, a positivity bias could be negative if you are completely disregarding any negative events in life. Also, there are things we already discussed, such as the impact bias or the illusion of control bias, that are important to make sure we address. Some other important biases to keep in mind are putting an overemphasis on past, present, or future events and also having misperceptions such as trying to read others' minds.

We will touch on ways to overcome these challenges, but just know we all need to beware of a wide spectrum of challenges. These are all things we can work against and develop abilities to overcome, but usually the priority is fighting too much negativity. Let's learn a little more about it.

In *Hardwiring Happiness* by Rick Hanson, Dr. Hanson outlines how our brain is hardwired to have a negativity bias.[73] This means our brains are naturally more likely to think about the negative side of things.

It's first important to see how our brains work. Let's review the relationship between the limbic system and prefrontal cortex. When dealing with (stimuli things in your environment that your brain has to process such as a friendly face, a source of danger, a text message, etc.), your brain reacts using a combination of two areas of the brain: the limbic system (fast reaction) and the prefrontal cortex (slow reaction).

---

[73] Rick Hanson, "Hardwiring Happiness FAQs," *Dr. Rick Hanson* (blog), accessed November 25, 2020.

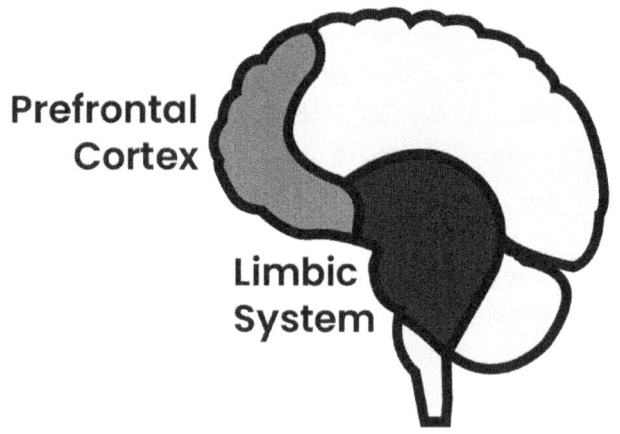

The limbic system, also known as the paleomammalian cortex, is a part of the brain that reacts quickly to stimuli.[74] I call it the "fast reaction" part because it is the part that rapidly reacts to threats and stimuli. It is called the "paleomammalian cortex," the ancient mammal part of the brain, because it is very similar in structure and function to other less-advanced mammals.[75] Basically, this part of the brain is our primitive "animal brain." It responds quickly to stimuli and is responsible for basic functions like driving us to eat when hungry and choosing to fight, flight, or freeze when faced with danger.[76] This part of our brain is critical for survival, but some parts of it are not necessary for survival as a human living in the twenty-first century.

---

[74] Andreas Komninos, "Our Three Brains – The Emotional Brain," The Interaction Design Foundation, accessed November 25, 2020.
[75] Ibid.
[76] Ibid.

The prefrontal cortex, or the slow reaction part of the brain, is what makes us different from the less-advanced mammals. This "executive" area of the brain controls rational thought and helps us separate between good and bad.[77] This area of the brain is what helps us realize what is actually a threat to our lives and what isn't.

In prehistoric times, the limbic system needed to constantly look for negatives: a lion in the field near you, a hostile member of your tribe, etc. This is what kept you alive. However, in the twenty-first century, our brains do not need to look for life-threatening threats nearly as often as we needed to in the past. But this doesn't change the fact that our brains still naturally try to screen out for negative things. This is why in 2001, psychologist Roy Baumeister found that people pay more attention to angry faces than to happy faces.[78] When someone glares at you, you are more likely to focus on angry ones than happy ones.

Unfortunately, in today's times, this can work to our disadvantage. Our brains are wired to focus more on the negatives than the positives in things. An example is if you're having a text conversation with a friend, and amidst a positive conversation, your friend mentions something critical about you. Most likely, you would remember the piece of criticism better than any positive pieces.

---

[77] Robert Morecraft, "Prefrontal Cortex – an Overview," ScienceDirect Topics, accessed October 3, 2020.

[78] Roy F. Baumeister, Kathleen D. Vohs, C. Nathan DeWall, Liqing Zhang. "How Emotion Shapes Behavior: Feedback, Anticipation, and Reflection, Rather Than Direct Causation – 2007," accessed November 11, 2020.

The negativity bias can be manifested in your life in many ways, through forms like social comparison, catastrophizing, black-and-white thinking, and mind reading. We will describe these challenges in detail with specific solutions in the next section, but let's talk a bit more about how this works in your brain.

Like we mentioned, the limbic system in our brain works much faster than the slower prefrontal cortex, which makes the response much more automatic and can make us overfocus on the negative. The amount that people focus on negative things can vary from person to person. This can be seen in what Dr. Hanson refers to as the "happy amygdala" and the "sad amygdala."[79] The amygdala is the portion of the limbic system responsible for emotional responses, and the sad vs. happy amygdala refer to how some people naturally have sad amygdalae, which are more prone to focus on negative stimuli (and therefore respond more often with stress and anxiety) as opposed to happy amygdalae, which are more optimistic and focus more on opportunities than difficulties.[80]

There are many reasons people can have sad amygdalae, and these can be both due to genetic presets and environmental influences on our lives. If you read this and say, "Oh great, I have a sad amygdala, tough luck," wait—there's hope! You can relearn how to have a happy amygdala. We will first talk about how we can overcome this using the concept of neuroplasticity.

---

[79] Rick Hanson, "Hardwiring Happiness FAQs," *Dr. Rick Hanson* (blog), accessed November 25, 2020.
[80] Ibid.

THERE'S HOPE: NEUROPLASTICITY

Like we mentioned in Section 1, your brain has the amazing ability to change itself through this process of neuroplasticity. In this process, you can literally change the structure of your brain in the same way that the taxi drivers changed the structures of their brains through their process. To combat our negative brains and our sad amygdalae, we must rewire the structure of our brains to be more positive by doing more positive activities later on in this section.

Before we get to the activities, however, I want to list out some benefits to having a positively rewired brain. Not only are the following benefits very interesting, but I hope these benefits will help motivate you enough to do these exercises so you can have the benefits of these exercises in your own lives.

BENEFITS TO POSITIVITY

Positive thinking has a myriad of benefits. By trying to rewire your brain to be more positive, you can see results that spread to all areas of life, including improved physical health, energy, immunity, improved relationships, improved performance in academics and careers, and an overall happier life. Some studies show that optimism even reduces the risk of heart attack by 35 percent.[81]

BECOMING MORE LUCKY

In terms of academics and careers, the following study shows how those who perceive themselves as "lucky" were far more likely to notice and take advantage of positive life

---

[81] Lisa Rapaport, "Optimism Tied to Lower Rates of Heart Attacks, Death," *Reuters*, accessed November 12, 2020.

events, compared to those who did not perceive themselves as lucky. Dr. Richard Wiseman ran a study consisting of a group of participants that labeled themselves as lucky and a group of participants that labeled themselves as unlucky.[82] Their job was to go through the newspaper and count the number of photographs in it. On average, the people who called themselves unlucky took around two minutes to count the photographs, while the people who called themselves lucky took only a few seconds. Why was this? Because the lucky people were able to see a message on the second page that said, "Stop counting—There are 43 photographs in this newspaper." This message took up half of the page and was written in type that was over two inches high. There was also another message halfway through the newspaper that said, "Stop counting, tell the experimenter you have seen this and win $250." Again, the unlucky people missed this message because they were still too busy looking for photographs. Wiseman believes this is due to the fact that personality tests show that unlucky people are generally much more tense and anxious than lucky people, and research has shown that anxiety disrupts people's ability to notice the unexpected.[83]

This is due to something known as the attentional spotlight, which means positive people tend to pay more attention to positive opportunities than negative people, influencing them to be more likely to capitalize on positive events in their lives than unlucky people. Basically, just thinking or

---

[82] Austin Fabel, "The Research Backed Guide to Being Lucky," Medium, February 26, 2018.
[83] Michael Shermer, "As Luck Would Have It," Scientific American, accessed November 11, 2020.

believing you are a lucky person subconsciously awakens your mind to look for more opportunities or "lucky" things.

However, on the converse, those who think of themselves as being "unlucky" will frequently miss amazing opportunities placed right in front of their noses, for the simple fact that their brains are hardwired to ignore lucky opportunities and instead look for misfortunes. If you think of yourself as an unlucky person, you will likely experience more misfortune, and if you think of yourself as a lucky person, you will likely find more lucky opportunities.

Su'a says, "What you feed grows. This is a principle of the mind. Where you choose to put your thoughts will have a tremendous impact on your performance, so choose wisely. Train your mind to find the diamonds in the rough, look for possibilities, and focus on solutions. If you want to start changing what you do, start changing what you think."[84]

OVERCOMING CHALLENGES THROUGH INCREASING FRUSTRATION TOLERANCE AND RESILIENCE

One other benefit to optimism is developing resilience to trials, also known as frustration tolerance. You can develop high frustration tolerance by choosing to act instead of giving up in the face of trials.

With the negativity bias, we naturally default to having low frustration tolerance (LFT). This is when you entertain a lot of irrational, pessimistic thoughts in the face of trials. If our

---

[84] Justin Su'a, *Mentally Tough Teens: Developing a Winning Mindset*, First Edition (Springville, UT: Plain Sight Publishing, 2014), chap. 1, Kindle.

frustration tolerance is low, we prematurely give up when we confront roadblocks, convincing ourselves it is impossible to attain the goals we are working on.

This is in contrast to high frustration tolerance (HFT), which is a characteristic of optimism. When we develop a high frustration tolerance, every time we hit a roadblock, we keep working and trying new solutions until we find one that gets us through the barrier.

Developing high frustration tolerance is an excellent way to increase your well-being levels so you are able to develop an optimistic approach to negative events, and learning to be more optimistic will improve our frustration tolerance.

LEARNING OPTIMISM

If you think you are naturally more of a pessimist (as many of us are), don't fret, because in line with the process of neuroplasticity, there is a large branch of research supporting a concept known as "learned optimism." Dr. Martin Seligman, the previously mentioned founder of positive psychology, pioneered the field with his research on learned helplessness and learned optimism.[85] With his studies on dogs learning to give up when faced with difficult tasks, he showed that animals and humans have the ability to learn pessimism and also learn optimism.[86] We can use this knowledge to be careful of not learning to be pessimistic, but instead to focus on positivity.

---

[85] Courtney Ackerman, "Learned Helplessness: Seligman's Theory of Depression (+ Cure)," PositivePsychology.com, March 24, 2018.
[86] Ibid.

The next chapter will teach us the activities that we can do to allow us to learn optimism and hardwire positivity in our brains.

TAKEAWAYS FROM CHAPTER 2A:

OUR BIASED BRAINS

1. Our brains can influence us to see things that are different from reality, often showing things in a more negative light than they really are.
2. Our brains are biased toward negativity in part because of evolutionary advantages to pay high attention to negative things in our environment, and also because the limbic system in our brains (that reacts to negative things) acts more quickly than the rational prefrontal cortex of our brains.
3. The amount that our brains are biased toward the negative can vary, but the important thing to realize is that no matter how negatively biased your brain is, you can begin rewiring your brain by incorporating positivity activities in your life.
4. A positive mindset can improve almost all aspects of life, increasing your ability to overcome challenges and even experience more luck in your life.
5. You can learn optimism through these activities in the next chapter.

CHAPTER 2B:

REWIRING OUR BRAINS AGAINST BIAS

Dr. Rick Hanson suggests doing a variety of activities to work against negative biases we have in our thought processes.[87] In order to rewire our brains and work against our innate biases and cognitive distortions, the first thing to do is to become aware of our thoughts. Once we are aware of our thoughts, we can then manage them. The two main approaches I would like to share are cognitive behavioral therapy (CBT) and acceptance and commitment therapy (ACT). These two approaches both teach us how to become more aware of our thoughts and how unhelpful thoughts can affect us, but they differ in the way they teach us to manage our thoughts.

Dr. Brett Merrill, a counselor specialized in working with young church member students at BYU Counseling and Psychological Services, told me his take on both of these

---

[87] Rick Hanson, "Hardwiring Happiness FAQs," *Dr. Rick Hanson* (blog), accessed November 25, 2020.

approaches. CBT teaches us how our thoughts, feelings, and actions are connected, and when these thoughts are unhelpful or negatively biased, it can teach us how to challenge these thoughts, with the end result of changing our behavior. Merrill says that because of the vast amount of research that supports it, his graduate training emphasized CBT. CBT is a recommended approach for working with a range of emotional and behavioral problems such as depression, anxiety, and phobias, as research supports CBT's effectiveness against these sorts of challenges. Merrill used this approach frequently when working with teenagers in substance abuse programs, as it is effective for skill building and changing unwanted behaviors. He uses CBT for more straightforward concerns such as depression or anxiety.

ACT is a newer "third wave" therapy approach that Merrill and many of the other BYU counselors use when dealing with BYU students. Like CBT, it also teaches us to be aware of our thoughts, but it is different in the sense that instead of fighting or feeling guilty for our thoughts, ACT teaches us to embrace our thoughts and build psychological flexibility. This is done by responding to unhelpful thoughts in an exploratory manner using mindfulness and learning how to direct our attention to the present moment. ACT is popular in use when working with young people who do not have serious pathology. This includes people who are not struggling with clear diagnoses such as relationship or sexual concerns, and for people who work well with thinking abstractly and dealing with metaphors.

Both Merrill and many experts in the field do not say that one approach is better than another or that one conflicts with another. Merrill tends to keep both styles separate and allows the student he meets with to select the method to use. He asks the student, "There are two evidence-supported ways to approach this concern. One is to find ways to think more rationally about the concern, and the other is to learn how to tolerate discomfort, while finding ways to align our values with our actions. Both work very well. Do you have a preference on which direction we take in here?"

The effectiveness and usefulness of both CBT and ACT are found across different psychological disciplines. Martha Knudson, the executive director of the Utah State Bar Well-Being Committee, says that a hybrid approach of both techniques can be useful depending on the circumstance. She states that telling CBT-style affirmations to yourself can be very helpful, but "if you know that your affirmations are BS, then using an ACT-based approach of accepting the way you are might be more helpful to yourself."

Su'a also mentions that both CBT and ACT have their own uses, and he states that it is a matter of preference whether one is used or not. He states that if you think to yourself, "I'm stupid," it can be helpful to immediately combat against it and tell yourself you aren't stupid. However, for other people, it might be more beneficial to approach your thought like you are viewing a cloud in the sky, telling yourself, "Oh, that's interesting, I'm having a thought that I'm stupid." For Su'a and his clients, he believes the approaches he uses are up to personal decision.

The most important thing to realize from both of these approaches is that you are separate from your thoughts, and your thoughts do not control you. While CBT teaches you to dispute negative thoughts and ACT teaches you to investigate them in your mind, both teach you to disconnect yourself from them and realize that the thoughts are not in control of your behavior.

Now that we've learned about both types, we will do activities from both of these types of approaches, and when you use them, you can decide which of them work best for you. Whichever approach you decide is best for you, the first step for both of the processes is to get a clear picture of what thoughts are helpful and what thoughts aren't helpful.

IDENTIFYING UNHELPFUL THOUGHTS AND TYPES

Dr. Paula Nagel, an educational psychologist and author of *The Mental Health and Wellbeing Workout for Teens,* states that some of the most unhelpful thought types that young people face today are social comparison, catastrophizing, black-and-white thinking, personalization, mind reading, and emotional reasoning.[88] In addition to these, I am also going to add a couple other challenges that other experts recommend managing.

SOCIAL COMPARISON

Comparing yourself to others is a normal and natural thing, but it becomes unhelpful when we only look at the negatives of ourselves in comparison to others and make unrealistic and unfair comparisons (like comparing yourself to celebrities). When you leave these kinds of thoughts unchecked,

---

[88] Paula Nagel, *The Mental Health and Wellbeing Workout for Teens : Skills and Exercises from ACT and CBT for Healthy Thinking,* First (London, UK: Jessica Kingsley Publishers, 2019), chap. 2, Kindle.

your mental health levels can decrease, and you can find yourself feeling as if you aren't good enough.

CATASTROPHIZING

Bad things happen to everybody, and sometimes being proactive about these and planning for these ahead of time can be a wise thing to do. However, your thoughts can be a problem if you think about most situations ending in the worst-case scenario. This is a prime example of the negativity bias, where you become fixated on the chance that things will end in catastrophe. You will know it's a problem when you overestimate the likelihood that something bad will happen, and you underestimate your ability to cope with the negative effects of something bad that happens.

BLACK-AND-WHITE THINKING

This is also known as all-or-nothing thinking because it doesn't allow room for any other possibilities. Sometimes, it makes decision-making simple to think of things in black-and-white terms, but this is not a healthy way to approach all aspects of life. For example, if you fail a test, black-and-white thinking tells you that because you failed the test, you must be a failure and will never be a success.

NEGATIVE FILTERING

Negative filtering happens when you look at the world through "gloomy goggles" and only filter out the negative things from all the positive things around you. For example, if someone gives you a compliment, you might think, "She's only saying that because she feels sorry for me."

PERSONALIZATION

This is also called over-owning it because you take ownership over all the bad things that occur in events. You know this is a problem if you hear yourself saying things like, "This is all my fault," "I'm to blame," or "Why me?"

MIND READING

Mind reading is a cognitive fallacy many of us do too often. Mind reading is when we assume we know what other people are thinking. Since none of us actually have the superpower to be able to read others' minds, we are often wrong in what we assume other people are thinking. Goob, from the story at the beginning of the chapter, showed us a prime example of doing unhelpful mind reading when he assumed that every other kid in the hall hated him. You will know your mind reading is unhelpful if you realize you are always second guessing what other people think, you replay interactions with others over and over, or you quickly jump to conclusions about other people.

EMOTIONAL REASONING

Emotions are a very important part of our lives, and being in touch with them is very healthy. However, when our emotions take control, it can stop us from being able to look at all aspects of an event. When you have feelings that give you permission to do things that you wouldn't rationally do, that could be telling you that you are emotionally reasoning.

RUMINATION

Thinking about challenges is normal, but when you think about negative things in an endless loop that never gets resolved, this is an unhelpful thought process known as rumination. Think of rumination as being like a cow that never stops chewing on the same chunk of grass, over and over. While we might think that endlessly thinking about the same thing over and over will help us resolve our challenges, it is actually worse for us to continue dwelling on these things.

PERCEIVED LONELINESS

It turns out that loneliness is more subjective than objective: Hawkley and Cacioppo tell us about the threat of perceived loneliness on our mental well-being.[89] In their study, they found that one of the largest challenges that we face as young adults and teenagers is much more about our perceived loneliness—how lonely we think we are—compared to how lonely we actually are. For example, an eighty-six-year-old lady that lives alone with a couple cats may feel less lonely than a fifteen-year-old boy that interacts with dozens of people his same age every day. When you feel lonely even though you are constantly interacting with others, you may be a victim of perceived loneliness.

STRESS AND FEAR

Stress and fear are natural responses by our limbic system and our negativity bias. We've all had times when we were afraid of looking bad, messing up, not doing well on a test, talking to someone you like, or disappointing your parents. Stress and fear are normal in small amounts, but they become unhelpful when they cause you to freeze instead of act.

---

[89] Louise C. Hawkley and John T. Cacioppo, "Loneliness Matters: A Theoretical and Empirical Review of Consequences and Mechanisms," *Annals of Behavioral Medicine: A Publication of the Society of Behavioral Medicine* 40, no. 2 (October 2010).

Now that we have discussed a variety of negatively biased thoughts, let's practice tracking these. After learning how to identify times when we think in unfair and unhelpful ways, we can then use several strategies later on in the chapter to replace these thoughts with positive thoughts.

BUILDING AWARENESS THROUGH WRITING AND JOURNALING
The first thing to do with managing your thoughts is to be aware of them, and the best way is to look at them from afar. Talking out loud to yourself or to someone else is a good way to do this. Another way we can do this is by writing and journaling. Su'a stated that journaling is important because it helps you look at your thoughts, not through your thoughts. Writing about yourself and your feelings has been shown in numerous studies to benefit health, emotional adjustment, and well-being.[90] Writing about yourself can help you enhance your emotional regulation skills because it gives you an opportunity to learn more about yourself and have insight into and restructure your priorities, motivations, and values. This can help you put your life experiences and goals into a healthy pattern and help you realize you have a sense of control over your life.

ACTIVITY 2.1: IDENTIFYING UNHELPFUL THOUGHTS
Jack, a young church member, said his therapist suggested he list thoughts and thought processes throughout the day and pay attention to any thoughts that are inaccurate, or give you permission to do something that goes against your morals. These are what you can identify as unhelpful

---

[90] Harvard Health Publishing, "Writing about Emotions May Ease Stress and Trauma," Harvard Health, accessed November 20, 2020.

thoughts that you can work on. So, here are the simple steps to doing this:

1. Schedule a day to do this activity.
2. Get a small notepad and pen that can fit in your pocket or create a new note on your phone.
3. Throughout the day, list as many thoughts as you can notice. If by the end of the day you haven't written much down, it's okay to just write in one big chunk. Write down some of the biggest things on your mind. Don't worry about spelling or grammar, just write as much as you can. Write down your worries, your concerns, your aspirations, and anything else you can think of. If you find yourself struggling to write your feelings down, try writing with your non-dominant hand.
4. After you are done with this list, read through the notes that you took and mark the unhelpful thoughts. These are the types of thoughts that we covered previously, or in general are inaccurate or overly negative. For example, take notes of times that you say, "I'm stupid" or "I'm worthless."
5. Keep these lists, as these are the thoughts that we will learn how to manage in the next activity. These are the kinds of thoughts that we will be working on this chapter. Go over these with an accountability partner.

After identifying thought processes you have, the next step is to deal with them in a way that is right for you. With these lists, we can manage them first with CBT approaches such as the internal locus of control and the ABCDE method, and then we can try to manage them from an ACT mindfulness approach.

THE CBT APPROACHES: THE INTERNAL LOCUS OF CONTROL AND THE ABCDE METHOD

In order to use the ABCDE approach, we first need to decide what is within our realm of control to change and what isn't. We will do this by dissecting our list with a locus of control activity. Let's learn about the locus of control first.

INTERNAL LOCUS OF CONTROL

During an interview I had with Dr. Gary Vatcher, a marriage and family therapist who specializes in working with missionaries in the field, he shared several cognitive behavioral approaches he uses to help young people rewire their brains. The first thing he helps his clients develop is an internal locus of control. Having a clear perspective on what we can and can't control is key to overcoming control-related biases.

He stated that locus of control refers to the degree to which individuals believe they can control the events and circumstances of their lives. This concept could be looked at as a continuum going from internal locus of control to that of an external locus of control. Those who lean more toward the internal side of the continuum tend to believe they are the authors of their fate. These are people who fight their brain's negativity bias, as they are more positive about their abilities and their control over life. They don't look to others for their successes and failures in life but rather, they assume responsibility for the results they achieve, whether good or bad, based on the effort they apply to whatever it is they are working on. They generally have a strong belief in themselves and their ability to achieve their goals and overcome obstacles and challenges.

People with an internal locus of control have more of a growth than a fixed mindset. Dr. Carol Dweck, a professor of psychology and the author of *Mindset*, tells us that individuals that realize their mental state is able to grow as opposed to stay fixed are able to experience a multitude of benefits, including increasing their intelligence.[91] When we have a growth mindset, we realize that setbacks in life are not as serious as they seem, because setbacks are all opportunities that we can grow or learn from.

While it should be our goal to have a more internal locus of control (as we surprisingly have much more influence over our life than many of us think), it is also important to realize that we realistically cannot control everything in our lives. For things that are outside of our control, like traumatic events and circumstances, we can't control the fact that they occur, but we can accept the events and take control of the way we react to them. This is what we want to focus on: building our locus of control internally, and then using this to change the structures of our brains.

The concept of the locus of control is well illustrated by the Alcoholics Anonymous Serenity Prayer which states:

> God, grant me the serenity to accept the things
> I cannot change,
> Courage to change the things I can,
> And wisdom to know the difference.[92]

---

[91] Mindset Works, "The Growth Mindset – What Is Growth Mindset – Mindset Works," Mindset Works, accessed November 20, 2020.

[92] Reinhold Niebuhr, "Serenity Prayer," Celebrate Recovery, accessed November 23, 2020.

As the Serenity Prayer states, our goal is to be able to discern what we can change and can't change, accept things we can't change, and do our best to change the things you have control over. The degree to which we have an internal locus of control is very much related to the way we think and the actions we take in response to our thoughts. Every time we recognize a negative thought and combat it, we strengthen our internal locus of control. Basically, we prove to ourselves that we have influence over thoughts in our heads to combat unhelpful thoughts and strengthen helpful thoughts.

The key is to learn to identify when our beliefs are rational or irrational, as irrational beliefs are not only unhelpful, but they immobilize us and stop us from being able to act. Conversely, healthy or rational thoughts tend to lead us to proactive behavior. If we believe in ourselves and the fact that we can accomplish much more than we think, it becomes easy to motivate ourselves to take action on our goals.

Also, having "wisdom to know the difference" between what we can change and what we can't change is very important. In *Mentally Tough Teens*, Justin Su'a tells us to focus on what we can control. He says, "It's easy to get caught up in who's bigger, stronger, faster, smarter, or better looking than you. The key is to focus on what you can control. You'll never be able to change other people, so instead of worrying about them, focus on yourself. Create the habits you need to be successful in the future. Strive to give your best effort. These things are always in your control."[93]

---

[93] Justin Su'a, *Mentally Tough Teens: Developing a Winning Mindset*, First Edition (Springville, UT: Plain Sight Publishing, 2014), chap. 1, Kindle.

There will be times when you rationally can't control things. Usually, the problem is that we don't believe in ourselves enough or understand how much we can actually do. We will all lose, experience pain, deal with unfriendly people, and feel lonely. You might have bad teachers, coaches, or parents, but when you take the responsibility on ourselves and have a can-do mindset, we are able to take advantage of our internal locus of control. When you face situations like these, rather than complaining about circumstances or life events, you can practice accepting them and then focus on working on what you can control.

ACTIVITY 2.2: IDENTIFYING WITH AN INTERNAL LOCUS OF CONTROL

1. Get your lists of thoughts from Activity 2.1.
2. Go back through your lists (if you can do this with a partner, great!) and identify things that you have control over and what you don't have control over from both your helpful and unhelpful thoughts. You should now have a total of four lists. Remember, you can do much more about things than you think. All the things that are within your control can tell you that you have an internal locus of control. Before you quickly throw things into the "outside of your control" list, see if you are playing the blame game. See if there are things that you have influence over and use your maturity and character to take responsibility over them.
3. Helpful thoughts within your control are activities you can use to make goals and plans to achieve them (reference back to the section on goals to see how to set them), and things outside of your control are things that you will make goals and plans to learn how to accept.

4. Unhelpful thoughts that are within your control are thoughts we will dispute in the ABCDE activity. We will make goals and plans for unhelpful thoughts that are outside of our control.

STRATEGIES TO DISPUTE NEGATIVE THOUGHTS

As we discussed in the previous chapter, our brains are wired to be negatively biased. Here are some strategies to help us manage negative thoughts to learn optimism and begin regularly hardwiring positivity in your brain.

ABCDE MODEL

The ABCDE model is a way to learn optimism by disputing irrational thoughts. Martin Seligman developed this model after Ellis's ABC model.[94] The original ABC model is a way to become aware of negative thoughts, by helping you identify the thought's activating event (A), beliefs related to that thought (B), and the consequential feelings and behavior (C). To the ABC model, Seligman adds disputation (D) and energization (E).

Disputation centers on generating evidence to counter negative beliefs in general, or the causes and implications of an event. Disputation also means reminding yourself of any potential usefulness of moving on from the adversity. For example, if someone cut you off while you were driving, you can dispute a negative thought toward the driver by telling yourself, "I am overreacting. I don't know what situation he is in. Maybe he is on his way to his daughter's piano recital

---

[94] Habits for Wellbeing, "Learned Helplessness and the ABCDE Model," accessed November 20, 2020.

and is running late. I'm sure I have cut people off before without meaning to, so I should really cut him a break. I am not in a hurry anyway."

Over time, responding with the ABCDE model will change your feelings to be more hopeful and positive. Successful disputation leads to energization, the E in the ABCDE model. After successfully disputing a negative thought, you will be energized, and you should actively celebrate the positive feelings and sense of accomplishment from overcoming a negative belief.

If you can practice this skill early in your life, you will better deal with adversity you will encounter as you get older. The repeated practice of ABCDE will change your brain's structure and thinking pattern to ingrain optimism in you, and pretty soon it will be automatic to think positively instead of in our negatively biased ways. Here is the exercise you can incorporate into your lifestyle routine:

ACTIVITY 2.3: ABCDE MODEL FOR DISPUTING NEGATIVE OR IRRATIONAL BELIEFS

Next time you recognize a negative thought, try this exercise. It is easiest to do this writing down on a worksheet (you can use the space below for practice or download some worksheets from www.firmnessofmind.com) or in your journal. It is an excellent idea to go through these steps with a partner.

A = **A**ctivating event (e.g., your friend doesn't want to hang out with you):

B = **B**eliefs related to activating event (e.g., "I am a worthless person"):

C = **C**onsequential feeling and behavior (e.g., you feel depressed and lack desire to do anything):

D = **D**isputing the irrational beliefs (e.g., "This belief is absurd! I am worthy of love and friendship. There are many examples of times that I am loved and worthy. It is better that I don't worry about this belief so I can get on with finding another friend to hang out with or a different activity I can enjoy."):

E = **Energization** (savor the good feeling of successfully disputing a thought and celebrate this achievement!):

Repeat this exercise as often as necessary, especially at times when you feel like you are overwhelmed by negative thoughts and feelings.

A key principle to remember is that the ABCDE model only works if you believe your disputations. As Martha Knudson stated, giving yourself BS affirmations will not be effective. If you find that you are trying to convince yourself of something completely unbelievable (use the help of a friend, family member, or counselor to see if this is really true), then it is something you need to learn to accept. The ABCDE model might now work well if you are denying reality by disputing something that is rational.

STRATEGIES TO ACCEPT NEGATIVE THOUGHTS USING THE ACT MINDFULNESS APPROACH
Sometimes when we have negative thoughts or feelings, a useful approach is to learn how to accept them as opposed to disputing them. This can work well for thoughts and feelings that we don't want to challenge, such as thoughts that we realize are true. Also, positivity can only go so far when we refuse to fully feel our full spectrum of emotions.

When I asked Dr. Tal Ben-Shahar about choosing to only feel our positive emotions, he told me, "It is unhealthy to suppress painful emotions and only entertain positive emotions. This is toxic and in the long run will lead to much unhappiness. The key to happiness is first allowing in unhappiness."

I understand if you are confused because I started out telling you that you should dispute negative thoughts and feelings and now it seems like I'm telling you to do the opposite, to accept your negative thoughts and feelings. The difference lies in the fact that you want to dispute negative thoughts that have occurred because of false or irrational beliefs. When you have negative thoughts that occur because of things that may be true, acknowledging them is alright. It is also very important to not suppress or numb these feelings but allow yourself to feel them and curiously inspect them. Remember, this is not me encouraging you to wallow in your negativity and throw yourself a pity party, but to fully feel your emotions to the extent that you can healthily move on from them. When deciding to what point you should dispute negative thoughts versus accepting them and allowing them to pass by naturally, the key is to try and look at your thoughts as clearly as possible. This can be done by speaking your thoughts out loud, writing them on paper, or talking to a loved one or professional.

In the case you discover that you want to try an acceptance and commitment (ACT) approach to negative thoughts and feelings, here are some things to keep in mind. We can realize that our thoughts may or may not be true, important, or wise, and that we don't have to obey or be afraid of our thoughts, no matter how negative they may seem. Your goal is to realize that you aren't your thoughts, and thoughts are simply words or pictures that pass through your mind like cars passing by on the street.[95]

To reach this point, try the following activity:

---

[95] Russ Harris, *The Illustrated Happiness Trap*, 1st ed. (United States of America: Shambhala Publications, Inc., 2013), 97.

ACTIVITY 2.4: ACT MINDFULNESS FOR MANAGING NEGATIVE THOUGHTS AND FEELINGS

Next time that you realize you are experiencing negative thoughts or emotions, try following this process that Dr. Russ Harris suggests in his book *The Illustrated Happiness Trap*. Harris calls the combination of these three components of mindfulness, and this kind of approach can be just as effective as CBT to help with anxiety symptoms.[96] The steps in the process follow:

1. Defusion: This means you unhook yourself from unhelpful thoughts. The key in this step is to help your brain realize that the thoughts you have aren't who you are. A way you can do this is by framing your thoughts in bizarre ways to tell your brain that you are separate from your thoughts. Here are some ideas:
    a. Sing the negative thought you have to the tune of a song like "Happy Birthday" or "Oh My Darling Clementine."
    b. Imagine that a cartoon character is saying these words.
    c. Write your thoughts down in an interesting and comical font or imagine that it is written in this kind of font.
    d. Label your negative thought as a story, and tell yourself, "I see, my brain is telling myself the (insert negative thought) story again."

2. Expansion: This means you make room for unhelpful thoughts and feelings, letting them flow through you

---

[96] Lisa Rapaport, "Optimism Tied to Lower Rates of Heart Attacks, Death," *Reuters*, accessed November 12, 2020.

instead of them sweeping you away. Here are the steps to follow for expansion:
  a. Observe how the uncomfortable feelings move through your body. Are they still or moving? How deep do they go? Where are they strongest or weakest? Find the sensation that stands out the most and observe it with curiosity and openness.
  b. Take some slow, deep breaths. Breathe into and around the sensations in your body and make room for them.
  c. Allow the sensations even if you don't like them. Say "thanks, mind!" to any resistance.

3. Connection: This means that you fully live in the present instead of dwelling on the past or worrying about the future.
  a. Wake up and notice what's happening around you.
  b. Ground yourself in the present by using all of your senses to be in the moment: see the sights around you, listen to the noises around you, feel the sensations of your body sitting in your seat.

The next time you notice yourself having unhelpful or negative thoughts, this mindfulness process might be a good way for you to manage these emotions. In addition to this approach, this next section gives us a variety of other activities to learn optimism in the face of unhelpful thoughts and feelings. The following section will teach us how to rewire our brains through gratitude, cultivating optimism, and positively responding to stress, fear, and rumination.

GRATITUDE EXERCISES

Gratitude is one of the most effective ways to combat negativity. The following are ways that you can express gratitude.

ACTIVITY 2.5: GRATITUDE LETTER

One way to express gratitude is through writing a gratitude letter. There is a lot of research surrounding gratitude letters. One study showed that writing and presenting a gratitude letter to someone special can boost happiness levels for up to a month after doing it![97] Regardless if the effects last up to a month or not, it definitely can help to write a gratitude letter. First, it helps you realize how lucky you are to have benefited in so many ways from the acts of another person. Second, it helps you focus on the good things in your life vs. the negative things. Third, it strengthens your relationship with said person and helps emphasize it in a positive light. We will discuss the importance of relationships more in Section 4, but if you had to choose one thing, positive relationships with other people are perhaps the largest contributors to our happiness.

ACTIVITY 2.6: GRATITUDE JOURNAL

A gratitude journal is also an excellent way to keep track of gratitude. You can do this by writing down several things you are grateful for, whether it be friends, family, or your favorite musical artist. Dr. Sonja Lyubomirsky told a group of subjects to do the following activity:

"There are many things in our lives, large and small, that we might be grateful about. Think back over the events of the

---

[97] Sonja Lyubomirsky and Jaime Kurtz, *Positively Happy: Routes to Sustainable Happiness*, 1st ed. (United Kingdom: Positive Acorn, 2008), chap. 3, Kindle.

past week and write down on the lines below up to five things that happened for which you are grateful or thankful." [98]

Lyubomirsky had her participants do this activity either just once a week, or three times a week, over the course of six weeks. She found that those that expressed gratitude felt happier, more satisfied with life, and spent more time exercising. They also reported fewer negative physical symptoms like headaches, coughing, and nausea.[99]

In addition to writing these in a physical journal, you can download many apps that can help you keep track of gratitude on a regular basis. My favorite is an app called Happyfeed, which reminds you every night to think of three different positive events of the day. It allows you to write down something you are grateful for and provides prompts to help you think of ideas if you have trouble thinking about what to write. Finally, it allows you to share things you are grateful for with groups that you choose, whether it is your accountability partners, or friends and family. Sanvello and Daylio are also excellent apps I use that help me keep track of my feelings and write things that I am grateful for.

ACTIVITY 2.7: PRAYER OF GRATITUDE
Prayer is also an excellent way to express gratitude. When you pray, whether this is in the morning, throughout the day, before you sleep, or at church, try and focus more on things you are grateful for as opposed to things that you

---

[98] Ibid.
[99] Ibid.

are asking for. When you focus on giving thanks, you will surprise yourself at how blessed you actually are.

CULTIVATING OPTIMISM ACTIVITIES

In addition to gratitude, these are activities that help us cultivate optimism by continuously conditioning our brains with positive influences. We'll take a look at positivity exercises like the positivity ratio, affirmations and validation, the positivity box, and savoring.

THE POSITIVITY RATIO

The ratio for improvement is at least three positives to every piece of feedback, with some studies suggesting ideal ratios as high as 5.6 positives to every 1 criticism.[100] The bottom line is that humans all function best when they think they are doing well, which happens when they are given more positive feedback than negative feedback (we will talk about this again in Section 3 so you can apply this ratio in your relationships). This also applies to the way you talk to yourself: The more positive feedback you give yourself (whether in your thoughts, writing, or self-talk), the better version of yourself you will be.

Regardless of your events, you can frame the world around you to be positively uplifting by focusing on the positives. The following activities will give us ways to improve our positivity ratios. Remember to keep the ratio of positives in your life much higher than the negatives in your life.

---

[100] Jack Zenger, "The Ideal Praise-to-Criticism Ratio," *Harvard Business Review*, accessed November 20, 2020.

AFFIRMATIONS AND VALIDATION

In an interview with Dr. Luc Hansen, a BYU grad and psychiatric fellow specializing in working with adolescents overcoming mental and emotional trauma, he stated that compared to any medicine he prescribes, affirmations and validation can be just as effective or more effective in rewiring your brain. On the same topic of neuroplasticity we discussed earlier, he told me that we all have "positive tracts and negative tracts of neurons. If you experience PTSD or are depressed, these tracts become neurologically prominent. PTSD actually causes a cartilaginous buildup in the brain, creating a negative wiring of neurons. In the same way that diabetes shows physical change in the pancreas or alcoholism causes cirrhosis in the liver, there is actual scarring in the brain after mental and emotional trauma." To rewire these negatively wired tracts, we can force ourselves to exercise new positive tracts, and affirmation and validation are key ways to do this.

Dr. Gary Vatcher, the marriage and family therapist who specializes in working with missionaries, gives us guidance on how to use affirmations to fight against our brain's negativity bias. He tells us that affirmations are used to help us learn to control what we focus on. In some ways, our brain operates like a computer. The brain tends to act on whatever we program it to do based upon the thoughts and images we feed it. If we focus on negativity, the brain acts on that thinking by helping us to feel miserable, dumping a chemical called cortisol into our system. Conversely, if we control what we focus on and entertain very positive thoughts and images, the brain dumps positive chemicals, such as serotonin into our system.

While we may have a habit of looking at the negative things in life, we are not compelled to continue that pattern. We can certainly train ourselves to take control of what we feed our brains.

You can choose some of the following affirmations from Dr. Vatcher or come up with your own. If you chose to do the latter, try to begin most of your affirmations with "I …" or "I am…" Try to keep your affirmations as brief as possible. Avoid focusing on the things you are striving to overcome, but rather, focus on the outcome you intend on making happen. For example, avoid saying things such as "I am no longer overweight" and change that to "I am now healthy and fit." If you say "I am no longer overweight," the brain will continue to see a picture of you as being overweight.

One caveat about using affirmations is that your behavior must match your affirmation. For example, if you are telling yourself that you are healthy and fit, but you are eating the wrong kinds of food on a regular basis and living a very sedentary lifestyle, you will be creating a dichotomy within yourself. Your thoughts and actions won't agree with one another.

When your actions don't follow your thoughts, you create a confusing environment for your brain. The brain will tend to disregard the intended affirmation. You can clear up this confusion by doing small, attainable actions that align with your thoughts. The idea is that you begin experiencing some positive changes in your life, which will then validate the affirmation you are presenting to your brain. You are basically proving to yourself that you can accomplish whatever you set your mind to.

Memorize the affirmations that you want to instill in your brain and repeat them in your mind or out loud as often as you can throughout the day. If you say them out loud, do so with lots of vigor and energy. Even if you are just thinking them, try to imagine doing so with a great deal of enthusiasm. The brain tends to respond and act on emotion. If you say an affirmation without any emotional content, the brain will likely ignore it.

Don't be surprised if you start having thoughts such as, "These affirmations will never work or lead to any change." The brain's job is to protect you and maintain the status quo. It does not like change. According to the brain, doing anything different is a threat to your emotional stability and well-being.

Whenever you have any downtime during the day, use that time for repeating your affirmations. It could be while standing in line at the market or waiting for your order at a restaurant. It might be while you are getting ready in the morning for work or school. If you're driving somewhere, rather than listening to music or talk radio, spend some time going over your affirmations.

ACTIVITY 2.8: AFFIRMATIONS

Dr. Vatcher created this list of affirmations based off of what his clients found helpful. You can use affirmations from this list for the ABCDE exercise (Activity 2.3) by using them as disputations against negative thoughts. You can also recite these to yourself as a regular positivity exercise or post these affirmations in places for you to regularly see. Remember, recite affirmations that align your thoughts with your actions, as "BS affirmations" can be ineffective create conflict in your brain. Align your actions with your thoughts by doing the actions in small and manageable ways.

Mental Well-being

1. I am so positive that I am easily able to uplift really negative people.
2. I am the master of my thoughts and I only focus on positive, righteous, uplifting, and proactive ones.
3. I am the master of my moods.
4. I am full of gratitude for the many blessings and growth opportunities I receive.
5. I am the author of my moods.
6. I love the feeling of having complete control of my happiness.
7. I am very successful in helping others overcome their negativity.
8. I am always up for any challenge.
9. It is quite easy for me to stay focused on uplifting others.
10. I have such a positive and dynamic personality that it is easy to help others make positive changes in their lives.
11. I have truly learned that I am the author of my outcomes.
12. I achieve incredible goals in my life.
13. I am always led by the Spirit.
14. I always choose to be happy, regardless of the state of mind of others.
15. I am a force for good.
16. I have an abundance of energy and enthusiasm.
17. I always maintain a "can do" attitude.
18. I always turn problems or challenges into growth promoting experiences.

19. I love my life and the daily opportunities to expand my horizons.
20. My life has great meaning and purpose.
21. I can easily see the hand of the Lord in my life.
22. I am incredibly successful in achieving all my goals in a timely manner.
23. I take massive action on every goal I set.
24. What others call problems I call growth opportunities.
25. I am totally self-disciplined.
26. I am an incredibly happy and humorous person.
27. I have total confidence in myself.
28. I am incredibly resourceful in solving problems and overcoming challenges.
29. In all areas of my life I do way more than anyone could ever expect of me.
30. I take total responsibility for my thoughts, feelings, and actions.

Spiritual Well Being

31. I am a very righteous and spiritual being.
32. I am open to and daily receive personal revelation and I always act on it.
33. I serve the Savior with all my heart, might, mind and strength.
34. I have achieved complete and permanent mastery over my thoughts.
35. I always strive to live the life of a celestial being.
36. I always strive to keep every promise, covenant, and commitment I make.

Physical Wellness

37. I am in incredible physical shape.
38. I exercise vigorously every day but Sunday.
39. I always strive to follow my daily exercise ritual.
40. I eat healthy and wholesome foods every day.
41. I eat in moderation.
42. I love eating foods that help build my health.
43. I always stay within my ideal weight.
44. I love the feeling I get from being fit.

Affirmations for Learning

45. I love learning new things.
46. I am easily able to stay focused on the things I am studying and learning.
47. I easily retain the things I learn.
48. I am a voracious reader.
49. I continue to grow and progress through continuously studying new material.
50. I love keeping up with new innovations by continuing to educate myself.

Social Affirmations

51. Because I am always so positive, people love being around me.
52. I always look for and find the good in others and in myself.
53. I have total confidence in myself when interacting with others.
54. I am a master communicator.

55. I am extremely effective in helping others resolve their own issues.
56. I have a very scintillating personality.
57. By allowing myself to be happy, I inspire others to be happy as well.
58. I have an active sense of humor and love to share laughter with others.
59. My personality exudes confidence. I am bold and outgoing.
60. I love serving and being a friend to others.

Other Useful Affirmations

61. I am always extremely positive and optimistic.
62. I have an iron will to always choose the right.
63. I always strive to live up to my own high standards and to those that the Lord has set.
64. I always keep a prayer in my heart and totally maintain positive and uplifting thoughts.
65. I love the feeling I get from taking total control of my life.
66. I take total responsibility for my thoughts, feelings, and actions.
67. I am becoming more like the Savior every day.
68. I completely let virtue garnish my thoughts unceasingly.
69. I always maintain a humble countenance.
70. I always listen for and follow the promptings of the Holy Ghost.
71. I read, ponder and liken the scriptures unto myself every single day.
72. I am always so confident in myself, totally relaxed, and perfectly calm.
73. I am totally obedient to the commandments of God.

74. My life belongs to the Lord and I always use my agency to do His will.
75. I actively use the power of the Savior's atonement in my life on a daily basis.
76. I am always filled with gratitude for the countless blessings I receive from the Lord each day.
77. I always face my fears head on and I always conquer them.
78. I have mastered my life and have completely overcome the things of the world.
79. I have an incredible ability to stay totally focused on whatever it is I am studying.
80. I always persevere and persist in following through on my goals even in the face of setbacks.
81. I love a good challenge as it always presents me with an opportunity for growth.
82. Wonderful things unfold before me.
83. I always choose to find optimistic and resourceful ways of dealing with challenges.
84. I sleep soundly, deeply, and beautifully every single night.
85. This day brings me great joy.
86. Today will be a gorgeous day to remember.
87. I have developed a laser-like focus.
88. I follow my positive dreams no matter what.
89. I feel joy and contentment in this moment right now.
90. I awaken in the morning feeling happy and enthusiastic about life.
91. My heart is overflowing with joy.
92. I rest in happiness when I go to sleep, knowing all is well in my world.
93. I expect to be successful in all of my endeavors. Success is my natural state.

94. I easily find solutions to challenges and roadblocks and move past them quickly.
95. Mistakes and setbacks are stepping stones to my success because I learn from them.
96. I feel powerful, capable, confident, energetic, and on top of the world.
97. I am totally relaxed and calm under any circumstance or challenge.
98. My personality exudes confidence. I am bold, courageous, and outgoing.
99. I love change and easily adjust myself to new situations.
100. I always fill my mind with positive and nourishing thoughts.
101. I possess all the qualities needed to be extremely successful.
102. Creative energy surges through me and leads me to new and brilliant ideas.
103. My ability to conquer my challenges is limitless; my potential to succeed is infinite.
104. Today, I am brimming with energy and overflowing with joy.

ACTIVITY 2.9: POSITIVITY BOX

Dr. Hanson recommends doing a positivity box to hardwire positivity into your brain. The positivity box is simple: find a box that you can keep by your bed. Something as simple as a shoebox is fine, or if you want to use a special box, then great! Make sure it is large enough to hold around 365 small pieces of paper. Every day (or as often as possible), write a small positive thing down and put it in the box. The purpose is to rewire your brain to look for positive things in your life. The goal is to change your label of yourself as an unfortunate or normal person, to making yourself realize that you are actually a very fortunate person! Also, when you run into a rough patch in the future or feel down about yourself, opening the box and reading over some of the positive things that have happened in the past can help boost your current mood; reminiscing about positive past events releases happy hormones such as oxytocin in your bloodstream, helping boost your mood.

ACTIVITY 2.10: POSITIVE VISUALIZATIONS
Another activity you can do to cultivate optimism is imagining being in a happy situation. Imagine being with a happy family or group of loved ones. Imagine spending time with them and imagine the ways that they speak to you or encourage you. Imagine laughing with them and them hugging you.

Whenever Hanson had negative thoughts about traumatic events in his childhood, he imagined a happy time, when he was watching over a friend's Welsh Corgis. He imagined how it felt to lie on the ground while the Corgis ran up to him and licked him while he was on the ground. To practice, think about some happy memories and write them down here.

HAPPY VISUALIZATION 1:

HAPPY VISUALIZATION 2:

Now, you have some memories to think back on when you need to cultivate optimism. Try planning in two-minute-long positive visualization activities into your lifestyle routine.

ACTIVITY 2.11: BEST POSSIBLE FUTURE SELF

One thing you can do to demonstrate your optimism for the future is write about your "best possible future." Dr. Lyubomirsky describes how to do this activity in her own words:

"To encourage optimistic thinking, Laura King created the 'best possible selves' activity, in which participants imagine that their life has gone as well as possible in a variety of important domains. For example, you might think of your life in ten years and visualize having a house in the country, a supportive spouse, two children, and a fulfilling career as a journalist. You might state more specific goals too, like having completed a marathon or publishing in a particular magazine.

"Importantly, this activity is not asking you to describe your fantasy life. It should be positive but also attainable and realistic. Also, it is important that you aren't comparing your current self to some idealized version of yourself that you are falling short of—not surprisingly, doing this is likely to backfire and make you feel worse. Be sure to project into the future when doing this exercise!"[101]

Schedule in times to do this activity in your lifestyle routine. This will take at least ten minutes; don't try and rush through this one in two minutes.

---

[101] Sonja Lyubomirsky and Jaime Kurtz, *Positively Happy: Routes to Sustainable Happiness*, 1st ed. (United Kingdom: Positive Acorn, 2008), chap. 3, Kindle.

ACTIVITY 2.12: SAVORING

Dr. Rick Hanson also recommends doing savoring as a method of hardwiring optimism. While negative experiences can weigh heavily on your brain and stick around in your thoughts for a long time, you can fight back against those by stretching out your positive thoughts as much as possible.

Next time you have a positive experience like a nice meal or a nice nature walk, schedule at least two minutes to maximize the positivity of the experience. Get rid of distractions, slow down, and focus on every tiny feeling or emotion. Let it really sink in all five of your senses.

ACTIVITY 2.13: POSITIVE REFRAMING

If there are things in your life that you dislike but must do (such as homework, part time jobs, extracurriculars, etc.), you can turn these from negative experiences to more positive ones by reframing them. For example, instead of trudging through your math homework, you can try thinking of it as a fun and challenging puzzle that also sharpens your mind. Change your attitude and have fun! Take two minutes to write down ways here that you can change your attitude on some of these things and turn them into fun things:

THINGS YOU DISLIKE:

WAYS TO CHANGE YOUR ATTITUDE AND REFRAME THEM TO BE FUN:

POSITIVELY RESPONDING TO STRESS, FEAR, AND RUMINATION

We all face stress and fear in many forms in our daily lives. People today are thought of as being more stressed now than in any other time, and stress is considered one of the biggest factors in shortened lifespan.[102] This doesn't mean we should give up—all this means is we should make sure we make these types of activities a priority in our lives.

Many young people experience high amounts of stress and fear right before a big event, like a test, sporting event, musical or theater performance, speech at church, or missionary lesson. Stress can cause a lot of negative impacts on your body, but interestingly enough, if you treat stress the right way and change the way that you label it in your mind, stress can actually be transformed into something that changes your performance for the better. Let's talk about activities we can do in the face of things like stress, fear, and rumination.

ACTIVITY 2.14: MAKING STRESS YOUR FRIEND

After I returned from my mission, the transition to college life was stressful. I started school in the middle of the school year, and since I couldn't find an open apartment in time, I had to sleep on a pad under my friend's bed in a freezing apartment in the middle of the winter. I was painfully awkward and had trouble fitting into normal life, so my roommates often teased me. I also had no idea of what to study in college as a major or what to do for a future career. I was

---

[102] Brian Mastroianni, "Why Americans Are More Stressed Today Than They Were in the 1990s," Healthline, accessed November 20, 2020.

pretty overwhelmed. I decided to meet with a counselor at BYU, and he told me to watch the "How to Make Stress Your Friend" TED Talk by Dr. Kelly McGonigal.

In this TED Talk, McGonigal states that stress can negatively impact your performance and physical health, causing an increase of stress chemicals in your body and other negative responses.[103] However, she states that if you simply relabel stress in your mind as something else, like excitement, your brain's physiological response completely changes.[104] Your blood vessels widen, your breathing slows, and the "nervous" energy you have can then be applied to be positive excitement that you can use to solve problems better or perform better overall.[105] Basically, stress is only bad for you if you tell your body stress is bad for you.

After watching this, I treated my stressful situation as an "exciting" time. After treating it like I was on an adventure, I realized that my stress and fear began to change into positive energy. I continued to practice treating stressful times like finals week or interviewing with lots of companies during recruiting seasons as being exciting. In the following years, I realized that this reframing made me perform much better, reach all of the goals that I wanted, and left me with no regrets. I felt like I performed to the best of my abilities during these times. Now, I honestly look back to times like finals week or recruiting season as fun and exciting times, where I was very focused and achieved a lot.

---

[103] Kelly McGonigal, "Kelly McGonigal: How to Make Stress Your Friend | TED Talk," Ted Conferences, accessed November 20, 2020.
[104] Ibid.
[105] Ibid.

Try to reframe your stress or fear as excitement. Take two minutes to talk out loud to yourself or write down ways to relabel stress as your friend. You will be surprised to see what happens.

ACTIVITY 2.15: TAKE A TIMEOUT

Justin Su'a tells us that "in sports, when the pressure is on and there is little time left, coaches will call a timeout to give their team the game plan, slow down the momentum, and offer some words of encouragement. Great athletes know that when the game speeds up, that's the perfect time to slow down. Same thing in life! If you find yourself buried in homework assignments, practice, rehearsals, church obligations, and other activities, rather than speeding up, slow down. You might be saying to yourself, 'I'm too busy to take a time-out!' My response is simple: you can't afford not to."[106]

When you take a timeout before a stressful event, there are a couple things that you can do to make you effective.

1. Remember what you can control. Dr. Craig Manning, a professor of performance psychology at BYU, teaches us that it is important when approaching stressful and important events to focus on your performance instead of the outcome. You can't try and control some things like the outcome of a sports match, but you can control your ability to give it your best shot. Take two minutes to tell yourself (either out loud, to a buddy, or on paper)

---

[106] Justin Su'a, *Mentally Tough Teens: Developing a Winning Mindset*, First Edition (Springville, UT: Plain Sight Publishing, 2014), chap. 1, Kindle.

what you are in control of and what you aren't in control of. Focus on what you can control.
2. Take a breather. A deep breath is a great tool for calming your nerves as it will relax your muscles and quiet your mind.

   a. For at least two minutes follow this process: Breathe in through your nose for ten seconds, hold it for ten seconds, and then let it out of your mouth for ten seconds. This will slow your heart rate down and ground you in the present.

   b. Make sure to breathe using your diaphragm (watch for your stomach to move, not your chest or shoulders) and pay attention to your breath: how does it feel for your stomach to move? How does the air feel to come in through your nostrils and into your lungs, how does it feel to hold it in your belly, and how does it feel to let it out of your mouth?

3. Change the way you're looking at your circumstance. Ask yourself what you can learn from the situation, what you did to prepare for this moment, how this is going to make you stronger, and when you have accomplished something difficult in your life before.

ACTIVITY 2.16: DISTRACTION FROM RUMINATION

Sometimes, your stress and fear can be unmanageable to the point of causing you to ruminate. If you remember from the start of the chapter, rumination is when you constantly think in unhelpful and unresolvable loops.

In his TED Talk "How to Fix a Broken Heart," Dr. Guy Winch shared this example of how to fight rumination using distraction. Winch shared a story of how his best friend and identical twin brother was diagnosed with a very aggressive form of cancer.[107] He recounts the story below.

"The urge to ruminate can feel really strong and really important, so it's a difficult habit to stop. I know this for a fact, because a little over a year ago, I developed the habit myself. You see, my twin brother was diagnosed with stage 3 non-Hodgkin's lymphoma. His cancer was extremely aggressive. He had visible tumors all over his body. And he had to start a harsh course of chemotherapy. And I couldn't stop thinking about what he was going through. I couldn't stop thinking about how much he was suffering, even though he never complained, not once. He had this incredibly positive attitude. His psychological health was amazing. I was physically healthy, but psychologically, I was a mess. But I knew what to do. Studies tell us that even a two-minute distraction is sufficient to break the urge to ruminate in that moment. And so each time I had a worrying, upsetting, negative thought, I forced myself to concentrate on something else until the urge passed. And within one week, my whole outlook changed and became more positive and more hopeful."[108]

In the same way Winch used distraction to fight rumination, you can as well. Next time you experience something tough and you can't get it out of your mind (whether it be a death in the family, a divorce, breakup, financial trial, or other traumatic event), take a step back, and follow this process:

---

[107] Guy Winch, "Guy Winch: How to Fix a Broken Heart | TED Talk," Ted Conferences, accessed November 20, 2020.
[108] Ibid.

1. Recognize your rumination and take action as soon as you can.
2. Distract yourself. For at least two minutes, engage in an activity that puts your mind in a different setting. Get up, move physical locations, and do something different: call a friend, exercise, read a book, or watch a movie.
3. Later on, acknowledge the way that you were thinking. Instead of being afraid of your negative thoughts, pretend to be a scientist: Treat your thoughts with curiosity, and try to understand the reasons that you fell into your rumination.
4. Record your reaction and how distraction helped you to remind yourself and reinforce in your brain that this was a successful way to approach this issue in the future (Feel free to use journaling or talking to a trusted friend in order to keep track of your thoughts).

A study of rumination among children and adolescents in the Netherlands showed that individuals who allowed themselves to be distracted from their sources of trauma reported much lower depression and anxiety scores, so the bottom line is that distraction is a great tool.[109]

TREATING YOURSELF WITH SELF-COMPASSION
To combat negative thought patterns like social comparison, catastrophizing, black-and-white thinking, and perceived loneliness, self-compassion exercises are some of the best things to do. Plan many of these in your regular lifestyle routines.

---

[109] Jeffrey Roelofs et al., "The Influence of Rumination and Distraction on Depressed and Anxious Mood: A Prospective Examination of the Response Styles Theory in Children and Adolescents," *European Child & Adolescent Psychiatry* 18, no. 10 (October 2009): 635–42.

Dr. Kristin Neff, probably the world's most renowned self-compassion researcher, tells us about the incredible benefits of self-compassion in her TED Talk "The Space Between Self-Esteem and Self Compassion."[110] She says that when we want to improve, many of us think that it is best to be harder on ourselves to improve, and that being easy on ourselves is a way to be self-indulgent.[111] However, her research indicates this does more harm than good, as people respond best to a higher ratio of positive encouragement than to negative criticism.

Imagine this situation: A daughter comes home to her parents feeling discouraged after receiving a poor grade on her math test. Her parents then react by telling her, "Wow, you are so stupid. I can't believe you got this bad of a grade. You are terrible." Seems harsh, right? However, we often speak to ourselves in the same negative way when we are going through tough times. While criticizing ourselves might work in the short term, it is very demotivating in the long run, and the girl who was criticized in our example would likely give up math in the long run.

That's because self-criticism releases tons of the stress hormone cortisol, which causes our brains to shut down.[112] Self-compassion on the other hand releases opiates (feel-good neurotransmitters) that help you manage unhelpful emotions and perform better in the future.

---

[110] Kristin Neff, "Self-Compassion Videos by Kristin Neff," *Self-Compassion* (blog), accessed November 20, 2020.

[111] Ibid.

[112] Kristin Neff, "The Physiology of Self-Compassion – Kristin Neff," *Self-Compassion* (blog), accessed November 20, 2020.

With self-compassion, we can constantly give ourselves positive feedback, as it teaches our brains to get in the habit of constantly reaffirming ourselves. When I interviewed Ashley Kuchar, a returned missionary who served in Poland, a former collegiate basketball player, and a PhD student under Dr. Kristin Neff, she said that self-compassion is positively impactful in every aspect of your well-being.

Kuchar used the following example to illustrate how a self-compassionate approach could help in missionary work. Say there was a time when you didn't talk to someone on the street because you were scared. If your companion was very hard on you for not talking to the person, then in the long run, you would associate talking to people with negativity, and you would be less motivated to do it in the long run. However, if you told your companion, "I'm kinda scared, we need to take a break and come back to this a little later," and she met you with compassion, then you would be more likely to want to do it in the future.

To use self-compassion in your own life, Kuchar tells us these three main principles that we need to follow in our compassionate activities:

1. Self-kindness: This means we are warm to ourselves instead of harshly critical or judgmental. When you are in emotional distress or pain, instead of criticizing yourself, speak to yourself as if you were a friend. Don't worry too much about over-indulging in being nice to yourself—you have to give yourself compassion because it is what you need to feel better.

2. Common humanity: Another thing to realize is that self-compassion is not the same thing as self-esteem. Self-esteem tells us how we are different from others. Self-compassion emphasizes common humanity, which tells us how we are the same as others. Everyone makes mistakes; it's all part of the plan. We shouldn't be surprised when bad things happen, as they happen to everyone else.
3. Mindfulness: We can't ignore our pain and feel compassion for it at the same time. We need to be mindful and acknowledge our pain and negative feelings without being so caught up in the negativity that we get swept away. She says, "If you have a sliver and avoid it, it won't get better. You need to acknowledge your pain, put ointment on it, and let it heal." However, we shouldn't dwell on them too much. If our thoughts are like a train, jumping on the train will cause you to go in circles. Mindfulness is like watching the train, you're not avoiding them or clinging to thoughts, but you are watching them and observing them.

ACTIVITY 2.17: TREAT YOURSELF LIKE YOU WOULD TREAT A FRIEND

Next time you're facing a challenge, walk yourself through these steps:

1. Write down how you are feeling and the way that you talk to yourself. See if you are talking to yourself in the way a friend would. If not, be kinder to yourself.
2. Mammals respond best to warmth, gentle touch, and soft vocalizations. Talking to yourself or touching yourself in a gentle and warm manner will release opiates that will help you feel better.

ACTIVITY 2.18: EMPHASIZE COMMON HUMANITY AND DECREASE COMPARISON

Comparing yourself to others is natural, but like we learned, comparing yourself to others is a characteristic of self-esteem, not self-compassion. Don't use other people as measuring sticks to emphasize differences, but instead, compare similarities between people. Humans evolved as social creatures, which means we thrive on connection between others.

Su'a reminds us, "You're going to have your bad acne days, and sometimes parts of your body will seem too big or too small. But that's not the worst part—while you're so busy beating up on yourself, you're putting other teens on pedestals, thinking they are 'gorgeous,' 'perfect,' or 'better' than you. The reality is that they're human too! And chances are that they're comparing their weaknesses to your strengths as well."[113]

The *American Idol* finalist and popular singer David Archuleta also emphasizes the importance of not comparing yourself to others. Fame and media exposure influenced mental challenges and anxiety in his life as well, impacting his family life and mental health. No matter who you are, he states, "You have to take care of yourself, even if you're not as popular or hip as Chris Brown. You can still find happiness, you can find balance, you can find confidence in who you are—without being someone else."[114]

---

[113] Justin Su'a, *Mentally Tough Teens: Developing a Winning Mindset*, First Edition (Springville, UT: Plain Sight Publishing, 2014), chap.1, Kindle.

[114] Herb Scribner, "David Archuleta Opens up about 'PTSD,' Mental Health in New Yahoo Interview," *Deseret News*, November 28, 2018.

Comparing yourself to others is a key reason young people suffer from perceived loneliness. It can be easy to feel like you are alone, and this can lead you to interpret other intentions as selfish or not toward our benefit. Seeing commonalities between others as opposed to differences is a key part of not feeling alone.

Tal Ben-Shahar also tells us the importance of giving ourselves permission to be human. He says, "When we accept emotions—such as fear, sadness, or anxiety—as natural, we are more likely to overcome them. Rejecting our emotions, positive or negative, leads to frustration and unhappiness. We are a culture obsessed with pleasure and believe that the mark of a worthy life is the absence of discomfort; and when we experience pain, we take it to indicate that something must be wrong with us. In fact, there is something wrong with us if we don't experience sadness or anxiety at times—which are human emotions. The paradox is that when we accept our feelings—when we give ourselves the permission to be human and experience painful emotions—we are more likely to open ourselves up to positive emotions."[115]

Do the following activities when you struggle with common humanity or social comparison:

1. In order to cultivate common humanity and decrease perceived loneliness, Dr. Kristie Lemmon of the DBT Network of Utah suggests to "read other's stories of struggles, not to compare, but to remind yourself that

---

[115] Tal Ben-Shahar, "7 Lessons On Earning The Ultimate Currency: Happiness," *Positivity Daily* (blog), February 10, 2015.

others are struggling to. I remember being on bedrest when I was pregnant and reading some blogs of other women on bedrest the same time I was. Reading their stories helped me not feel so alone and helped me feel compassion for all of us who were scared we would lose our babies and who were uncomfortable lying in bed day after day."[116] If we do feel isolated, look for connection and common ground where we can find it. Find ways to create emotional bridges with those that aren't like you, as this can pick you up when you're depressed and you don't want to connect with others.

2. In addition to reading stories of other peoples' struggles, you can do a regular connectedness exercise. In your journal, write down a list of people you feel like you are connected to. Try to schedule two-minute times throughout the day to do this. Write down how you feel when you think about these people and write down ways they make you feel connected to them. Also, write down ways you make them feel connected to you. Connection is something that is critically important to our health.

3. In Activity 2.1: Identifying Unhelpful Thoughts (Chapter 2b) where we learned to take inventory of our unhelpful thoughts, we can identify our thoughts of social comparison. We can then manage these through disputations like the ABCDE approach, or we can do an ACT mindfulness approach like in Activity 2.4: ACT Mindfulness for Managing Negative Thoughts and Feelings (Chapter 2b).

4. Try and limit sources of comparison, whether this is media use or people that make you feel this way. I can

---

[116] Kristie Lemmon, "Guidepost #2: Cultivating Self-Compassion through Common Humanity," *Kristie Lemmon* (blog), April 19, 2018.

remember times in my life where I had significantly higher well-being, and these are times where I had limited social media use because I had taken a break from it, was busy doing other things, or was out in nature where I think about problems of comparison far less often than if I am living my normal day-to-day life.
a. Take a break from social media for a set time. After getting over the initial FOMO stage, you will be surprised to see how your mental well-being improves.
b. In addition to taking breaks from social media, try and do other things that decrease your usage, such as deleting the app and using a web browser instead, or using social media only for pre-planned purposes instead of mindless scrolling.
c. When you are using social media, try and unfollow or hide accounts or content that make you feel like comparing yourself to others.

ACTIVITY 2.19: COMPASSIONATE CHAIR ACTIVITY

This is an activity from Courtney Ackerman of PositivePsychology.com. This is a way to exercise self-compassion by using three chairs. The activity follows:

"Think of something that has recently caused you to criticize yourself. Each chair in front of you represents a different perspective to help you understand your self-criticism. The first chair represents a voice of self-criticism. The second chair represents the emotionality or sensation of feeling judged. The last chair takes the perspective of a supportive friend or wise counselor. Your job is to play the role of each voice represented by the respective chairs. There's no need to feel silly. Learn through accessing different perspectives.

Part 1

"First, sit from the perspective of the inner critic. Now, express out loud in words or sound how you think about the issue that you have been dwelling on. For example, 'I hate that I am so lazy and can't seem to get anything done.' Try to understand the tone you use. Notice the emotions your words evoke. Notice your posture or general demeanor.

Part 2

"Now move to the chair that represents the sensation of being judged (by yourself). Express out loud in words or sound how it feels to encounter criticism. For example, 'I feel hurt' or 'I do not feel supported.' Notice the same things you did before (your tone, emotions, posture, etc.).

Part 3

"Now, engage with yourself in a dialogue between the last two perspectives (the critical voice and the emotion voice). Try to understand how each perspective feels.

Part 4

"Next, move to the chair that represents the friend or wise counselor. Drawing on a sincere sense of compassion, confront the critical voice and the critiqued voice. Address both perspectives out loud. What do you say? What advice do you give? How do you relate to each perspective from a more detached point of view? Notice your tone and demeanor. Allow yourself enough time to express everything you need to from each perspective. Make sure you leave time to reflect on the experience. Try to understand how you think, and how you could benefit from the perspectives you explored. How does that inform your inner critic and your experience with self-compassion? Ultimately, you are already capable of using a more supportive voice. Next time you find yourself being negative and self-critical, try to locate the compassionate voice."[117]

ACTIVITY 2.20: MINDFULNESS FOR SELF-COMPASSION
As we learned earlier in this chapter about the effectiveness of mindfulness in managing emotions through Activity 2.4: ACT Mindfulness for Managing Negative Thoughts and Feelings (Chapter 2b), it is also a critical part of self-compassion. Feel free to follow the ACT mindfulness activity in order to do this. Practicing meditation is also an excellent way to practice mindfulness and build self-compassion.

Research has shown how meditation improves levels of compassion, altruistic behavior, relationship quality, attention and memory skills, and even improved immune system functioning.[118] Meditation also will decrease the rate of the aging of your brain cells.[119] It's a good idea on many levels.

---

[117] Courtney Ackerman, "16 Compassion Focused Therapy Training Exercises and Worksheets," PositivePsychology.com, December 1, 2017.

[118] Gaëlle Desbordes et al., "Effects of Mindful-Attention and Compassion Meditation Training on Amygdala Response to Emotional Stimuli in an Ordinary, Non-Meditative State," *Frontiers in Human Neuroscience* 6 (November 1, 2012).

[119] Elissa Epel et al., "Can Meditation Slow Rate of Cellular Aging? Cognitive Stress, Mindfulness, and Telomeres," *Annals of the New York Academy of Sciences* 1172 (August 2009): 34–53.

The easiest way I like to meditate is by using apps or guided meditations. Try and download apps like Insight Timer, Headspace, Sanvello, and Calm—they have free trials and student discounts. You can also find many guided meditations for free online on websites like YouTube.

TAKEAWAYS FROM CHAPTER 2B:

REWIRING OUR BRAINS AGAINST BIAS

1. To positively rewire our brains, the main methods psychologists employ today are cognitive behavioral therapy (CBT) and acceptance and commitment therapy (ACT). Both teach us how to healthily manage our unhelpful thoughts by first being aware of them, but CBT focuses on disputing unhelpful thoughts while ACT focuses on being mindful and accepting them.
2. Both approaches have their benefits and uses, and we will practice both of them. From there, you can decide which activities fit best with your needs.
3. As the goal of both approaches—and rewiring our biases—begins with awareness of our thoughts, we can begin by going over the major types, which are social comparison, catastrophizing, black-and-white thinking, personalization, mind reading, emotional reasoning, rumination, perceived loneliness, and stress/fear.
4. Journaling is a great way to recognize when you have any of the unhelpful thoughts listed above. After listing and identifying our unhelpful thoughts, we will learn ways to manage them.

5. The CBT method of managing your thoughts centers on you recognizing your ability to have control and influence over your thoughts and to dispute unhelpful thoughts.
6. The ACT method helps us to be mindful and accept thoughts instead of arguing against them. Activity 2.4 teaches us a three step process to the ACT method, which consists of defusion, expansion, and connection.
7. In addition to ACT and CBT, we can rewire our brains through gratitude, cultivating optimism, positively responding to stress/fear/rumination, and treating yourself with self-compassion. There are fifteen activities in each of these areas, so definitely go back in the chapters to see what kinds of things you can implement into your lifestyle routines.

MATERIALS LIST FROM CHAPTER 2B:

REWIRING OUR BRAINS AGAINST BIAS

- Journal or notebook to write out your thoughts
- Pocket memo pad or small notebook to track thoughts and feelings throughout the day
- Shoe box and small pieces of paper for the positivity box
- Thank you cards for gratitude letters
- Three chairs (or any sort of seat) for Activity 2.19: Compassionate Chair Activity (Chapter 2b)
- Soft mat for mindfulness meditation (Put in your room or by your bed for to remind you to take time to do this activity)

CHAPTER 2C:

MANAGING CHALLENGES TO THE HAPPINESS BALANCE

Last chapter, we listed many ways to overcome the bias of our brains toward the negative. Now, we will discuss other challenges to the balance of our mental well-being. Like we mentioned in the introduction, happiness is dependent on the balance between present pleasure and future meaning or purpose. This chapter will give us a reminder on things that challenge the happiness balance and will lead into the next chapter, which will give us specific activities to work on these.

Let's do a brief review on what we've learned in the introduction on happiness. Pleasure is also known as positive emotion, and the key to happiness and well-being is balancing positive emotion in the present with future purpose. Dr. Martin Seligman says the "route to well-being is hedonic—increasing positive emotion. Within limits, we can increase our positive emotion about the past (e.g., by cultivating gratitude and forgiveness), our positive emotion about the present (e.g., by savoring physical pleasures and mindfulness) and our positive emotion about the future (e.g., by building hope and optimism)."[120]

So, we need to learn how to balance positive emotion and future purpose and, like Seligman said, we can do this by building positive emotion for the past, present, and future. We will learn to integrate this into our happiness balance, first by going back to the archetypes of happiness listed in the hamburger model. You may remember what these were from the introduction, but let's have a high-level refresher so we can then work on activities specific to each of these burgers:

HEDONISM: JUNK FOOD BURGER

Ben-Shahar states, "The experience of present benefit and future detriment defines the hedonism archetype. Hedonists live by the maxim 'Seek pleasure and avoid pain.' They focus on enjoying the present while ignoring the potential negative consequences of their actions."[121] This lifestyle was described as being like a junk food burger, which tastes good at the time you eat it, but makes you feel sick and is bad for your health in the long run. This happens when you are overly focused on the present.

---

[120] The University of Pennsylvania, "PERMA™ Theory of Well-Being and PERMA™ Workshops | Positive Psychology Center," accessed October 2, 2020.
[121] Tal Ben-Shahar, *Happier* (McGraw-Hill Education (India) Pvt Limited, 2007), chap. 1, Kindle.

Hedonism aims to satisfy desires. You can compare satisfying desires to giving into the "natural man," as the scriptures often put it. This is when you give into the primitive tendencies that your brain has, such as animalistic desires for pleasure or the fight-flight-freeze response that your limbic system controls.

The big factor that stops you from getting lasting happiness from hedonic experiences is the concept of hedonic adaptation, which means that over time, humans tend to adapt to many pleasurable circumstances. Our activities will teach us how to fight against hedonic adaptation, help us to overcome overly hedonistic behavior, and help us to pair meaning to our hedonic tendencies.

RAT RACE: VEGGIE BURGER

The rat race burger is the healthy veggie burger that tastes bad but is meant to benefit your health in the long term. This is when you overemphasize things that are unpleasant. This could be like taking too much time away from your family to make the incremental dollar at work, or regularly sacrificing your sleep so you can be more productive in school. We will learn activities to overcome the rat race by focusing more on the present, seeking pleasure from our actions, and getting out of rat race activities.

NIHILISM: WORST BURGER

This is the rat poison burger, which is a burger that gives you no present pleasure or future benefit. It tastes bad and is terrible for your health. This is when you have little to no focus on both present pleasure and future meaning. Nihilists feel helpless—as if no matter what you do, you have no control over life or happiness and nothing really matters. We will focus on activities that help you to find both pleasure and purpose in your lives.

Now that we have gone over the archetypes in our lives, let's talk about how we can manage the challenges that can come up in each of these types of burgers. As we mentioned, the key is knowing how to balance pleasure and meaning, and the challenges come up when you either are too focused on present pleasure, too focused on putting off gratification to the future, or not being interested in pleasure or benefit at all. First, let's talk about challenges with hedonism.

OVERCOMING THE HEDONISTIC JUNK FOOD BURGER

There are a variety of challenges related to hedonism. These include hedonistic behavior and hedonic adaptation. Let's talk about some examples of hedonistic behavior one by one, and about ways to manage these.

ACTIVITY 2.21: MANAGING SHADOW COMFORTS AND NUMBING BEHAVIORS

Pleasure is inherently good and important to maintaining the happiness balance. However, hedonistic pleasure seeking is unhelpful when you pursue desires to the point that they lose meaning. Examples of these are behaviors like "shadow comforts," which Dr. Brett Merrill describes as temporary comforts that give you fleeting pleasures that disappear as fast as a shadow. There's nothing wrong with enjoying shadow comforts, such as eating a tasty dessert, but it becomes unhelpful when pursuing these temporary comforts becomes your goal. Other examples of temporary pleasures are focusing on objects or material possessions. Material possessions in particular do not lead to lasting happiness, unless they are purchases directly connected to a source of continuous meaningful experience.[122]

When pursuing endless comforts is your goal, you will confront the law of diminishing marginal returns: Your fifth ice cream cone is not going to be as tasty as your first cone. You will slowly become numb to the enjoyment you experience, as humans naturally adapt to circumstances and material possessions due to hedonic adaptation.

It is also detrimental to turn to these sorts of behaviors to numb uncomfortable feelings. If you are feeling lonely, sad, tired, or anxious, turning to shadow comforts may help you feel better in the short term, but will not help you learn how to manage your emotions.

You can learn how you can attach pleasurable behavior with mindfulness and a sense of purpose through these tips:

1. Mindfulness: This is a way to overcome hedonic adaptation. When you purposefully eat an ice cream cone, do it for the enjoyment of the experience as opposed to doing it to numb emotions. Take several minutes to savor it; ground yourself in the present. Remove distractions as you eat it and focus entirely on the experience of eating the ice cream. Take in all the tastes and textures.
    a. Plan this savoring exercise into your lifestyle routines.
    b. You can prevent hedonic adaptation to these experiences by intentionally spacing them out. Enjoy your

---

[122] Erash Emamzadeh, "Materialism=Happiness?," Psychology Today, accessed November 20, 2020.

pleasurable experiences and record them in your journal to relive the experience again. Looking back on favorable pleasurable experiences are ways to extend the meaning of these events.

2. Attaching purpose: Merrill tells about how he gains lots of pleasure from movies like *Star Wars*. He is able to make this pleasure more meaningful by deciding to watch *Star Wars* together with his friends and his family, which turns a pleasurable experience into a meaningful activity that deepens relationships.
   a. Find ways that you can attach a sense of meaning or purpose to activities that give you pleasure. See what values you listed from Activity 1.2: Values List (Chapter 1c) and then see how you can combine them with what gives you pleasure.
   b. Try to limit purchases that provide short-term pleasure and little meaning, such as spending money on possessions that do not support important values. You can quickly adapt to material possessions.

ACTIVITY 2.22: ANGER AND EMOTION MANAGEMENT

Like I stated in the introduction of this chapter, we all have a "battle" in our brains of survival responses from our primitive brains being regulated by the logic of our rational brains. Anger is an example of a "fight or flight" response our brains have that can get out of control. This can be a form of hedonism in the sense that you give into your present desire of acting out instead of doing the more difficult thing of managing your emotions.

When you act in anger, it actually causes you to shut down your cognitive abilities.[123] While I attended BYU, my professor, Dr. Sarah Coyne from the School of Family Life, shared with our class how unresolved anger over the course of several minutes can actually cause you to descend to the cognitive level of a young child and can make you act in many unwanted and irrational ways. Coyne recommends doing the following when you are in an upset circumstance. Try practicing this process so you can apply it to the next time you are angry:

1. Recognize when you are losing your rationality. When you feel your anger rising, immediately identify the fact that your rationality is decreasing.
2. Communicate your state. For example, if Coyne identified that she was getting frustrated with one of her children, she would tell her child, "Mommy needs to take a break. I will be back after I have a timeout."
3. Take time to cool down. Coyne likes to retreat to the bathroom where she can turn on the fan for white noise and take time to be alone.

LAZINESS AND FINDING A SENSE OF PURPOSE

Laziness can be a form of hedonism when you are afraid of feeling the discomfort necessary for doing activities that have future purpose but may not be as pleasurable in the moment. A key way to overcome this kind of discomfort is by setting goals. Like we mentioned in the chapter on goals, these give us a sense of purpose and improve the quality of our lives.

---

[123] Sarah N. Garfinkel et al., "Anger in Brain and Body: The Neural and Physiological Perturbation of Decision-Making by Emotion," *Social Cognitive and Affective Neuroscience* 11, no. 1 (January 2016): 150–58.

Ben-Shahar has stated that because we are a future-oriented species, goals actually help us live longer. He says, "Studies have shown that the mortality rate rises by 2 percent among men who retire right when they become eligible to collect Social Security, and that retiring early may lead to early death, even among those who are healthy when they do so."[124]

If you feel like you aren't moving forward in life, setting goals can help you achieve purpose and meaning. This is critical to generate the satisfaction, that is part of the happiness equation.

To achieve things that are purposeful, it is normal to experience a bit of discomfort. You don't want to deny all present pleasure while trying to achieve your goals (that goes into rat racer territory, which we will talk about next), but you will need to exercise a certain amount of grit in order to achieve your goals.

To exercise goal achievement, refer back to the sections on goal setting in Chapter 1c, or go to the practice Activity 1.3: Lifestyle Routine Worksheet. Remember that it is critical to be intentional about your goals. Do things you truly believe will make you happier. Su'a says when you are forced to do things, our "motivation tends to dip. Own your motivation by attaching a purpose to everything you do. Developing the habit of thinking, speaking, and acting on purpose and with purpose will help you take the driver's seat of your own life and reap the benefits of acting rather than being acted upon."[125]

---

[124] A. C. Shilton, "You Accomplished Something Great. So Now What? (Published 2019)," *The New York Times*, May 28, 2019.

[125] Justin Su'a, *Mentally Tough Teens: Developing a Winning Mindset*, First Edition (Springville, UT: Plain Sight Publishing, 2014), chap. 1, Kindle.

ACTIVITY 2.23: NAVIGATING SEXUAL FEELINGS

I included this activity in this section because there are times when purposeless sexuality can be considered hedonistic, but I want to make sure that I put this activity into proper context. Knowing how to navigate sexuality can be a complex and confusing topic for young people in the church. However, here is some advice from some experts on the topic.

First, Dr. Brett Merrill from BYU Counseling and Psychological Services states that he prefers to use an ACT approach when working with clients that are trying to manage unwanted sexual behavior. For the most part, this has to do with behavior like pornography usage and masturbation. Merrill uses an ACT approach as opposed to a CBT approach because sexuality is inherently a healthy and important part of all of our lives. None of us would be alive if it weren't for sexuality, and sexuality is a wonderful way to express love and deepen marriages. Basically, the important thing with these feelings is to understand that they are natural and healthy parts of our lives but also be aware of and discern between desired and undesired behavior.

Also, focusing too much on a forbidden nature of sexuality can exacerbate your perceptions of sexuality or any hedonistic activity. An example is mentioned by Dr. Jennifer Finlayson-Fife, a sex therapist specializing in working with members of the church. She gives an example in her podcast that if you repeatedly tell children never to eat chocolate cake, then the one thing on their mind will be chocolate cake.[126]

---

[126] Jennifer Finlayson-Fife, "Ask a Mormon Sex Therapist Part 6 on Rational Faiths," Dr. Jennifer Finlayson-Fife, accessed November 25, 2020.

Ben-Shahar also illustrates the consequences of focusing too much on limitation with the same example of chocolate cake: When he decided not to eat cake at his birthday because he was living a strict dietary regimen for his elite level of squash playing as a youth, the obsession over the forbidden nature of the cake drove him to wake up in the middle of the night to eat almost the entire cake.[127] Make sure we do not obsess or place an overly forbidden nature to things like sexuality or any other type of hedonistic behavior. In order to avoid obsession with hedonistic behavior, it's important to approach our thoughts and feelings with mindfulness. Feel free to reference Activity 2.4: ACT Mindfulness for Managing Negative Thoughts and Feelings (Chapter 2b) to help you manage these feelings, or follow the advice of Dr. Daley below.

Dr. Dan Daley, a psychologist at Utah Valley Hospital and a positive psychology professor at BYU, gives us advice on managing undesirable behavior such as pornography usage or risky sexual behavior. He states that lust or objectification of people can be dehumanizing and potentially be harmful for relationships. So, at times you recognize undesired behavior, it is important to follow an action plan you make for yourself. Daley recommends some of the following activities as actions against undesirable behavior:

1. Identifying and reconceptualizing undesirable thoughts
2. Recognizing and minimizing triggers (feelings in your brain that cause you to not think rationally and act out)
3. Creating counter thoughts for undesirable thoughts

---

[127] Karl Niebuhr, "Using the Path of Least Resistance to Build New Habits — Excerpt from The Happiness Advantage," Karlbooklover, accessed November 21, 2020.

4. Filling life with positive activities such as physical exercise (this releases dopamine, a chemical that makes you feel pleasure)

OVERCOMING THE RAT RACE VEGGIE BURGER

The rat race burger is the veggie burger that tastes bad in your mouth but is good for your health in the long term. People who follow this style of life are those who are on a continuous cycle of postponing pleasure for a future purpose, but never take the time to enjoy the present. They are victims of the arrival fallacy, or the "I will be happy when…" mentality. They think they can't be happy until they have a certain event occur in their life, but as we learned from previous chapters, happiness from events or accolades doesn't last, which we saw from Tal Ben-Shahar's short-lasting pleasure he gained after winning the Israeli national squash championship.

Rat racing falls in line with perfectionism and overachievement, as people who are on the rat race try to do all they can to stick to an unrealistic ideal. Examples of rat racers are missionaries who tract every day (including on the preparation day, which is meant for rest) and people who try to be perfect in every aspect of following the Gospel. Tracting and trying to live the Gospel are both excellent things, but doing these at an unrealistic and unsustainable level can cause you to be unable to hold it up and eventually flip out.

One way to overcome the rat race veggie burger is through proper goal setting. Refer back to Chapter 1c to review tips on how to do this. Remember that the key parts of successful goal-setting requires setting goals that focus on your strengths yet are a balance of pleasure and meaning.

When reviewing goal setting, the main thing to beware of is singular, arrival-oriented goals. The problem with these is after you complete arrival-oriented goals, you might feel a loss of purpose after completing them. That's why Ben-Shahar teaches us that concurrent goals are critical in order to counteract the effects of the arrival fallacy.[128] Concurrent goals are simply multiple goals we progress toward at the same time. That way, after we complete a goal, we have other goals to work on to give us a continued sense of purpose. When we set goals for our lifestyle routines, it is okay to progress in multiple areas at once, but it is important we keep them simple and do not overdo ourselves.

Another way to find pleasure in the journey is by being engaged in pursuits you are both good at and find intrinsic meaning in. You can find pursuits that provide both of these by discovering your character strengths.

ACTIVITY 2.24: CHARACTER STRENGTHS
We all have the ability to do many things, but should we all go to medical school? Dr. Daley tells us we can't just base career choices on aptitude, we must also do something we are fulfilled in. True fulfillment is achieved when do things that align with our character strengths or positive parts of our personalities that impact how we think, feel, and behave.

Doing things we are good at is very important for our well-being; in fact, self-determination theory states that in order to be truly motivated and happy, we must feel

---

[128] A. C. Shilton, "You Accomplished Something Great. So Now What? (Published 2019)," *The New York Times*, May 28, 2019, sec. Smarter Living.

competence in our pursuits.[129] Self-determination theory states that as humans, we have three basic needs to thrive: autonomy, relatedness, and competence. We will get into the concept of autonomy in Chapter 2d: Spirituality and the Mind and relatedness in Chapter 5a: Benefits of Being Active in Our Communities, but let's first get into competence. Competence is considered one of our needs for happiness and motivation because we have the innate need of feeling like we are doing things that we are skilled at. Feeling competent also comes with a feeling of being engaged in something intrinsically meaningful. Finding our character strengths helps us determine life directions that both provide meaning and an expression of our skills.

Dr. Daley shared a story of his journey through finding his character strengths. He told us how he began at the University of Utah studying chemical engineering and realized that although he performed well, he was never happy taking these courses. After discovering he had character strengths in helping people and withholding judgment, he decided he should pursue a career in psychology. Since he made this decision, he has been extremely happy and fulfilled with his career.

When deciding upon life pursuits we go after, it is critical we gain pleasure by doing things we are both good at and that mesh well with our personalities. To find out your character strengths, visit https://www.viacharacter.

---

[129] C. K. John Wang et al., "Competence, Autonomy, and Relatedness in the Classroom: Understanding Students' Motivational Processes Using the Self-Determination Theory," *Heliyon* 5, no. 7 (July 1, 2019): e01983.

org/reports?source=character-strengths-page or Google "character strengths report." This will take you to a test that you can take (it costs $10 for youth and $20 for those over eighteen), but this will be some of the best money that you spend in your life. This test was made by psychologists including Dr. Martin Seligman at the University of Pennsylvania and was produced with extensive research. The character strengths you find from this test can help you engage in efforts truly meaningful and enjoyable to you and can help you with decisions regarding things like careers or courses of study.

MAXIMIZING AND SATISFICING

Another way to live like a rat racer is to be a maximizer instead of a satisficer. Dr. Barry Schwartz, a psychology professor at Swarthmore College and the author of *The Paradox of Choice,* teaches about maximizing and satisficing. Maximizing is a life strategy whereby individuals faced with a number of choices try to find the absolute best option possible.[130] Satisficing, on the other hand, is when you stop searching for better alternatives once you find an option that is good enough. Schwartz's studies found that satisficers were happier than maximizers. An experiment that illustrated this phenomenon showed that people were happier with their car choice when they picked one car out of a few cars, as opposed to picking one car out of a whole catalog of cars.[131]

---

[130] Cassie Shortsleeve, "Tips to Get Better with Decision Making Process – Furthermore," Furthermore from Equinox, accessed November 20, 2020.

[131] Barry Schwartz et al., "Maximizing versus Satisficing: Happiness Is a Matter of Choice," *Journal of Personality and Social Psychology* 83, no. 5 (2002): 1178–97.

The maximizer mindset is similar to the rat race mindset because the maximizer tries to get the best possible outcome in many aspects of life. However, those who are happiest are those that choose to stick with what is good enough.

Dr. David Burns, a therapist and the author of *Feeling Good*, tells us to "dare to be average."[132] Stretching yourself beyond your abilities or trying to get the very best thing for the sake of it being the best thing can steal your joy. Being realistic with yourself and choosing to be average can be the decision for you if you feel like you are an unhappy maximizer or are living in a rat race.

But what if it gives you pleasure and meaning to be the best at something that you love to do? Angela Duckworth, the author of *Grit*, states that in order to be happy, there can be a mix of maximizing and satisficing. When I asked her what the balance was, she told me this is mostly a personal decision, but you want to satisfice in most things in life. For example, Duckworth said there are many things she likes to do, including jogging, cooking, and being a psychologist. However, she lives a happier life when she satisfices in most areas. She is still just as fast as she has ever been with jogging, and she has no intention to be the best jogger in the world. She tries to improve her cooking when she can, is happy with the moderate progress in her cooking skills. However, she tries her hardest and is very gritty about being a great psychologist and achieving her top-level goal of "using psychological science to help children thrive."

---

[132] Greg McKeown, "Today, Just Be Average," *Harvard Business Review*, October 30, 2013.

Duckworth does offer a word of caution when maximizing in certain areas. She states, "One lesson that gritty people struggle to learn is that it really isn't a gritty thing to work so hard without break or balance that you end up being isolated from family or fail to develop friendship. To play the long game, you have to learn to take breaks or some sort of a sabbath."

ACTIVITY 2.25: SATISFICING
To help combat unhealthy maximization or being stuck in the rat race, following these steps can help you learn to be happy in your satisficing.

1. Set requirements of what you need to be satisfied and how much you need to put in to get what you want.
2. Pursue options that meet your requirements.
3. Stop pursuing after you meet your requirements.
4. Enjoy the option that you satisficed for.

ACTIVITY 2.26: FLOW
The final way to find pleasure in the journey toward your goals is to experience flow. Mihaly Csikszentmihalyi, a psychologist, former WWII prisoner, and the developer of the term "flow state," says that flow is "a state in which people are so involved in an activity that nothing else seems to matter; the experience is so enjoyable that people will continue to do it even at great cost, for the sheer sake of doing it."[133] You can reach this state when your skills match the level of challenge. Having flow states in our lives is important, because if you remember, feeling competence in our regular activities (from

---

[133] Mike Oppland, "8 Ways To Create Flow According to Mihaly Csikszentmihalyi [+TED Talk]," PositivePsychology.com, December 16, 2016.

self-determination theory) is critical for us to be motivated and satisfied in our pursuits. Rat racers do not experience flow because they engage in pursuits that do not give them pleasure in doing the activity. Make sure you regularly have flow experiences in your life and check and see if your activity follows these requirements for flow:

1. Complete concentration on the task
2. Clarity of goals and reward in mind and immediate feedback
3. Transformation of time (speeding up/slowing down)
4. The experience is intrinsically rewarding
5. Effortlessness and ease
6. There is a balance between challenge and skills
7. Actions and awareness are merged, losing self-conscious rumination
8. There is a feeling of control over the task[134]

OVERCOMING THE NIHILISM BURGER

If you find yourself in a nihilistic state, first just know that I am truly sorry. I am very sorry to hear that you are going through a time where you feel hopeless, like there is no point in doing thing and nothing gives you joy. I have had times when I have felt like this after challenges in my life. If you have experienced a traumatic event like the loss of a loved one, an end of a relationship, or any other negative life change, you may feel like you will never be able to recover. When facing these challenges, the first thing to do is make sure that you are taking proper emotional first aid. Take time to grieve and fully feel your emotions and treat yourself with compassion.

---

[134] Ibid.

Throughout your life, you will have dreams, and it is part of life that some of your dreams will die. Dr. Daley shared how his dreams died several times in his life, including how his life dream of becoming a pro golfer died when he was told to not even try out for the U of U golf team and his dream of getting into grad school died when he was rejected from every single one that he applied to. After getting rejected from grad schools, he drove to a park by himself, parked his car, and broke down in tears. After devoting his life to his dreams, he was told he wasn't good enough, and he felt like a failure.

However, whenever dreams die, you can always find a new dream. Over time, Daley developed a new dream to become a psychologist. Since becoming a psychologist, he has discovered that his second dream did not take second place to his first dream—it ended up becoming better than the first dream.

If you've had a dream die, you too can create a new dream and rediscover purpose and pleasure in life. Here are some tips in creating new dreams:

ACTIVITY 2.27: CREATING A NEW DREAM
1. Like Daley took time to cry in the parking lot by himself, take the time you need to grieve. However, beware of morbid reflection, as this can be a barrier to your recovery. Take time to be aware of and mindful of your feelings. Try Activity 2.4: ACT Mindfulness for Managing Negative Thoughts and Feelings (Chapter 2b) and fully explore your emotions and thoughts.

2. Take the time to find a sense of purpose. Start by doing things that you love with people that you love and be compassionate to yourself in the process.
    a. When you are ready, refer to goal setting tips in Section 1c and align them with your character strengths that you found in Activity 2.24: Character Strengths (Chapter 2c)
    b. Plan in plenty of happiness boosters. Ben-Shahar tells us, "Whether at work or at home, the goal is to engage in activities that are both personally significant and enjoyable. When this is not feasible, make sure you have happiness boosters, moments throughout the week that provide you with both pleasure and meaning. Research shows that an hour or two of a meaningful and pleasurable experience can affect the quality of an 'entire day, or even a whole week."[135]
    c. Remember your inherent spiritual worth. We will talk about this more in the next chapter, but remember that you are valued on a spiritual level and that, no matter what, God loves you. Take time to revisit your spirituality and find a sense of purpose in it.

3. Meeting with a mental health professional can be very helpful in the process of finding a new dream.

---

[135] Tal Ben-Shahar, "7 Lessons On Earning The Ultimate Currency: Happiness," *Positivity Daily* (blog), February 10, 2015.

TAKEAWAYS FROM CHAPTER 2C:
MANAGING CHALLENGES TO THE HAPPINESS BALANCE

1. In addition to learning how to overcome biases to rewire our brains, it is also important that we balance pleasure and meaning.
2. To have a refresher on what this looks like, we will follow the hamburger model looking at the hedonism burger, the rat race burger, and the nihilism burger.
3. In order to overcome the hedonism burger, the main challenges are to attach purpose to our activities and also overcome hedonic adaptation.
4. The activities we have listed to overcome hedonism are overcoming shadow comforts and numbing behavior, anger, laziness, and navigating sexual feelings.
5. Overcoming the rat race burger lies in to learning to find pleasure in the journey as opposed to just focusing on the destination.
6. Activities to help us overcome the rat race burger include finding our character strengths, satisficing, and flow.
7. Overcoming the nihilism burger entails finding a sense of purpose and pleasure in life.
8. Overcoming nihilism is difficult, but when our dreams die, we can learn how to make new dreams.

CHAPTER 2D:

SPIRITUALITY AND THE MIND

———

As many young members of the Church have been told from a young age, spiritual sources are an essential place to turn toward for strength and support. Many mental health professionals both in and out of the Church tout the benefits of spirituality on your well-being.

In addition to that, many church leaders have told us about how important it is to invest in your mental well-being. General Conference talks like Elder Jeffrey R. Holland's "Like a Broken Vessel" share how your faith in God can help you respond to mental and emotional challenges. In this talk, Elder Holland encourages us to be proactive with our mental well-being through doing things such as seeking professional help if necessary.

Many aspects of spirituality can help you with your mental well-being. Let's take a look at what we have learned in

Sunday School and also how research suggests we exercise our spirituality.

THE GOSPEL OF JESUS CHRIST TEACHES US PRINCIPLES THAT FOCUS ON OBTAINING TRUE HAPPINESS

In *The Family: A Proclamation to the World*, we learn that happiness "is most likely to be achieved when founded upon the teachings of the Lord Jesus Christ."[136] In this chapter, we will learn about how teachings in the Gospel tell us to focus on happiness principles that research also happens to support.

First, the gospel teaches us the importance of having a sense of purpose and identity. We have all learned in Sunday School about being children of God and that our purpose is to be like God and follow the example of Jesus Christ. The Book of Mormon also teaches us our purpose in life is to have joy, and that we can achieve it through following the aptly named "Plan of Happiness."

We learned about our worth in the doctrine of the atonement—that no matter who we are or what we've done, we are worthy of love because we are God's children. Christ has atoned for our sins solely because we have innate value for who we are.

As we learned in the previous chapters, a sense of purpose and meaning is a key part of the happiness balance, and living a deeper spiritual purpose fulfills this. Lyubomirsky

---

[136] The First Presidency and Council of the Twelve Apostles of The Church of Jesus Christ of Latter-day Saints, "The Family Proclamation," The Church of Jesus Christ of Latter-day Saints, accessed November 22, 2020.

states that a "belief in a deity, an afterlife, and a system of understanding the origin and purpose of the universe can imbue your life with a sense of broader meaning. Because most major religions invoke some sort of ultimate, transcendent state, having the goal of getting to heaven or achieving nirvana, for instance, gives you a goal that helps give life meaning and structure. You are constantly striving for something. Also, it is a great comfort to know that a benevolent force is looking out for you and loves you unconditionally. This is especially true during trying times. Religious belief helps people make sense of and cope with tragedy."[137]

In terms of our identity, Ben-Shahar states how we must experience some form of inherent worthiness in order to lead a happy life.[138] We must feel worthy for simply existing. We are loved and valued independent of our actions and accomplishments. Spiritual beliefs like the Gospel of Jesus Christ helps us to have this inherent worthiness that is critical to well-being.

A key part of our sense of purpose is the doctrine of agency, which gives us the ability to have control over our actions in life. This falls right in line with what we have learned about developing an internal locus of control. Dr. Gary Vatcher tells young people that we have influence over our own lives, that we can apply the concept of agency to ourselves and decide to take actions in our own hands for our well-being.

---

[137] Sonja Lyubomirsky and Jaime Kurtz, *Positively Happy: Routes to Sustainable Happiness*, 1st ed. (United Kingdom: Positive Acorn, 2008), chap. 4, Kindle.

[138] Tal Ben-Shahar, *Happier* (McGraw-Hill Education (India) Pvt Limited, 2007), chap. 12, Kindle.

The ability to choose is also a key component of self-determination theory, which we first brought up in "Chapter 2c: Managing Challenges to the Happiness Balance" when we discussed the importance of engaging in pursuits that allow us to use our competence. Like we said, self-determination theory states that as humans, we have three basic needs to be truly motivated and happy: autonomy, relatedness, and competence.

We will talk more about relatedness in "Chapter 5a: Benefits of Being Active in Our Communities," but now we will focus on the importance of autonomy. The importance of autonomy is that people need to feel like they have choices and can determine the direction of their lives. The Gospel teaches us we have the choice between good and evil, and we can make decisions ourselves.

Also, the Gospel teaches us to focus on higher purposes, as opposed to the pursuit of material possessions that do not provide lasting happiness. Christ teaches us in Matthew 6:19-20 to not "lay treasures upon earth, where moth and rust doth corrupt, and where thieves break through and steal," but to instead to lay up "treasures in heaven, where neither moth nor rust doth corrupt, and where thieves do not break through nor steal." By living in pursuit of values instead of materials, we will be in the pursuit of things that are truly meaningful.

A relationship with God also helps us to live a life of optimism. Throughout the scriptures, we are frequently encouraged to express gratitude to God, and being able to pray to God allows us to focus on the good things in life as opposed to the bad things.

There are also many ways that living the Gospel improves parts of our lives such as our physical health, relationships, and our communities. We will expand upon these more in the next sections, but let's look at some ways that we can improve our mental well-being from a spiritual perspective.

ACTIVITY 2.28: IMPROVING MENTAL WELL-BEING THROUGH SPIRITUALITY

1. Strengthening a sense of purpose, identity, and worth
   a. Pray for confirmation or the comfort that comes from having a spiritual purpose in God's plan, having an identity as a child of God, and innate worth regardless of your actions.
   b. Read scriptures or other gospel literature that strengthen your sense of purpose, identity, and worth. Reading scriptures under the topic of the atonement is a great place to start.
   c. Receive a patriarchal blessing, or if you have one already, study it regularly. In this you can find a variety of strengths and gifts that you can use to determine a sense of purpose. If you find repeats in both your patriarchal blessing and your character strengths assessment, consider these as your "super strengths" that you definitely need to use on a regular basis.

2. Practice using your agency
   a. Use spiritual guidance to help you at times you need direction in life, especially in discerning what is within your control and what is out of your control.
   b. When you receive inspiration or revelation, choose to use your agency to act on it and strengthen your

ability to take control of the things within your sphere of influence.
c. When you discover things outside of your control, pray to have the strength to accept and be at peace with them.

3. Focus on things of a spiritual rather than material nature
   a. Try to decrease the amount of time, energy, and money that you spend on increasing or improving the material goods you own.
   b. Use the extra time to invest in your spirituality. Take more time to study the scriptures, pray, and receive revelation.

4. Cultivate optimism in a spiritual context
   a. Try and increase the portion of your prayer focused on giving thanks and expressing optimism.
   b. Throughout the day, give frequent prayers of gratitude for the little blessings you encounter in your life.

5. If having difficulty in developing spirituality:
   a. If you are having issues with developing your personal spirituality or having a crisis of faith, know that you are not alone and are actually part of the norm. Professional counselors deal with young people like us that have faith crises all the time. It is common to have these challenges.
   b. Talk to your bishop, a trusted church leader or friend, and guide yourself by study and prayer to find spirituality in your life. Just know that God loves you and wants you to be happy.

TAKEAWAYS FROM CHAPTER 2D:

SPIRITUALITY AND THE MIND

---

1. Spirituality is very important for our mental well-being, and much of what we've learned in Sunday school is actually backed by positive psychology.
2. The Gospel of Jesus Christ teaches many important principles for living a happy life including having a purpose and identity, the ability to choose, pursuing values over materials, and living a life of optimism.
3. The activities in this chapter will help you to improve your mental well-being through spirituality. Activities include ways to strengthen a sense of purpose, identity, and worth. They also help us to practice using our agency, focusing on the spiritual over the material, optimism, and developing spirituality in general.

SECTION 3: EXERCISES FOR THE BODY

Now, after discussing exercises we can do for our minds, the next sphere of influence is on the body. The body houses the mind, and it is essential to do the right physical activities to make sure our mental well-being is in the right place.

Dr. Ben-Shahar tells us to "remember the mind-body connection. What we do—or don't do—with our bodies influences our mind. Regular exercise, adequate sleep, and healthy eating habits lead to both physical and mental health."[139]

Mental health is directly linked to our physical health, and we will learn how exercise, sleep, and nutrition can help our bodies build the ideal amount of happy chemicals to help us reach a higher well-being baseline.

---

[139] Tal Ben-Shahar, "7 Lessons On Earning The Ultimate Currency: Happiness," *Positivity Daily* (blog), February 10, 2015.

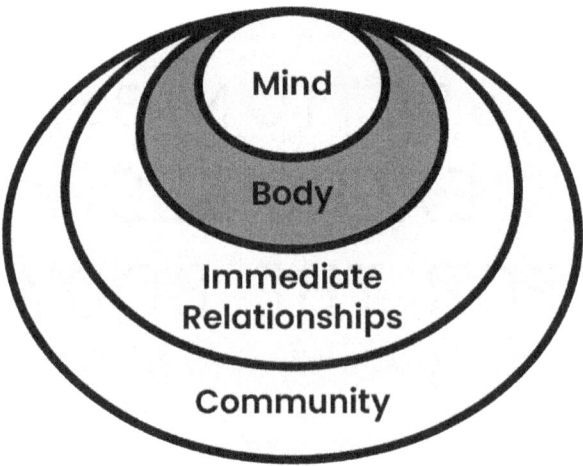

Spheres of Influence

We will now discuss the "Body" sphere of influence.

On that same vein, the state of unhappiness can cause real health problems that can be seen in our bodies. Dr. Daley tells us that unhappiness can even influence health problems such as hypertension, heart disease, and diabetes. This shows a very real and simple scientific principle: The state of your physical body is directly linked to the condition of your mind and the way you think. An important thing to note is how certain practices are essential to supporting a firm mind. If you truly want to live to the full level of your happiness, you must live principles that keep your body in a good state to support a healthy mind.

Studies show that these principles of exercise, sleep, and nutrition can be even more effective to boost your mood than antidepressants.

While these are things you have heard your whole life, very few people actually do all of these to the necessary level or at the regular frequency to actually reap the psychological benefits. Dr. Dan Daley said the first thing he makes sure his patients do is to get these three things in order before they move onto pharmaceutical treatment. Without a healthy diet, regular exercise, and sufficient sleep, your body cannot have the necessary base to allow your brain to function at the very basic level it needs.

It is no wonder the Word of Wisdom focuses on the importance of proper nutrition and care of your body. The health benefits of the Word of Wisdom are supported by numerous studies. Living the Word of Wisdom is definitely a good idea!

INTRODUCTION TO NEUROTRANSMITTERS

You know how I said that things like exercise, sleep, and nutrition can be more effective to boost your mood than taking pharmaceuticals like antidepressants? Let's learn more about why this is. First off, your mood is highly dependent on a variety of chemicals in your body called neurotransmitters. These chemicals are ways that your nerve cells communicate with each other and send messages, and these are what influence you to feel different emotions and feelings.

For example, if you are faced with a threat to your life (or are watching a movie that makes you feel scared), your body will release adrenaline, which makes your heart beat faster, your senses sharpen, and the blood flow to your muscles increase. These chemicals are enacted to help your body enact a fight or flight response to help you stay alive in a potentially life-threatening circumstance. Other neurotransmitters you might have heard of include serotonin (helps stabilize mood), dopamine (makes you feel pleasure), and oxytocin (produces the feeling of being in love).

The way and the amount your body naturally produces these chemicals can vary from person to person. Some people have genetic predispositions to create more happy chemicals, and some people have genetic predispositions to create less happy chemicals. Our genetic predispositions are not things we can control. However, we still do have control over a significant portion, and this has to do with optimizing the healthy production and balance of these chemicals.

One big neurotransmitter that we will talk a lot about is serotonin, as this neurotransmitter plays a role in mood stability, happiness, mental focus, and many bodily functions.[140] Low serotonin amounts are also linked to depression.[141]

Some people use drugs like antidepressants or stimulants to influence their neurotransmitter levels and, subsequently, their thoughts and feelings. For example, if they are sad, they can take Prozac, an antidepressant that increases serotonin, or if they are tired, they can take caffeine, which stops our brains from binding to neurotransmitters that make us tired. While drugs can be helpful for those that are facing severe

---

[140] Debra Rose Wilson, "Serotonin: Facts, Uses, SSRIs, and Sources," Medical News Today, accessed November 18, 2020.
[141] Ibid.

clinical challenges, the majority of people can achieve healthy levels of neurotransmitters and healthy levels of thoughts and feelings by taking care of their bodies. Getting proper exercise, sleep, and nutrition can do just as good or sometimes a better job than drugs.

Let's start by looking how exercise helps us increase the chemicals that are critical in improving our well-being levels.

CHAPTER 3A:

PHYSICAL EXERCISE

In 1999, several researchers at Duke University conducted the SMILE study (Standard Medical Intervention versus Long-term Exercise), testing the effectiveness of pharmaceutical antidepressants compared to exercise.[142] They gathered 156 participants who had been previously diagnosed for major depressive disorder (aka clinical depression), meaning they had serious struggles with depression and other related issues such as insomnia, eating disorders, and suicidal ideation. They set them in three different experimental groups: a group that was to take antidepressants (Zoloft) without exercise, a group to take antidepressants with exercise (three times a week, thirty minutes of exercise), and a group that only exercised (three times a week, thirty minutes of exercise). The majority of the subjects experienced decreased depression levels.

The study took a look at the participants six months after the study. They found that in the medication group, 38 percent of the over 60 percent that got better went back to being

---

[142] James A. Blumenthal, Patrick J. Smith, and Benson M. Hoffman, "Is Exercise a Viable Treatment for Depression?," *ACSM's Health & Fitness Journal* 16, no. 4 (2012): 14–21.

depressed. In the exercise and medication group, there was a relapse rate of 31 percent. The exercise only group had a relapse rate of only 9 percent after six months.

What this tells us is that first, even a moderate amount of exercise can be just as effective at decreasing depressive symptoms as antidepressants. Second, those who implement a regular exercise routine are much less likely to go back to being depressed than if they took an antidepressant.

This does not mean we can and should do away with psychiatric medication for those who have severe levels of depression, as people with major depressive disorders often require a little bit of medication to get to the point to start exercising, but we can see we need to take exercise seriously because it works.

There are thousands of studies that support the usefulness of exercise on anxiety, depression, ADD, and ADHD. Exercise seems like a miracle drug, and some might even think that it is like taking an antidepressant, but actually, not exercising is more like taking a depressant.

Today, many people are at a high risk for increased mental and emotional challenges because of their lack of exercise. As humans, we weren't made to be sedentary and sit in front of screens all day. In fact, our ancestors in hunter-gatherer societies probably walked close to seven miles a day, which is much more than the average person today, especially since the advent of the digital age.[143]

---

[143] Barbara King, "The Anthropology Of Walking," NPR.org, accessed November 16, 2020.

This is why Dr. Daley tells his clients to exercise regularly before he tells them to try taking antidepressants. This is not only because of the basic necessity and effectiveness of exercise (it is what our bodies are meant to do), but also because a growing body of research is beginning to show how antidepressants have many downsides. Studies have shown how antidepressants may be overprescribed in America, create a wide variety of side effects, and have limited efficacy that can largely be due to placebo (the placebo effect is when a treatment is effective at relieving symptoms due to your belief in the treatment, regardless of its true validity).[144]

In addition to just depression, exercise has been found to greatly improve other aspects of our lives including increases in school performance and decreased levels of bullying and violence in schools.[145] Exercise has been said to be like a hit of Prozac and Ritalin, as it releases chemicals that are like a drug that can make you feel better and help you focus.[146]

Exercise also prevents cognitive decline that occurs during aging. If you are a younger person, you can invest in your future mental health now. Exercise helps build your prefrontal cortex and hippocampus, making it break down slower and therefore decrease the risk of Alzheimer's or mental

---

[144] Brendan Smith, "Inappropriate Prescribing," American Psychological Association, accessed November 16, 2020.

[145] Amelia R. Turagabeci, Keiko Nakamura, and Takehito Takano, "Healthy Lifestyle Behaviour Decreasing Risks of Being Bullied, Violence and Injury," *PLOS ONE* 3, no. 2 (February 20, 2008): e1585.

[146] Carey Goldberg, "Why To Exercise Today: It's Like Prozac Plus Ritalin," CommonHealth, accessed November 16, 2020.

disease.[147] You can push back cognitive decline by ten to fifteen years and decrease risk of Alzheimer's by 50 percent, and if you are older and haven't begun, you can still do it now—the healing and benefit can begin as soon as exercise occurs.[148]

ACTIVITIES TO HELP US EXERCISE

So now, I hope you understand how important exercise is for your overall happiness and well-being. Now, let's discuss ways we can implement exercise in our lifestyle routines and overcome any challenges that are stopping us from exercising.

If you find yourself in the category of not regularly exercising, there are a variety of reasons that you are unable to exercise. This could include:

1. Not knowing how to exercise
2. Not liking exercise
3. Not making time for exercise
4. Not exercising because of physical limitations

We will discuss these reasons one by one.

---

[147] Mary Ellen Lytle et al., "Exercise Level and Cognitive Decline: The MoVIES Project," *Alzheimer Disease & Associated Disorders* 18, no. 2 (June 2004): 57–64.
[148] Ibid.

CHALLENGE: NOT KNOWING HOW TO EXERCISE

First, for those who are not sure how to exercise, exercise can be much simpler than many people think. There are several things that you need to keep in mind for exercise.

Make little changes to move more every day. Start small if you are new to exercise and review how often you get exercise in on a regular basis.

The goal is to get your heart rate up. While society wants you to think that the main goal of exercise is to change the way your body looks through burning calories, losing weight, or building muscles (don't get me wrong, this can be healthy), the most important reason you should exercise should be for the health benefits of exercise. Dr. Daley says that in order to access these benefits, it is important to do aerobic exercise, or exercise that increases your heart and breathing rate. These activities like running, walking stairs, squats, and burpees use major muscle groups like in your legs and back. These may not have dramatic weight-loss or muscle-building effects but going from no activity to a moderate level of activity will dramatically increase the release of mood-boosting and mentally-sharpening hormones and improve your physical health.

Traditional exercise like going to the gym is great, but it's also a good idea to begin doing exercise that you can do continuously for the rest of your life. Gyms are generally used by younger people or people with higher fitness levels without physical limitations. However, much of the population does not fit into this group, and as a result, many of these people do not get enough exercise for health benefits.

ACTIVITY 3.1: TIPS FOR IF YOU DON'T KNOW HOW TO EXERCISE

1. Add up as much movement as possible throughout the week. A study from Queens University states that getting a cumulative amount of 150 minutes of exercise a week can be beneficial for your cardiovascular health whether it is in big chunks several times a week, or in little bits every day.[149] (However, keep in mind this is just talking about cardiovascular health. You will get the most mental and emotional benefit if you are able to have some sort of exercise every day). A great way to do this is to make a goal for number of steps each day in your watch or app.
2. Schedule in "nontraditional exercise." You can make significant changes to your health without a gym membership if you do little things such as intentionally parking further away from the store or making a rule to never take the elevator. Taking the stairs and walking faster during your usual path are also ways to get more exercise.
3. Make a goal to add exercises in breaks during your day. Between work calls or in between Netflix episodes, do nonstop burpees, squats, lunges, or dance moves to just get moving. If you regularly have a phone call, try going for a walk as you talk, or if you prefer to stay inside, pace inside your home or apartment. If you have to regularly check emails, reply to text messages, or do reading, try doing this while pedaling on a stationary bike.

---

[149] Canadian Science Publishing, "Total Amount of Exercise Important, Not Frequency, Research Shows," ScienceDaily, accessed November 17, 2020.

4. If you eventually build up to a higher fitness level, you can begin combining nontraditional exercise forms (above) with other forms. The benefits of increased exercise can start from as little as twenty-three minutes a day, which leads to twelve hours of better mood.[150] Doing up to an hour of some form of exercise also will lead to even higher levels of mental and physical health.
5. Be careful to not overdo it, as this can either make you dread exercise as a chore or can injure you and prevent you from continuing exercise. Make sure to add stretches and warmups to your exercise routine. Listen to your body, and if you are unsure, talk to your accountability partners, do your research, or talk to a professional.

CHALLENGE: NOT LIKING EXERCISE

If this is the case for you, start in small ways that makes exercise more pleasant or at least manageable. Like I mentioned previously, work it into your regular routine. Try turning something routine into an opportunity to be active.

ACTIVITY 3.2: TIPS FOR IF YOU DON'T LIKE EXERCISE
1. If there are activities you like to do, try mixing them with exercise. Try saving your favorite music or audiobook to only be used for when you go for a walk or jog. This will make you look forward to exercise time. If you love watching TV, save an episode to watch it while you sit back and pedal on a stationary bike or walk on a treadmill. This can work with almost anything you like

---

[150] Jeff Haden, "Exercise Scientists Say One 23-Minute Workout a Week Is Nearly as Effective as Three--but There Is One Catch," Inc.com, March 27, 2020.

to do on your phone, whether it is spending time online, watching funny videos, or listening to music. If you have a scripture-reading or gospel study routine, listen to the scriptures or conference talks as you walk or do exercise.

2. Get people involved. Create a list of many friends or acquaintances to walk or jog with, so at times when you want to go exercise, the chance of one of them being available increases. It can be a really fun and great way to get closer with your friends by talking while walking or going on a hike. It also can be safer to do activities outside like walking or jogging when you are with friends or buddies.

3. If you happen to like a sport, you can kill two birds with one stone. Join Facebook groups, intramural teams, classes, or group messages of people that like to play frisbee, basketball, soccer, tennis, swimming, hiking, skiing, rock climbing, or other activities. If you are new to these activities, join them anyway! It can be an awesome way to make new friends, build talents, and create a new lifestyle that will improve your life. If you are a college student, luckily, most colleges offer some sort of exercise class. These are fun ways to make exercise part of your schedule.

4. Gamify exercise. Download an app like Fitocracy or Strava, where you can level up and track progress with your friends and peers. Also, you can make exercise fun by doing dance-related workouts. It can be as simple as breaking it down to your favorite music in a private location like your room or downloading a dance app to follow along to a planned Zumba-like routine. Apps like Jog.fm will track your running pace and match it to a song with a similar pace. If there is something you do like watching TV, make a game with your friends.

For example, if you are watching an action movie, every time there is an explosion, you have to do five burpees.
5. Try and relabel the way you perceive exercise. Refer to it in a positive light. Say, "I get to spend time with my friends" or "I get to have a chance to boost chemicals in my body to make me happier and nicer to my loved ones" or "I am so lucky that I get to do something that boosts my mood."
6. Pay close attention to how you feel on days that you exercise vs. days you don't exercise. The difference may be subtle, but after paying attention closely, I have noticed that I improve in pretty much all aspects of my life. Science supports all of this, of course. I find that I am in a more cheerful and less irritable mood after returning from exercise and I am able to focus better, sleep better, be a better friend/family member, and even have better digestion. When I returned from my mission with stress-related digestive issues, my gastroenterologist suggested that I exercise more regularly. After doing this, I noticed a substantial improvement in my stress-related symptoms.

CHALLENGE: NOT MAKING TIME FOR EXERCISE
To address these concerns, we can apply the same principles we talked about in Chapter 1c on keeping up lifestyle routines. Here are some other tips to remember when making your plans:

ACTIVITY 3.3: WAYS TO SCHEDULE EXERCISE IN
1. Remember to keep it positive. As discussed in the goals section, there are two types of goals: approach goals and avoidance goals. Approach goals are goals that focus on "dos" vs. avoidance goals, which focus on "don'ts." Examples of approach goals are like "make time to walk

with friends" or "watch my favorite show while cycling." Examples of avoidance goals include "don't miss exercise more than twice a week" or "don't stop for a breather during the jog." Research shows that approach goals are much more motivating and sustainable in the long run than avoidance goals, so make sure to do this. Write your goals down in a journal or on a post it note, as writing things down makes you much more likely to do it.
2. Keep it interesting! Have a full arsenal of activities you can choose from, such as doing a hike with friends over the weekend, walking to school on some weekdays, and going to the gym or playing sports on some days.
3. If you have difficulty fitting it in your schedule, do all that you can to decrease the activation energy to start your activity. For example, it can seem inconvenient to have to change, go exercise, and then shower after. Try lining them up in a convenient way, make it as streamlined as possible. For example, you can wear your exercise clothes to bed so you don't have to change the first thing in the morning, and have your shoes and socks ready the night before to put them on instantly. If you have the thought to go for a quick jog but only have a thirty-minute window, throw on some clothes in a few minutes, jog for ten minutes, and then clean-up/shower/change in twenty minutes. It is definitely worth the time to get ready and clean-up to get in a ten-minute jog, especially considering the benefits you can gain. Everyone can make thirty minutes in their day, especially since most people our age spend a couple hours a day doing things such as scrolling through social media or watching TV. Cut those activities down by a quarter and make time to exercise!

4. Like I have said many times before, get friends involved. Not only will it be more fun and more safe, but having friends that invite you or include you in their regular routines can help you exercise more often.
5. If you stop for a bit, don't worry about it. Just start it again! Treat yourself as you would treat a friend.
6. If you ever think, "I have too much studying to do" or "I am too tired to do it," remember that exercise can be a great energizer to get blood flowing to your brain for a boost of energy. Exercise releases chemicals in your brain that are similar to stimulant drugs like Ritalin for ADD/ADHD or caffeine. Plan two-minute breaks in between studies or work to do burpees, jumping jacks, or pushups to get a mental boost of energy. It is very worth the several minute investments of exercise while you study, as it will make you more effective than if you didn't take the time to do it.

CHALLENGE: NOT EXERCISING BECAUSE OF PHYSICAL LIMITATIONS

If you are injured or are facing challenges that make exercise difficult, do whatever you can! If you can swim a little bit or do stretches or only exercise certain parts of your body, a little bit is infinitely better than nothing at all. Ask your doctor for their recommendations on exercise, and there are many online resources you can find to get more ideas.

ACTIVITY 3.4: OTHER PHYSICAL "EXERCISES" TO IMPROVE WELL-BEING

1. Body scanning is a way you can detect and manage stress or tension in your body. Whether you are sitting at your desk, on the bus, or lying in bed, you can close

your eyes and focus on different areas in your body. Begin with the top of the head and focus on individual parts of the body, moving down to your face, jaw, neck, and all the way down to your toes. You can flex or tense your muscles, feel what is going on in that part of your body, and feel the stress dissipate as you relax the muscles. This is also a great way to practice mindfulness, awareness, and grounding in the present. Plan two-minute body scans into your lifestyle routines.

2. Yoga uses many aspects of body scanning and is a great addition to exercise routines as it helps with your body's flexibility. It also helps you practice mindfulness, awareness, and grounding in the present. Look up yoga moves that you can do for two minutes just to get the hang of it, and you can combine this with body scanning if you want. I like to do a position called Child's Pose before I go to bed, as this is a great way to gently stretch your lower back.

3. Incorporating physical touch in your life is an excellent way to release mood-boosting chemicals in your body. You do not need to have a romantic partner to do this. The effects of physical touch can be noticed from as short as a ten-second hug every day, as this will release endorphins that make you feel better.[151] If you're a macho tough guy like me (just kidding), screw social norms and get more physical touch in your life to improve your health. Hug your friends, roommates, and family members. Give your loved ones a pat on the back. Even placing your hands on yourself such as

---

[151] Marangeli Lopez, "Study: A 10-Second Hug Can Make You Healthier, Happier," *NEWS10 ABC*, January 21, 2020.

on your chest or your arms, in a self-hugging motion, is shown to boost these chemicals in your body.[152] As you do this, you can speak reassuring words to yourself and imagine a supportive friend, family member, or role model doing this to you. To further highlight the importance of physical touch, studies have shown how lack of physical touch leads to decreased quality and length of life, such as in a study of infants in orphanages that actually died without being touched, or how groups that receive less touch (such as elderly men) experience quicker cognitive decline.[153] So try and find ways to incorporate touch in your life and realize that this can help other people. Give your grandparents or elderly members of your ward a hug or pat on the back if you can—it can make a big difference. Plan a daily eight-second hug into your lifestyle routine. Even better, plan in two minutes a day to cuddle with or hold a loved one or pet. If you are by yourself, hugging or placing your hands on your body can also give you these positive effects.

4. Spend time outside in nature. Many studies tout the benefits of being in nature, and some studies document the risks of "nature deficit disorder." Whether the benefits claim to come from distancing yourself from negative messages, taking time to be mindful, or spending time in the sun, there is no doubt that something about

---

[152] Kerstin Uvnäs-Moberg, Linda Handlin, and Maria Petersson, "Self-Soothing Behaviors with Particular Reference to Oxytocin Release Induced by Non-Noxious Sensory Stimulation," *Frontiers in Psychology* 5 (January 12, 2015).

[153] Andrew Reiner, "The Power of Touch, Especially for Men (Published 2017)," *The New York Times*, December 5, 2017, sec. Well.

being in nature is good for you.[154] Plan to spend at least two minutes a day in nature. This could be stopping to rest by some trees in the park during your walk, or even sitting in your backyard for a short moment. You can combine this with other exercises like meditating or journaling.

---

[154] Richard Louv, "No More 'Nature-Deficit Disorder,'" Psychology Today, accessed November 23, 2020.

TAKEAWAYS FROM CHAPTER 3A:
PHYSICAL EXERCISE

1. Chemicals your body produces, called neurotransmitters, are largely responsible for the moods and emotions we feel.
2. People use drugs like antidepressants or stimulants to influence their neurotransmitter levels and subsequently, their thoughts and feelings, but taking care of your physical body through exercise, sleep, and proper nutrition can do just as good or sometimes a better job.
3. Even a moderate amount of exercise can be just as effective at decreasing depressive symptoms as antidepressants. Also, those who implement a regular exercise routine are much less likely to return to being depressed than if they took an antidepressant.
4. Exercise can also help us perform better in school, improve our relationships, and decrease our rate of cognitive decline.
5. There are several reasons people don't exercise: not being sure how to exercise, not liking it, not being able to make time for it, or being unable to do it because of physical limitations.
6. If you don't know how to exercise, don't like physical exercise, can't make time for physical exercise, or have limitations to physical exercise, this chapter has a variety of activities and resources to help you exercise.

7. There are other helpful physical "exercises" you can do that help your well-being, such as body scanning, yoga, spending time in nature, or having enough physical touch in your life. These are all proven ways to improve your happiness levels.

CHAPTER 3B:

SLEEP

Sleep is the next piece of the puzzle that is critical for our mental health. It is profoundly important for your mental wellness, as many of your neurotransmitters are manufactured during your sleep.[155] People who don't sleep well suffer on many levels. Even losing just one hour of sleep over a few days can have an effect; it can lead to a decrease in performance, mood, thinking, physical appearance, and put you at risk for many diseases.[156] Getting regular, adequate amounts of sleep is critical.

As Dr. Daley puts it, "The positive aspects of the Word of Wisdom may be compromised when there is sleep deprivation." You can exercise as much as you want and eat as healthily as you want, but your health will be severely affected without adequate sleep. In order to be happy, we must get enough sleep.

---

[155] Mohammed A. Al-Abri, "Sleep Deprivation and Depression," *Sultan Qaboos University Medical Journal* 15, no. 1 (February 2015): e4–6.

[156] Johns Hopkins Medicine, "Sleep/Wake Cycles," Johns Hopkins Medicine, accessed November 18, 2020.

SLEEP AND YOUR BRAIN

Recent studies have also debunked myths such as "some people can function on only five hours a sleep a night," showing that while the effects aren't immediate, sleep deprivation releases proteins in the blood that greatly increase your risk of Alzheimer's and other neurological problems.[157] You may not see the effects right away, but over time, you are killing your brain cells little by little every time you deprive yourself of sleep.[158]

Sleep deprivation is linked to mental challenges such as depression and mood disorders.[159] This is largely due to the fact that your brain produces many neurotransmitters during your sleep, which are critical for you to have stable and positive emotions.[160]

Sleep deprivation in young people is also linked with higher risk of suicide.[161] As suicide is one of the leading causes of preventable death for people ages fifteen to thirty-four, it is unquestionable that we should prioritize our sleep, as our lives literally depend on it.[162]

---

[157] Ehsan Shokri-Kojori et al., "β-Amyloid Accumulation in the Human Brain after One Night of Sleep Deprivation," *Proceedings of the National Academy of Sciences of the United States of America* 115, no. 17 (24 2018): 4483–88.

[158] Melanie Haiken, "Lack Of Sleep Kills Brain Cells, New Study Shows," Forbes, accessed November 18, 2020.

[159] Al-Abri, "Sleep Deprivation and Depression."

[160] Ibid.

[161] Erin Digitale, "Sleep Disturbances Predict Increased Risk for Suicidal Symptoms, Study Finds | News Center | Stanford Medicine," Stanford Medicine News Center, accessed November 18, 2020.

[162] Ibid.

THE IMPORTANCE OF SLEEP WHILE YOU'RE YOUNG

Dr. Daley says young people are especially in danger of having issues related to sleep deprivation. He said how one study showed how the average college student only slept four to five hours a night. As a result of this, college students experienced skin aging at a rate similar to the elderly. The study showed that over a four-year period, these college students had skin that aged equivalent to sixteen years over the course of their four-year college career. Numerous other studies show how young people can age significantly and decline in their appearance and health from not getting enough sleep.[163]

Throughout your teenage years and early adulthood, your brain is forming and the rest of your body is growing. Experts suggest a range of eight to ten hours of sleep while you are young, and this varies from person to person.[164] Also add in the fact that young adulthood is the time when you go through the biggest life changes and emotional roller coasters, and you will see that you need all the emotional support that you can get. Sleep provides this emotional support and stability that will help you in the challenges that occur in perhaps the most pivotal time of your life.

SHARPENING YOUR MIND

In addition to putting your mind in a healthy place to handle emotions and thoughts healthily, adequate sleep is also critical for your ability to perform cognitive tasks such as learning, memorizing, and solving problems. As this skill is critical for schoolwork, work, and extracurricular tasks

---

[163] University Hospitals Case Medical Center, "Sleep Deprivation Linked to Aging Skin, Study Suggests," ScienceDaily, accessed November 25, 2020.
[164] Alex Dimitriu, "Sleep for Teenagers," Sleep Foundation, April 17, 2009.

such as learning music, playing sports, or doing dance moves, you definitely want to have your mental abilities at the top of their game.

Sleep plays a critical role in this process as a lot of research shows how your mind works through solutions to problems you haven't solved as you sleep, and sleep is also the time when your brain stores short-term memories into long-term storage.[165] This just shows how important it is for you to get your sleep, especially if you're a student. So, the next time you think forgoing sleep will help you for a big test or presentation, the best strategy is to sleep regularly and prepare for your big day ahead of time as opposed to cramming the night before. Also, do not pull all-nighters! All-nighters are extremely traumatic on your health. Not only will they throw off your sleep schedule, but they will also trigger changes in the body that can eventually lead to obesity, diabetes, and dangerous health issues.[166]

SLEEP AND RELATIONSHIPS

As we stated how sleep produces neurotransmitters that are critical in regulating our moods, we can now take a look at how sleep affects our interactions with others.

Have you ever heard of the saying, "Never go to bed angry"? Relationship experts such as Dr. John Gottman state that this is actually a myth and bad advice. The longer you deprive

---

[165] Ut Na Sio, Padraic Monaghan, and Tom Ormerod, "Sleep on It, but Only If It Is Difficult: Effects of Sleep on Problem Solving," *Memory & Cognition* 41, no. 2 (February 2013): 159–66.

[166] Katherine Lee, "Study Reveals Why All-Nighters May Be So Dangerous for Your Health," Everyday Health, accessed November 18, 2020.

yourself of sleep, especially during a conflict, the more your cognitive abilities decline and your ability to rationally solve a conflict diminishes.[167]

This is largely due to the fact that sleep deprivation weakens our rational brain and makes us go into the fight-flight response of our amygdalae much more quickly. One study shows how sleep deprivation causes us to have much more emotional responses in the face of challenges.[168] So it is important to keep this in mind when we sacrifice our sleep because responding to criticism in school, at work, or in our relationships will be greatly compromised if we don't sleep enough.

WHAT IF I CAN'T AFFORD TO CUT DOWN MY SLEEP TO DO ALL THE THINGS THAT I NEED TO DO?
Prioritize your sleep and cut down your overachievement. We learned about how overachievement is not a sustainable route to happiness in Section 2, and you will have a happier life overall if you have a healthy chemical balance and achieve enough than if you achieve more but have a worse chemical balance.

Getting enough sleep is difficult for many young people, as today, more than ever, young people are busy. Being busy is generally a healthy thing, as involvement in many extracurricular activities can help you later on with your success

---

[167] David Khalaf, "It's Okay to Go to Bed Angry," The Gottman Institute, August 30, 2018.

[168] Seung-Schik Yoo et al., "The Human Emotional Brain without Sleep--a Prefrontal Amygdala Disconnect," *Current Biology: CB* 17, no. 20 (October 23, 2007): R877-878.

in life.[169] We all have many things going on—school, sports, dance, clubs, friends—and if you are a high school student enrolled in an early morning seminary program, you can pretty much kiss a good night's sleep goodbye.

For example, if you are a high school student going to seminary in the morning, you may have to wake up as early as 5 a.m. and then go to bed at around 8 p.m. to get the eight to ten hours of sleep recommended for teenagers. Given the average schedule of a high schooler in America, it is very difficult and almost unheard of to go to bed at 8 p.m. I remember never waking up refreshed in the morning before early morning seminary, as I would often go to bed closer to midnight every night and would never complete a full and healthy sleep cycle.

To address this, make going to bed early a priority! Avoid staying up late to cram before a test or project. If you have too many things that take up your time such as instrument practice, sports teams, or other extracurriculars, Dr. Daley says cut things down. Your health depends on it, and sleep is a priority. If early morning seminary is too hard to sustain, try and find ways to do makeups or alternatives.

It is important to keep these considerations in mind, especially if you are a high school student, as your teenage years are a critical time for the formation of your brain and other key life decisions. Without ample sleep during this time, you are much more prone to having emotional instability, which makes handling the challenges of a teenage life even more difficult.

---

[169] Angela Duckworth, "What Are Kids Really Learning from Their Extracurricular Activities? Practice and Character," *The Philadelphia Inquirer*, sec. News, accessed November 18, 2020.

THE IMPORTANCE OF A SLEEP SCHEDULE

It is important to sleep on your normal cycle. Research shows that you can significantly decrease depressive symptoms if you go to bed and wake up around the same time every day, from weekdays to weekends.[170] Sleep does not have cumulative effects in the same way exercise might. For example, sleeping small amounts on weekdays and catching up on the weekends is not the same as sleeping the same amount every day, even if you get the same number of hours in both situations. It is much better for your health to sleep as much as you need every day, and not have the need to catch up.

If you have an irregular sleep schedule and make it up with napping, that's good—getting in naps when you are tired is better than not sleeping at all. However, Dr. Daley says it is important to note that if you try and make up through just naps, naps are only effective during the first twenty-four hours of initial deprivation. Without that nap, the sleep deprivation damage will cause more serious and long-term effects.

Daley also tells us to remember that the quality of sleep you gain decreases greatly when you go to bed later. You don't produce as many good neurotransmitters when you push your sleep cycle back, as many of the healthy neurotransmitters are produced during your last several sleep cycles as you sleep. If you go to bed later and start your sleep cycle later,

---

[170] Sarah Cummings, "5 Sleep Tips That Can Help with Depression | NAMI: National Alliance on Mental Illness," National Alliance on Mental Illness, accessed November 18, 2020.

the result is that you will cut off the important "end part" of your sleep cycle and lose many of the psychological benefits.

So, now that we have talked about the risks of cutting down your sleep, we now can get into activities we can do in order to improve our sleep.

ACTIVITY 3.5: GET ON A NORMAL SLEEP CYCLE
1. Ideally, you should be going to bed early enough that you can wake up refreshed without the use of an alarm clock. Make that a priority and a benchmark for how healthy your sleep patterns are.
2. Try to go to bed at the same time every day and wake up at the same time every day.
3. If you are having trouble making time for your optimal sleep schedule, cut down your commitments. When you say yes to things that take sleep away, you are also saying yes to decreasing your health and emotional stability. Do whatever you can to plan around your sleep. Sleep experts even suggest for young people and parents to advocate for later school start times for improved sleep.[171]

ACTIVITY 3.6: IMPROVING YOUR SLEEP QUALITY
1. Justin Su'a says, "For most teens, technology is the biggest thing stopping them from getting optimal sleep. Get off the video games, stop texting, and don't tempt yourself by charging your phone next to your bed; both you and I know you'll be on it all night."[172] Abstain from

---

[171] Alex Dimitriu, "Sleep for Teenagers," Sleep Foundation, April 17, 2009.
[172] Justin Su'a, *Mentally Tough Teens: Developing a Winning Mindset*, First Edition (Springville, UT: Plain Sight Publishing, 2014), chap. 1, Kindle.

media use or screen time at least a half hour before you go to bed and put it on silent mode. The blue light from screens affects your brain's ability to relax before sleeping, and even "night mode" on devices can still affect your sleep. Also, things that incite emotional responses such as social media, TV, or messages can produce chemicals in your body that make it harder to sleep. So, the best thing you can do is to put your phone away a good amount of time before you sleep. If you need an alarm in the morning, begin by training yourself with a real alarm clock so you can keep your phone outside of your room.
2. Darken your room. Get better blinds installed in your room and buy a sleep mask to cover your eyes.
3. Make your environment quieter. Buy earplugs to use or a white noise machine to ensure that no sounds will be keeping you up when you go to bed early.
4. Keep your room cool, as your body temperature cooling is a key signal to your body to have higher quality rest.
5. Avoid caffeine and energy drinks, especially in the afternoon and evening.
6. Make your room comfortable. Set up your bed with a supportive mattress and pillows.
7. Avoid reading or doing work in your bed—this makes your brain associate your bed and bedroom with work, as opposed to sleep. Have your brain associate your bed and bedroom with sleep, so do activities like work or studying outside of your bedroom if possible.
8. If tired and restless in bed, get up and do something that is not emotionally stimulating like reading scriptures or calming meditation. Writing in your journal can also help you manage restless thoughts or worries. Don't look at a screen.

9. Expose yourself to sunlight during the day (or if you live somewhere that isn't sunny, buy a happy light). Your sleep quality and serotonin production are dependent on exposure to sunlight, as sunlight triggers your serotonin levels during the day. Your serotonin levels help you follow your circadian rhythm (your natural sleep cycle), which helps you sleep more soundly at night.[173]
10. Get exercise during the day. Studies have shown that exercising during the day can help you have higher sleep quality at night.[174] However, try to avoid exercising right before you sleep, as this can give you a boost of energy and wakefulness that will need to subside before you tire.

CHALLENGE: BEING TIRED FOR STUDYING, WORK, ETC.

Many people turn to substances in order to help them overcome effects of tiredness. A lot of these "shortcuts" are much worse for you in the long run. For example, if you're tired, you may decide to drink an energy drink with caffeine. However, caffeine is a drug, a toxin, and bad for your health in the long run.[175] No wonder the Word of Wisdom advises against drinks like tea and coffee. If you really need to wake up during a slump in the day or need a boost of energy and focus, here are some healthier alternatives:

---

[173] Rachel Nall, "What Are the Benefits of Sunlight?," Healthline, May 25, 2018.

[174] Hideki Tanaka and Shuichiro Shirakawa, "Sleep Health, Lifestyle and Mental Health in the Japanese Elderly: Ensuring Sleep to Promote a Healthy Brain and Mind," *Journal of Psychosomatic Research* 56, no. 5 (May 1, 2004): 465–77.

[175] Cyril Willson, "The Clinical Toxicology of Caffeine: A Review and Case Study," *Toxicology Reports* 5 (November 3, 2018): 1140–52.

ACTIVITY 3.7: GETTING AN ENERGY BOOST WHEN TIRED

1. Get moving. Like we learned earlier, immediately after exercising, you can get a hit of energy-boosting chemicals and increased blood flow to your brain can make you more alert.
2. Use cold water. Plunging yourself is one of the best ways to reset your nervous system and also decrease depression, with zero toxicity.[176] Cover your face and head with cold water or take a cold shower. Drinking something cold can also help with this.
3. Listen to some pump-up music and clap your hands; this excites your prefrontal lobe and wakes you up.[177] I like to put on some intense EDM or dubstep (feel free to make fun of me) when I am getting tired, and this gets me excited and more alert.
4. Take a break to chat with someone or have an energizing conversation.
5. Work in a cool place. A hot room can make you feel groggy and sluggish.
6. Sit up or stand up. Hunching over collapses your chest and presses your diaphragm against the bottom of your lungs, hindering your ability to breathe easily. Sitting up straight or standing up allows you to breathe more fully, giving your brain more oxygen and the ability to concentrate better.[178]

---

[176] Nikolai Shevchuk, "Adapted Cold Shower as a Potential Treatment for Depression," *Medical Hypotheses* 70 (February 1, 2008): 995–1001.

[177] Mayumi Ikeuchi et al., "Research on the Frontal Lobe Activation Effect of Music Therapy – Effect of Listening Music on Frontal Lobe Activation by Using Near-Infrared Spectroscopy –," *Japanese Journal of Complementary and Alternative Medicine* 15.

[178] James Clear, "The Productivity Guide: My Best Productivity and Time-Management Tips," *James Clear* (blog), accessed October 4, 2020.

TAKEAWAYS FROM CHAPTER 3B:

SLEEP

---

1. Sleep is critical because sleep produces the chemicals in your body necessary to stabilize your mood and have positive emotions. People who don't sleep well suffer on many levels including decreased mood, thinking, and physical health.
2. Not getting enough sleep can contribute to depression and suicide, and the early years are critical for getting enough sleep. Sleep provides emotional support and stability that will help you in perhaps the most pivotal time of your life.
3. Sleep helps you perform better at mental tasks including creativity and memory, and shirking on sleep before big events is a bad idea.
4. Adequate sleep is also critical for our interactions with others, as we are less able to think rationally and interact positively with others when we are sleep deprived.
5. Prioritize your sleep at the sake of overachievement. We learned about how overachievement is not a sustainable route to happiness in Section 2. You will have a happier life overall if you have a healthy chemical balance and achieve less than if you achieve more but have a worse chemical balance.
6. It is critical to sleep in a regular pattern: sleeping the same amount every day, going to sleep at the same time,

and waking up at the same time every day. Disrupting this sleep pattern can be dangerous for your health.

7. This chapter provides activities and many ideas on how to get on a normal sleep schedule, improve your sleep quality, and get a healthy boost of energy without getting tired.

MATERIALS LIST FOR CHAPTER 3B:

SLEEP

- Alarm clock (not a phone) if you need one to get up in the morning
- Room darkeners like a sleep mask or window blinds
- Noise reducers like earplugs or a white noise machine
- Things to increase comfort while sleeping, such as sheets, pillows, blankets or mattress pad
- Happy light if you don't have enough natural sunlight during the day

CHAPTER 3C:

NUTRITION

Like we learned in health class, there are important food groups that are key to fueling your body and mind. We will get into those more in this section. First, let's discuss the importance of taking care of your mental well-being from a nutrition perspective. As we mentioned at the start of the chapter about the importance of neurotransmitters, you need the right nutrients for your body to make them. While exercise and sleep are key in producing neurotransmitters that are critical for your mood, proper nutrition is what provides the raw materials to build these chemicals in the first place. Nutrition is also critical in building the tissues that make up our brain and nerve cells.

Healthy foods are where your body gets the building blocks and fuel in order for you to maximize the production of happy chemicals. This chapter will teach us how to eat the right things in order to optimize our health. Also, notice how I referred to this section as "nutrition" as opposed to "diet." Sometimes, when we hear the word diet, we might think of something restrictive that says no to certain foods. While certain foods could be better or worse for you, I hope that you approach the reading of this section thinking of things to incorporate, with a lighter focus on things to cut out.

Like we mentioned in the exercise section, if you make goals for nutrition, make them approach-based as opposed to avoidance-based. Say "eat a green vegetable every day" as opposed to saying "give up chocolate for a month." Focusing on the negative is much more likely to make it stick in your mind, leading to less sustainable results and less healthy perspectives on food. Don't worry much about the don'ts, just focus on the dos.

So, now let's talk about the essential food groups for our mental health. We will first talk about micronutrients our body needs: vitamins and minerals. We will then go over the three basic macronutrients or building blocks that our body uses, which are fats, protein, and carbohydrates. We will close by discussing the importance of getting proper hydration and nutritional intake.

VITAMINS AND MINERALS

Adequate vitamins and minerals are key to keeping our many bodily functions healthy. These are essential micronutrients our body needs. We can get proper vitamins and minerals through supplements and having varied diets with lots of fruits and vegetables. The particular vitamin that we want to make sure you take is vitamin D. Dr. Daley says he recommends two basic things for proper mental nutrition: taking adequate omega-3 and vitamin D. We will get more into omega-3s later, but just know that given the research on vitamin D and omega-3s, everyone should be taking one every day to get the immense amount of health benefits that these offer.

According to Daley, vitamin D is very important for your well-being. Your mood is highly dependent on adequate vitamin D levels, as happy neurotransmitter production is based on this. Vitamin D is a big part in having stable mood and healthy well-being, and vitamin D deficiency is strongly linked to many mood disorders and mental illnesses.[179] In addition to its importance for your mental health, it also critical for your physical health. Vitamin D is very important for your teeth, bones, and organs, and vitamin D deficiency is linked to many other physical illnesses including osteoporosis, muscle weakness, and cancer.[180] Despite the huge importance of vitamin D to our mental and physical health, an estimated 40 percent of American adults are deficient.[181] Dr. Daley suggests having 2000–4000 IU of vitamin D every day to combat depression and mental challenges. Also, for your physical health, research indicates that if everyone took 2000 IU of vitamin D every day, cancer rates would decrease by 30 percent.[182]

In addition to taking vitamin D supplements, one way to also improve vitamin D levels is through sun exposure. Exposure

---

[179] Ibrar Anjum et al., "The Role of Vitamin D in Brain Health: A Mini Literature Review," *Cureus* 10, no. 7, accessed November 18, 2020.
[180] Ryan Raman, "How to Safely Get Vitamin D From The Sun," Healthline, April 28, 2018.
[181] Ibrar Anjum et al., "The Role of Vitamin D in Brain Health: A Mini Literature Review," *Cureus* 10, no. 7, accessed November 18, 2020.
[182] M. Rita I. Young and Ying Xiong, "Influence of Vitamin D on Cancer Risk and Treatment: Why the Variability?," *Trends in Cancer Research* 13 (2018): 43–53.

to the sun's UVB rays is what allows your body to synthesize vitamin D.[183] One thing you can do, if you live in a sunny climate, is to find ways to get ten to thirty minutes of direct sunlight a day, two to three times a week. Ways I like to do this are by going on walks with friends, going to the park, going fishing, or going jogging. Vitamin D can be synthesized from exposed parts of your body like your arms, hands, and face. If you have lighter skin, it takes less time to synthesize vitamin D (closer to ten minutes) and if you have darker skin, it takes more time to synthesize vitamin D (closer to thirty minutes).[184] Also, wearing sunscreen blocks the rays that your body uses to synthesize vitamin D, so you shouldn't wear sunscreen for the first ten to thirty minutes in the sun. However, anything past ten to thirty minutes can be dangerous to your skin (especially if you have lighter colored skin), as unprotected rays can cause sunburn, skin aging, and skin cancer.[185]

Vitamin D deficiency is also linked to geographical areas that do not have much sunlight. In my hometown of Seattle, Washington, many people experience seasonal affective disorder (SAD), which is a type of depression linked to changes with the seasons. Seattle in particular has high amounts of SAD because of the frequently overcast and rainy weather.

SAD occurs because of the lack of sunlight during fall and winter seasons, and this lack of sunlight influences decreased vitamin D production. This is a reason why

---

[183] Ryan Raman, "How to Safely Get Vitamin D From The Sun," Healthline, April 28, 2018.
[184] Ibid.
[185] Ibid.

doctors commonly advise Seattle residents to regularly take a vitamin D supplement (1000 IU) to ensure they have proper nutrition to maintain mental and emotional wellbeing without sunlight.

In addition to vitamin D deficiency, decreased sun exposure also increases depression because limited sunlight exposure decreases your sleep quality and your production of mood stabilizing neurotransmitters like serotonin. Serotonin is linked to boosting your mood, increasing productivity, and improving sleep, so if you want these benefits, being exposed to sunlight is an awesome way to do this.

In addition to vitamin D, there are several other vitamins and minerals that are important for mental well-being and mood. Vitamin B-9 (also known as folate or folic acid), magnesium, selenium, and vitamin C are all linked to improving mental well-being and preventing mental illness.[186] Fruits and vegetables (especially leafy greens) are excellent sources of these vitamins and minerals. You can also get these vitamins and minerals by taking supplements (pills or capsules), but the best overall benefit is from eating a variety of fruits and vegetables, as they can also provide phytonutrients that are important in promoting your overall physical health and preventing cancer, not to mention the fact that vitamins can be better absorbed when eaten as fruits and vegetables.[187]

---

[186] Dennis Relojo-Howell, "Vitamin Deficiency Can Affect Your Mental Health – Here Are 5 Supplements for Mental Health," *Psychreg* (blog), May 28, 2020.

[187] Harvard Health Publishing, "Should You Get Your Nutrients from Food or from Supplements?," Harvard Health, accessed November 18, 2020.

FATS

Healthy fats and oils are critical for our overall health and mental health. Your brain and neural tissue (what nerve cells are made of) are made up of fats and oils, and getting the proper fats is very important. The particular fats we want to prioritize are omega-3 fatty acids.

Omega-3 fatty acids are key compounds that make up neural tissue. Your brain development is highly dependent on the amount of omega-3s in your diet.

Jennifer, a young church member who struggled with depression, stated that a big reason she feels she has overcome depression was because of regular omega-3s in her diet. After seeing on a TV commercial about how fish oil can improve her mental well-being, she began to eat fish on a daily basis. While she saw no dramatic or immediate results, after a couple months, she realized her mental well-being had risen to the point that she no longer needed to take antidepressants to stay happy. While I don't promise that everyone will have the same experience as Jennifer, research supports how important omega-3s are for our mental health. Numerous studies show how omega-3s are very important for your mental health, as they can improve depression and help you recover from brain injury.[188]

Omega-3 supplements include fish or krill oil pills, and you can add omega-3s into your diet through the consumption of healthy fats from sources like fish, avocados, and nuts.

---

[188] David Mischoulon PhD MD, "Omega-3 Fatty Acids for Mood Disorders," Harvard Health Blog, August 3, 2018.

PROTEINS

Past Daley's top nutritional recommendations of omega-3 and vitamin D, several other nutrients are important for your mental health. Proteins are very important for your mood and mental health, as they are key in making neural tissues and mood-boosting neurotransmitters. Make sure you get enough protein in your diet, as proteins are made of amino acids (the building blocks of protein), and amino acids such as tryptophan help you restore serotonin levels in your body and can fight against depression.[189]

Meat is the best-known protein source, but try to limit the amount you consume. In line with how the Word of Wisdom guides, decreasing levels of meat in your diet is shown in many studies to decrease rates of cancer and other health issues.[190] Especially avoid processed meats like bacon, ham, and hot dogs, as they are Group 1 carcinogens, meaning that research links their cancer causing tendencies at the same level that research supports cigarettes causing cancer (I know, it's sad—I love these).[191] If you can, limit red meat like beef, lamb, and pork, as these are Group 2A carcinogens, which means that research says they probably cause cancer.[192] Also, something to keep in mind is that the livestock industry might create more greenhouse gases than the transportation industry (think cars, trains, planes, ships),

---

[189] NAMI Minnesota, "Nutrition And Recovery," NAMI Minnesota, accessed November 18, 2020.
[190] World Cancer Research Fund, "Meat, Fish & Dairy," World Cancer Research Fund, April 24, 2018.
[191] Ibid.
[192] Ibid.

with the majority of the impact coming from beef.[193] So, limiting the amount of red meat, especially beef, can be a great move for your personal health and the health of the planet. Even from a guy who loves meat, I try and limit it as much as possible.

Fish is generally linked to better health, as it is high in omega-3s and has research supporting how it decreases the risk of certain cancer types.[194]

But if possible, try and get as much of your protein from plant-based sources like legumes (beans, lentils, etc.), nuts, and whole grains, or dairy sources like Greek yogurt and cheese. Mixing these together in your diet will make sure that your body receives all the protein building blocks it needs to build your happy mood.

Another mental health benefit from a high-protein diet is that proteins have a lower glycemic index (lower impact on blood sugar levels) than carbohydrates, which means that proteins can help keep your mood more stable.[195] We will read more in this next section about how blood sugar levels are important for your mental and emotional state.

---

[193] Simon Worrall, "Eating a Burger or Driving a Car: Which Harms Planet More?," National Geographic News, March 11, 2015.

[194] World Cancer Research Fund, "Meat, Fish & Dairy," World Cancer Research Fund, April 24, 2018.

[195] Isa Kay, "Is Your Mood Disorder a Symptom of Unstable Blood Sugar?," University of Michigan School of Public Health, accessed November 18, 2020.

CARBOHYDRATES

One thing to keep in mind is maintaining healthy blood sugar levels. The main energy source for our brain is glucose, meaning we need to have supplies of blood sugar to be at the top of our mental game. Your body makes glucose out of the food we eat, and glucose is a simplified form of carbohydrates. It is therefore important that we incorporate healthy carbohydrates in our diets because they are a large source of energy for our bodies.

However, in order to have high levels of mental well-being, it is important that we have stable blood sugar levels. Studies show that fluctuations in blood sugar levels can affect your mood in critical ways. One study that may suggest the influence of blood sugar levels on behavior is a study that showed how judges were 65 percent more likely to give a pardon or light sentence right after breakfast and right after lunch. Right before lunch they were 0 percent likely to give a light sentence, and right before the end of the day (after a significant time after eating lunch), the likelihood to pardon dropped to 0 percent as well.[196] The study suggested that this was due to the fact that a drop in blood sugar influenced the judge's moods negatively, and as a result, gave harsher sentences when they were "hangry."

The concept of being "hangry" is a real thing: When we don't have enough fuel for our brain, our mood worsens, we become more emotionally unstable, and our body's ability to make rational or fair decisions decreases.

---

[196] Shai Danziger, Jonathan Levav, and Liora Avnaim-Pesso, "Extraneous Factors in Judicial Decisions," *Proceedings of the National Academy of Sciences* 108, no. 17 (April 26, 2011): 6889–92.

The best way to keep stable blood sugar levels is to eat foods that have low glycemic indexes, or a slower effect on raising blood sugar levels. It is important to make sure that the types of carbohydrates we consume are slow-digesting carbohydrates, as simple and refined carbohydrates can cause adverse effects to our health in a similar manner to sugars. We'll talk about the dangers of high-sugar diets in a second, but let's first talk about healthy carbohydrates you can eat. Healthy carbohydrates include whole grains such as quinoa, corn, brown rice, and whole wheat (if you are not sensitive to gluten). Other slow digesting carbs include sweet potatoes or legumes such as beans, peas, and lentils. Do a Google search for ideas on how to incorporate healthy carbs in your life.

SUGARS

Sugar is the basic building block of what makes carbohydrates. However, I want to discuss these in a separate section from carbohydrates, because eating lots of simplified carbohydrates and sugars can be problematic for both our physical and neurological health. Some sources of excess sugars are easy to identify, such as candy, desserts, and soft drinks, but also remember that refined carbohydrates like white flour act in almost the same way as sugar in your body.

Studies involving rats being fed high-sugar diets showed that they developed tumors much more rapidly and developed brain diseases like Alzheimer's much more frequently than other rats that had low-sugar diets.[197] Also, rats fed higher

---

[197] Matthew P. Pase et al., "Sugary Beverage Intake and Preclinical Alzheimer's Disease in the Community," *Alzheimer's & Dementia : The Journal of the Alzheimer's Association* 13, no. 9 (September 2017): 955–64.

sugar diets performed much worse at memory tests than other rats on low-sugar diets.[198]

It's not only rats that it affects. Sugar can cause a variety of studied effects on humans on areas like your mood, stress management abilities, depression risk, and cognitive abilities. For example, one 2017 study found that subjects who consumed a high amount of sugar (sixty-seven grams or more each day) were 23 percent more likely to receive a diagnosis of clinical depression within five years.[199] Even suddenly stopping sugar intake can create symptoms similar to withdrawal from a drug.[200]

While links between sugar consumption and cognition are still being researched, so far what science has found is that excess sugar is not great for your mental health in the long run.

HYDRATION

Cognitive function is also very dependent on proper hydration. Studies show that dehydrated people perform more poorly on mental tasks, and those that rehydrate after being dehydrated show an increase in subjective happiness, memory, motor skills, visual attention, and visual search.[201]

---

[198] Ibid.
[199] Anika Knüppel et al., "Sugar Intake from Sweet Food and Beverages, Common Mental Disorder and Depression: Prospective Findings from the Whitehall II Study," *Scientific Reports* 7, no. 1 (July 27, 2017): 6287.
[200] Ted M. Hsu et al., "Effects of Sucrose and High Fructose Corn Syrup Consumption on Spatial Memory Function and Hippocampal Neuroinflammation in Adolescent Rats," *Hippocampus* 25, no. 2 (February 2015): 227–39.
[201] David Benton, "Dehydration Influences Mood and Cognition: A Plausible Hypothesis?," *Nutrients* 3, no. 5 (May 10, 2011): 555–73.

Even mild dehydration of less than 2 percent of body weight (an amount of dehydration that occurs after normal exercise) has been shown to affect mental performance. Test subjects who experienced mild dehydration of 1.4 percent body mass (from walking for forty minutes on the treadmill at room temperature) found a deterioration in vigor, increased fatigue, greater total mood disturbance and increased difficulty to complete cognitive tasks and concentrate.[202] Brain imaging of these mildly dehydrated brains showed increased brain activity in areas mediating executive functions, suggesting that subjects may have had to increase the cognitive resources needed to complete the task when mildly dehydrated.

The moral of the story is to make sure to drink lots of water. This doesn't mean drink more sugary drinks or even artificially sweetened drinks—the best option for your health is to drink plain water.

HAVING A HEALTHY RELATIONSHIP WITH FOOD
It is important to realize the fact that our brains and bodies cannot function properly without the proper nutrition and having a healthy relationship with food. Many things in our world today can pressure us to feel like we need to look a certain way and we need to achieve this by decreasing the nutrition that our bodies receive. This is not a healthy decision because you can be a healthy individual without fitting into society's molds of body shape.

---

[202] Lawrence E. Armstrong et al., "Hydration Biomarkers and Dietary Fluid Consumption of Women," *Journal of the Academy of Nutrition and Dietetics* 112, no. 7 (July 2012): 1056–61.

Remember that this section tries to focus on approach-based goals to healthy nutrition vs. avoidance goals. The majority of what we talked about was about things to include in our nutrition, as opposed to things to leave out of our nutrition.

ACTIVITY 3.8: CREATING A BRAIN NUTRITION PLAN

1. Take in omega-3s and vitamin D every day. To strengthen the cue to take these, buy a pill organizer container that has the days of the week on it and put the pill container on your desk or by your sink so you can see it every day. If omega-3 pills give you stomach discomfort, try buying omega-3 or fish oil by the bottle; you can keep these in your fridge and they have lots of tasty fruit flavors. I promise, they don't taste fishy at all, and they are easily absorbed by your body. For omega 3-s, fish oil and krill oil are great sources, and vitamin D can be taken as a supplement, 2000–4000 IU depending on the amount of sun you get. Other dietary forms of omega-3 can come from fish, nuts, and seeds; dietary forms of vitamin D can be found in fish, egg yolks, mushrooms, and fortified foods like milk, soymilk, orange juice, and oatmeal. Leave out bowls or plates of fruits and vegetables on your desk, table, or counter, so it will be easy to grab a fruit or vegetable as you walk by. We are recommended to have five servings of fruits and vegetables every day, as they provide the vitamins necessary for your brain to function properly.

2. Make sure and eat protein at every meal. Try and get these from plant and dairy sources, and limit meat, especially processed meats. Increase the cue to eat these by buying plenty of protein-rich foods and keeping them at the front of your refrigerator. Put out bowls or jars with

nuts and seeds on your tables and at your desk so it will encourage you to snack on them as you pass.
3. Incorporate lots of healthy carbs in your life. Substitute your carbs with whole grain whenever possible, whether this is your bread, pasta, or cereal. Decrease the amount of sugar that you eat by decreasing cues to eat them: hide or get rid of sugary foods in your house.
4. Drink lots of water. Buy a refillable water bottle that you are proud of carrying with you everywhere. Personalize it and get some cool stickers to decorate it with things you like. Better yet, make customizable stickers online with favorite quotes, inspirational statements, or goals and values you want to live by, so every time you see it, you can be reminded. Keep it on your desk while you are at school or work, so you can always see it and drink from it while it's there. At home, put refillable water bottles in areas that you frequent like the living room and kitchen, so you will always be reminded to take a drink.
5. A key part of ensuring you get the proper brain nutrition is making it easy. Eating healthy is not always convenient. Meal prep is a great way to do this. You can pick one day of the week to cook and prepare all your food that you can pack with you to school or work. Maria, from the introduction, says that cooking healthy meals can be a chore for her, but she finds it easiest to eat pre-made frozen meals from Trader Joe's. These are healthy, tasty, and convenient, and she says this really allowed her to get the food that she needed. Maria also fulfills her fruits and vegetable goal by packing something easy like a carrot or apple with all of her meals she takes to school. It may be tempting to gorge yourself in a large meal every day for convenience sake, but it is healthier

overall and better for your blood sugar levels to eat small regular meals throughout the day. Plan in regular mealtimes and avoid eating large meals at one sitting. I notice that I get drowsy and sluggish after eating very large meals (think food coma), and I stay sharper when I eat in regular, small amounts.

TAKEAWAYS FROM CHAPTER 3C:
NUTRITION

---

1. Healthy nutrition is crucial in our mental well-being, as it provides the building blocks to make happy chemicals and our neural tissue.
2. The basic micronutrients we need for mental well-being are vitamins and minerals. The three basic macronutrients our bodies need are fats, protein, and carbohydrates.
3. Vitamins and minerals are very important to our mood and mental well-being. The most important vitamin that we should include for our mental well-being is vitamin D.
4. Fats are the main ingredient of our brains and nerve cells, and omega-3s are the most important types of fats for our mental well-being.
5. Proteins are a big ingredient of our neurotransmitters and are also great sources of low-glycemic energy. Try and get protein from a variety of sources and try and limit meat, especially in processed forms.
6. Carbohydrates are one of the main sources of energy for our brains, and slow-digesting carbohydrates are the healthiest way to go.
7. Be careful of eating too much sugar, as sugar is linked to a wide range of negative neurological effects.

8. Making sure you take enough food and water in your body will ensure that your brain will have what it needs to function.
9. The activity in this chapter suggests methods for building a brain nutrition plan.

MATERIALS LIST FOR CHAPTER 3C:

NUTRITION

- Omega-3 supplements
- Vitamin D supplements
- Plenty of healthy food
    - Vegetables
    - Fruits
    - Proteins
    - Carbohydrates
- Meal prep materials
    - Food containers
    - Pre-made meals
- Pill organizer
- Water bottle and stickers

SECTION 4: EXERCISES IN OUR IMMEDIATE RELATIONSHIPS

Now that we've worked on our thoughts and mind in Section 2 and our physical bodies in Section 3, the third sphere we are now focusing on is our immediate relationships.

We've already set the stage for this section throughout the book: I've mentioned many times about how important social support is for completing activities and for supporting well-being. Because of the importance of social support and relationships, this chapter might be the most influential on your happiness. In fact, numerous studies show that the number one predictor of happiness is the time we spend with people we care about and who care about us.[203]

---

[203] Tal Ben-Shahar, "7 Lessons On Earning The Ultimate Currency: Happiness," *Positivity Daily* (blog), February 10, 2015.

Spheres of Influence

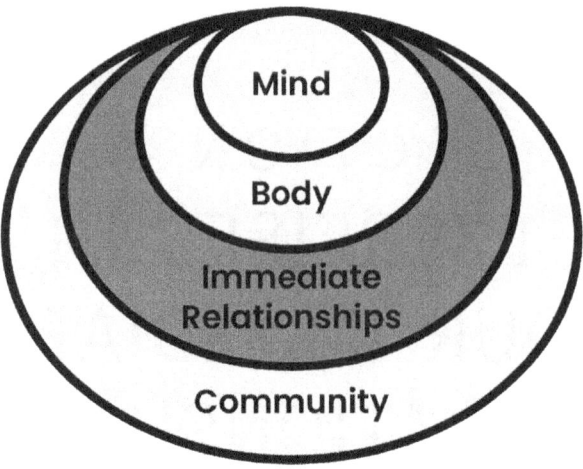

We will now discuss the "Immediate Relationships" sphere of influence.

This section will be split into two chapters: benefits from prioritizing your relationships and ways to deepen the quality of your relationships. You will learn that happiness is a two-way street—not only do you become happier from relationships, other people you are in relationships will become happier from your relationships as well.

As you go through this section, remember that the most important source of happiness may be the person sitting next to you. Make your relationships a priority, show your appreciation for others, and savor your time with the people you care about.

CHAPTER 4A:

BENEFITS FROM OUR RELATIONSHIPS

As my time at BYU came to an end, I realized that I really wanted to live with my brothers. Up until my final year of living in the college town of Provo, Utah, I had never had the chance to live with them together. Not only did I think it would be fun to spend time with my brothers, but I also felt like I needed a close support system of my brothers and best friends. I was going through a pretty stressful time in my life. I had just gotten out of a serious romantic relationship and I was also entering the recruiting season to find a post-graduation job. While I've had a pretty easy life so far and I know that these are mild challenges compared to what most people experience, I was still pretty overwhelmed.

After working out the details, we finally got an apartment with my brothers and one of our high school friends. Even though we had to overcome some obstacles to get it to work, it was one of the best decisions that I have ever made, because this was the start to one of the best years of my life.

No matter how hard, stressful, or difficult a day was, every day I would return to my apartment to see my brothers and roommate in the living room. We would all share the challenges and positives of our days and our lives, and we would laugh, make jokes, and connect, often over a tray of late-night nachos. My brothers and I would also frequently say a prayer together before we went to bed and have a nice long group hug.

On especially difficult or stressful days (such as after watching a disturbing horror movie), we would sit in a circle with our guitars, strum together, and sing along to as many songs that we could think of that matched the chords. We would also blast music and have random awkward dance parties to ourselves in our apartment, or if it was late at night, we would hop in a car and have a mini dance party in there. We deeply bonded and enriched each other's lives. What started out seeming like a potentially stressful and challenging year quickly turned into one of the best school years of my life, thanks to the fact that I prioritized and deepened my relationships.

Obviously, I have been incredibly lucky to not only have two brothers close in age to me, but to also have them live in my same college town. However, the principle I want to illustrate is that we can all tap into being our happiest selves if we prioritize connecting emotionally with people that we love. Let's take a look at studies that show how long-term happiness and longevity are related to having deep, healthy, and meaningful relationships.

STUDIES ON THE BENEFITS OF RELATIONSHIPS

A longitudinal study done by Harvard University showed that the most influential factor on our happiness is the quality relationships that we have in our lives. This study started in 1938, and over the years the researchers have taken a look at two groups of young men: highly educated Harvard students and working-class young men in the inner city.[204] Over the course of almost eighty years of this ongoing study, the researchers have taken a look at a myriad of factors such as income and education level, but they have found that the only thing different about those individuals that lived longest and reported the highest happiness levels were ones that had strong, close, and emotionally intimate relationships.[205]

QUALITY RELATIONSHIPS HELP YOU LIVE LONGER

There are other studies in addition to the Harvard longitudinal study that show how quality relationships can help you live longer. In a study by Harvard psychologist George Vaillant, you will have a higher chance of living longer if you have a friend that you can call at 4 a.m. to tell your troubles to, as opposed to someone who doesn't have a friend they can call at 4 a.m.[206] This could be for a variety of reasons, but having a friend close enough that you would feel comfortable calling in the middle of the night is probably someone you have spent a lot of time with. Spending lots of time

---

[204] Liz Mineo, "Over Nearly 80 Years, Harvard Study Has Been Showing How to Live a Healthy and Happy Life," *Harvard Gazette* (blog), April 11, 2017.
[205] Ibid.
[206] Designed to Thrive, "Fostering 4AM Friends," Designed to Thrive, accessed November 25, 2020.

with people that care about you has been shown to release plenty of feel-good neurotransmitters, which is something that decreases stress levels (a major factor in shortened lifespans).[207] Frequently interacting with people who love you can help you to increase healthy chemical levels in your body and build a healthy mental foundation.

To illustrate this point by looking at the other side, research indicates that a reason men on average live shorter lives than women is that men do not open emotionally as much in their relationships as women do.[208] This depends on social and cultural masculinity norms, but this shows how your life literally depends on the emotional closeness of the relationships you have. Like we mentioned in the previous sections, humans are social creatures. Our ancestors depended on their close relationships, as their cooperation and closeness with others is what helped them survive. For this reason, it is hardwired into our DNA to have this need to connect deeply.

SUPPORT FROM RELATIONSHIPS
Relationships can give us support in nearly all aspects of our lives. Relationship support can help you in areas we discussed in the previous sections like helping you reprogram the way you think, manage your thoughts, and talk to yourself. They can be partners for healthy habits of exercise, nutrition, and sleep, and can help keep you accountable to these.

---

[207] Lauren J.N. Brent et al., "The Neuroethology of Friendship," *Annals of the New York Academy of Sciences* 1316, no. 1 (May 2014): 1–17.

[208] Sarah K. McKenzie et al., "Masculinity, Social Connectedness, and Mental Health: Men's Diverse Patterns of Practice," *American Journal of Men's Health* 12, no. 5 (September 2018): 1247–61.

For example, people in our relationships can help our mental and emotional health by helping us healthily manage our thoughts and emotions. In the same way that you can tell yourself affirmations and be compassionate to yourself, you can also get affirmation and compassion from your close relationships. They can treat you with love, point out when your way of thinking is distorted, and keep you accountable.

Studies also show that you can do much better with sticking to routines if you have buddies to do them with. That is why learning can also be best in a class environment and achieving things can be most productive in teams—you are contributing to a collective energy.

RELATIONSHIPS CONTRIBUTING TO A SENSE OF PURPOSE
Like we mentioned in Section 2, having a sense of purpose is critical to living a life of well-being. Part of the reason that relationships help us live happy lives is that they help us define ourselves and give ourselves a sense of purpose.

We often define ourselves in terms of our relationships, calling ourselves friends, sisters, brothers, daughters, sons, mothers, or fathers. We also gain a sense of identity from spiritual relationships, calling ourselves children of God.

In addition to gaining a sense of identity from our relationships, we also can gain a sense of purpose through fulfilling our familial relationships. Dr. Daley mentioned the importance of providing for others' needs, as it can give you a sense of meaning and importance in life. Even something like owning a dog and feeling like you need to take care of its needs can give you a sense of purpose.

Also, a thing to note is that you don't need to feel like you have no purpose if you don't have certain types of relationships in our lives. Mainstream culture or even parts of church culture might make us feel like our value is dependent on relationship roles we take, such as whether we are in romantic relationships or whether we are able to live a life of mother or fatherhood.

Dr. Julie Hanks, a clinical psychotherapist who specializes in working with members of the church, tells us problems that can occur from idealizing some relationship roles over others. She gives the example of motherhood. She says, "Being a mother is an important aspect of my identity as an LDS woman, but it is not the entirety of my identity. While mothering my children is an important contribution, it is not the source of my worth. When we talk about motherhood as the defining aspect of a woman, the core of her identity, or the only valuable contribution, it can isolate and alienate women who are not able to, or who haven't had the opportunity to, or who have no desire to bear and raise children in this life."[209]

While a sense of identity from relationships can give us benefit, we shouldn't feel like our happiness is dependent on filling all types of relationship roles, because it isn't. We have inherent worth in our identities, and we can gain benefits from all types of healthy and beneficial relationships. The longitudinal Harvard study showed that the relationships that improved peoples' well-being were much more than just

---

[209] Julie Hanks, "How Idealizing Motherhood Hurts Mormon Women," *Dr. Julie Hanks* (blog), accessed November 21, 2020.

romantic or parental relationships; they were relationships between close friends, family members, and colleagues.[210]

Even though music, movies, and aspects of church culture may make you think that your happiness is limited if you are not in a relationship, married, or raising kids, just know that there are many more types of beneficial relationships you can have in your life.

RELATIONSHIPS ARE A TWO-WAY STREET

Research clearly shows that relationships benefit you. However, having relationships doesn't just benefit you; it also positively benefits the other member of the relationship.

American philosopher Ralph Waldo Emerson said, "It is one of the beautiful compensations of life that no man can sincerely try to help another without helping himself."[211]

When you ask for support from someone that cares about you, they get a boost of happiness from giving you support. When someone you care about asks you for support, you get a boost of happiness from supporting them. Therefore, it is a continuous cycle of positivity and happiness that occurs when you invest in relationships: The more you receive, the happier you are, and the more you put into a relationship, the more another person puts in (to a healthy extent). This is why people benefit so much from relationships.

---

[210] Liz Mineo, "Over Nearly 80 Years, Harvard Study Has Been Showing How to Live a Healthy and Happy Life," *Harvard Gazette* (blog), April 11, 2017.

[211] Ralph Waldo Emerson, "A Quote by Ralph Waldo Emerson," Goodreads, accessed November 25, 2020.

It is important to keep in mind, however, that you shouldn't cross the line into dependence on your relationships. Relationships are healthiest if you are a healthy and independent person who is able to provide for your own needs yet is able to enrich your own life and the lives of others by cultivating deeper relationships.

TAKEAWAYS FROM CHAPTER 4A:
BENEFITS FROM OUR RELATIONSHIPS

---

1. In the same way that living with my brothers and friend in college was foundational to my happiness, research shows that relationships are found to be the strongest factor in our happiness and longevity.
2. Relationships help us live longer, give us support, and give us a sense of purpose. One large indicator of how long you live is if you have a friend that you can call at 4 a.m. for help.
3. While culture may overemphasize romantic or parent-child relationships, we can get benefits from any type of close relationship.
4. Relationships are like a two-way street: They provide you social support and provide social support to others simultaneously.

CHAPTER 4B:

PRIORITIZING OUR RELATIONSHIPS

In order to fully gain the benefits of our relationships, we need to make sure we prioritize them. Dr. Clayton Christensen, a former Area 70 and Harvard Business School professor, said many people say that the things they value most are things like family or relationships.[212] However, he tells us that the true test to see how much you value things like these are by seeing how you allocate your resources of time, money, and effort toward them. If you want to make the goal of making healthy relationships at the top of your priority list, you need to take a look and see where most of your time, money, and effort are being spent.

Of course, we all have living necessities and academic and professional responsibilities, so we need to make sure our needs are being met and we are pursuing our life aspirations.

---

[212] Clayton Christensen, "Clayton M. Christensen Quotes (Author of The Innovator's Dilemma)," Goodreads, accessed November 21, 2020.

However, as soon as any of these areas begin to eat too much into your relationships, you may need to reconsider how you allocate your resources.

The next time you are faced with a decision between supporting a friend going through a tough time or putting in the extra hour of studying, remember that the research shows that the happiest people weren't the ones who had the greatest accomplishments or made the most money, but were the ones that prioritized relationships.

So, what are ways that we can prioritize our relationships? First, we need to make sure that we surround ourselves with good people.

SURROUNDING YOURSELF WITH GOOD PEOPLE

We have all been told how important it is that you select good friends. Like the *For the Strength of Youth* pamphlet emphasizes, it is critical to surround yourself with those who are uplifting and support your values.[213]

Make sure that those you surround yourself with are those who are healthy for you. If people have toxic or abusive tendencies toward you, stand up for yourself and demand that you are not treated in those ways. If they do not change, then those people are not healthy in your life. Don't expect those in your circles to be perfect, but they at least need to be genuinely interested in your well-being, open to feedback, and willing to improve.

---

[213] The First Presidency and Council of the Twelve Apostles of The Church of Jesus Christ of Latter-day Saints, "Standards for Youth," The Church of Jesus Christ of Latter-day Saints, accessed November 23, 2020.

Su'a says in *Mentally Tough Teens* to "surround yourself with people who will lift you to higher ground—people who are doers, not just talkers. When you are in the presence of greatness, it will make you want to get better, do more, and make positive changes to your life. Have the courage to walk away from those who are pulling you down, even if it requires standing alone."[214]

"THE GRASS IS GREENER" MENTALITY
While we mentioned it is important to surround ourselves with positive people and distance ourselves from harmful people in our lives, it is important to remember that all relationships take work, and you can't always assume that other people would be better friends, parents, siblings, or significant others than the ones we have. Beware of comparison in relationships and the "grass is greener" mentality. Dr. John Gottman mentions that this mentality can be a common issue in relationships. You can think of this as when people don't prioritize the healthy relationships or friendships they already have because the grass is greener on the other side.[215] It's fine to make new friends and deepen new relationships, but we need to remember to invest in our current quality relationships. As the scout rhyme says:

> Make new friends, but keep the old,
> One is silver and the other gold.[216]

---

[214] Justin Su'a, *Mentally Tough Teens: Developing a Winning Mindset*, First Edition (Springville, UT: Plain Sight Publishing, 2014), chap. 1, Kindle.
[215] Kyle Benson, "The Grass Is Greener Where You Water It," The Gottman Institute, August 17, 2017.
[216] Author Unknown, "Make New Friends (but Keep the Old)," Kids Environment Kids Health – National Institute of Environmental Health Sciences, accessed November 25, 2020.

It is important to show our loyalty in our healthy relationships by prioritizing what we have, especially if they are relationships that denote a level of long-term commitment such as family or romantic relationships. Gottman reminds us that the grass is greener where you water it, which means that instead of focusing too much on finding the greenest grass, try taking care of and watering the grass you already have. Maybe that will turn it green!

ACTIVITY 4.1: PERSONAL RESOURCE ALLOCATION INVENTORY
Here are some ideas below on ways that you can prioritize relationships with those around us.

1. Conduct a personal resource allocation inventory. Write down how much time, money, and effort you spend on a weekly basis on areas including work, school, mental exercises, extracurriculars, hobbies, relationships. See how much of your resources you allocate to these areas in your life and decide to invest more of your resources into your relationships.
2. Schedule regular times to connect with others. One thing I like to do is call my family on Sundays and catch up with them. Just being able to share thoughts and feelings among yourselves is a great way to make you feel whole and connected.
3. Say no to things. Every time you say yes to something that takes time like another episode of TV or another round of videogames, you are also saying no to things you could be doing in that time, such as calling a friend or checking up on a loved one. Don't be afraid to treat your time as precious and say no to things that may not be as influential to your happiness as building a relationship.

TAKEAWAYS FROM CHAPTER 4B:

PRIORITIZING OUR RELATIONSHIPS

---

1. If we want to get the full health and well-being benefits of relationships, we need to prioritize them.
2. We can do this by assessing how we spend our resources of time, money, and effort.
3. Make sure that you surround yourself with positive and supportive people in your relationships. Distance yourself from people who are toxic and abusive.
4. Remember that all relationships take work and beware of comparison in relationships and the "grass is greener mentality."
5. Activity 4.1: Personal Resource Allocation Inventory is a tool that can help us determine if we are properly prioritizing our relationships.

CHAPTER 4C:

DEEPENING OUR RELATIONSHIPS

As mentioned in the previous section, prioritizing our relationships is a way you can greatly improve your mental and emotional health. We now know how important that it is to build healthy relationships. However, some people may feel like the level of their relationships are not at the level of being able to call someone at 4 a.m. The way to gain full benefit from our relationships is by deepening them, and this chapter will teach us ways that we can deepen our relationships and make them more meaningful.

CULTIVATING CONNECTEDNESS AND INTIMACY THROUGH VULNERABILITY

One thing you can add into your conversations and your relationships is vulnerability. Brené Brown, a world-renowned professor, author, and vulnerability specialist, states that being vulnerable with others is key to cultivating connection. She describes that vulnerability is "uncertainty, risk, and emotional exposure."[217] Vulnerability is the unstable feeling we get when we step out of our comfort zone or do something that forces us to loosen control. A lot of us are afraid to put ourselves out there and prefer to keep our armor on in our interactions. However, keeping our armor on decreases the intimacy between others because it prevents us from truly expressing our feelings and being known.

While it may be difficult for many of us to open up and show our weaknesses and shortcomings with those who are close to us, taking the step to be authentic through vulnerability is a way to deepen relationships. Next time you think of weaknesses that you have and next time you face challenges, share these experiences with those close with you. You will be surprised at how your relationships can flourish through vulnerability. Here are some things you can do to cultivate vulnerability.

ACTIVITY 4.2: VULNERABILITY PRACTICE
1. Recognize that being vulnerable takes lots of courage. Take small steps (like asking someone what they are thinking) and congratulate yourself for your bravery when you do something vulnerable.
2. Let go of worrying about what other people think of you. You'll be surprised to see how most people are focused on their own internal struggles, not you.
3. If you are feeling overwhelmed, ground yourself in the present by taking two minutes to focus your attention on your breath and the sensations in your body.

---

[217] Taking Charge of Your Health & Wellbeing, "Daring to Be Vulnerable with Brené Brown," Taking Charge of Your Health & Wellbeing, accessed November 21, 2020.

4. Remember that no one is perfect, and review self-compassion exercises in Section 2 to remind yourself that you are enough.

ACTIVITY 4.3: ASKING FOR NEEDS FROM OTHERS

One potential barrier to deepening our relationships can be if we are afraid to ask for our needs. It can be scary to ask for needs as it makes us vulnerable, but remember that vulnerability leads to connection. Su'a says, "Asking for help isn't a sign of weakness. You don't have to live in quiet desperation. You don't have to suffer alone. Ask for help. Don't think that no one cares, because someone does. Nothing is wrong with you for having problems—everyone does. Get the help you need and conquer your problems."[218]

Practice asking for the things you need. Next time you find that you are facing a problem, ask for support. You can actually improve the lives of others by asking for their help, as service is a way that people can increase their happiness.

ACTIVITY 4.4: PROMOTE CONNECTEDNESS AND INTIMACY

These are activities that you can do to promote connectedness with others. This activity draws off the same connectedness activity in Activity 2.18: Emphasize Common Humanity and Decrease Comparison (Chapter 2b). Now, try to specifically use it to draw closer with those that are in your relationships.

1. Be open with deep feelings and emotional struggles that you have, and don't be afraid to share them with others.

---

[218] Justin Su'a, *Mentally Tough Teens: Developing a Winning Mindset*, First Edition (Springville, UT: Plain Sight Publishing, 2014).

Also, welcome and accept when people share their deep emotions and challenges with you. Be nonjudgmental and a good listener when people are vulnerable with you.
2. In your journal, write down a list of people that you feel like you are connected to. Try to schedule two-minute times throughout the day to do this. Write down how you feel when you think about these people and write down ways that they make you feel connected to them. Also, write down ways that you make them feel connected to you.

ACTIVITY 4.5: DEEPENING RELATIONSHIPS THROUGH CONVERSATIONS

Conversations are some of the best ways to deepen relationships with others. These are ways that you can deepen intimacy and can also be times to express vulnerability. Stephen R. Covey, a member of our church, a leadership coach, and the author of the best-selling book *The Seven Habits of Highly Effective People,* advises in his book to "seek first to understand, then to be understood."[219] He states that the way to build relationships well is to first listen and understand peoples' thoughts and feelings before sharing what you want to say.[220] This applies to any sort of conversation, whether this is a conversation sharing events of a day, or for resolving a stressful conflict.

In your conversations, begin by active listening. Active listening is a way to show that you are listening through actions such as body language and follow up questions. When you

---

[219] FranklinCovey, "Habit 5: Seek First to Understand, Then to Be Understood®," FranklinCovey, accessed November 25, 2020.
[220] Ibid.

are talking to people, show you are interested. Put your phone on silent or even put it in another room, a study showed that even a phone present on a table by people engaged in conversation made the participants of a conversation rate the owner of the phone less engaged in the conversation.[221] Definitely don't be looking at your phone, watching something else, or doing something else. This sends the message of "this conversation is not important" to the other conversation member, and also sends the message of "I don't think this other person is important."

If possible, face the person speaking. Make eye contact and give cues that you are listening such as nodding or grunting in affirmation. Don't be afraid of silence, and if someone pauses, don't be afraid to let them continue after gathering their thoughts. When they ask your opinion or you think it is appropriate for you to join the conversation, ask clarifying questions restating the gist of what the other person was saying to show that you have been listening to what they say. Then, they can tell you whether or not you were listening, and if you didn't understand things completely, they can help point you in the right direction.

Also, during your conversations, keep it in a positive tone as much as possible. If you have generally positive interactions with others, you will find that your relationships will go in positive directions, and your life will have positive tones overall.

---

[221] Veronica V. Galván, Rosa S. Vessal, and Matthew T. Golley, "The Effects of Cell Phone Conversations on the Attention and Memory of Bystanders," PLOS ONE 8, no. 3 (March 13, 2013): e58579.

Like we mentioned in the first sphere, it is critical that you talk to yourself in a ratio that is heavily skewed to having more positive encouragements than criticisms, of at least a 3:1 ratio (even more is better). In the same way that this is the way to bring out the best in yourself, keeping your interactions in this ratio will bring out the best in your relationships.

Dr. John Gottman, one of the world's most cited marriage researchers, did a study in a simulated "marriage lab" watching married couples interacting with each other, and his findings showed that he could predict which couples would get married with 94 percent certainty.[222] In general, couples that had more negative interactions than positive interactions with each other were the ones that were most likely to get divorced.

So, the lesson to learn from Gottman's studies is that for your relationships to flourish (whether that be between family, friends, coworkers, or significant others), you need to keep your interactions mostly positive. You can do this by having a regular talk ritual where you openly talk about your relationship and basically check the pulse on it to make sure that you are both positively interacting with each other.

While this may seem awkward or strange to many of you (when I first talked to some of my guy friends about how our relationship had been, it felt awkward and strained), my experience has shown me that over time, it gets easier and more natural.

---

[222] John Gottman, "Frequently Asked Questions – Research," The Gottman Institute, accessed November 23, 2020.

Finally, during your conversations, keeping things positive is also a very important thing. Whenever you can, try and smile and laugh, but remember to be genuine. Don't force something fake or mask underlying emotions.

GIVE AND TAKE: THE EMOTIONAL BANK ACCOUNT

As mentioned in the introduction, relationships help us live happier because we benefit from both receiving support and providing support. By healthily managing your interactions with others, you can deepen the quality of these relationships.

Covey described interactions between people as being like transactions in a bank.[223] As you serve someone else or actively listen to them, you make a deposit in their account. If you ask for a difficult favor or do something straining to someone else, this is a withdrawal from their account. [224]

Covey suggests that to keep your relationships healthy, you need to balance the withdrawals with deposits you make with other people.[225] Otherwise, a relationship can undergo difficulty if you ask for a favor from someone that you have built no deposits with. Think of how difficult it would be to call someone you don't know well at 4 a.m. to come over and help you in a difficult time; the people that would be willing to come to your home at 4 a.m. and help you will be those that you have already deposited a lot in their accounts.

---

[223] Todd Davis, "Take Stock Of Your Emotional Bank Accounts," Franklin-Covey, accessed November 26, 2020.
[224] Ibid.
[225] Ibid.

To create more deposits in others' bank accounts, try doing the following activities:

ACTIVITY 4.6: SERVICE

One of the best ways to deepen relationships with others is through service. Positive psychology research shows that one of the leading factors in becoming happier is living an altruistic life or focusing on serving others.[226]

People are emotionally affected when people sacrifice their time and effort for others, and this affects both the giver and the recipient. Studies also show how spending money on people you care about is more influential in boosting happiness than spending money on yourself.[227]

Teachings of the restored gospel also tell how serving others is critical to living happier lives. The Savior was a perfect example of living a life of service. He taught lessons like the parable of the Good Samaritan, emphasizing the importance of selflessness and service.

He also taught by example, spending most of his time ministering to and healing the afflicted and those rejected from society. We will go more into serving the community in the next section, but we can remember to serve others in order to improve the quality of our relationships.

---

[226] Stephen G. Post, "Altruism, Happiness, and Health: It's Good to Be Good," *International Journal of Behavioral Medicine* 12, no. 2 (June 1, 2005): 66–77.

[227] Elizabeth W. Dunn, Lara B. Aknin, and Michael I. Norton, "Spending Money on Others Promotes Happiness," *Science* 319, no. 5870 (March 21, 2008): 1687–88.

Dr. Gary Chapman, the author of the popular *5 Love Languages* book, talks about how acts of service are a key way to share love with people close to you, and that by both serving others and receiving others, we can deepen our relationships.[228] The Arbinger Institute mentions the importance of having an outward mindset, and shows that thinking outside of yourself and having a perspective centered on others is a way to have a more fulfilling life.[229]

So, try and exercise the service muscle in your life—the more you do it, the more natural and easy it is for you. In the same way that physical exercise gets more enjoyable and beneficial over time, service will have deeper effects when you do it regularly.

Ideas:

1. Next time you go to the home of a loved one, try and serve them as the first thing you do when you enter. Take out the trash, do some dishes, cook a meal, tidy up a mess, or help them with a chore in the home.
2. Next time you need a friend or family member to do something for you, think of something that you can help them with first, or help them with something immediately after they help you.

Look for things to help with as opposed to asking. Asking is an excellent way to think of service ideas, but serving

---

[228] Moody Productions Grooters, "5 Love Languages," The 5 Love Languages®, accessed November 25, 2020.

[229] The Arbinger Institute, "Free Supporting Resources | The Outward Mindset Book," The Arbinger Institute, accessed November 25, 2020.

others often has to be driven by more proactivity than anything else.

ACTIVITY 4.7: GRATITUDE IN OUR RELATIONSHIPS
Like we mentioned before, expressing gratitude is an instant and long-lasting mood booster. I'm going to reiterate some of the activities I listed earlier, but ones that are more focused on relationships. You can go back to that section to learn details on how to do these but writing gratitude letters to those close to you is a great way to deepen relationships and make deposits in their emotional bank accounts.

Throughout conversation, expressing gratitude is an excellent way to bring positive tones to the relationship. In the same way that you might begin a prayer with gratitude or include gratitude throughout a prayer, try interspersing gratitude in different parts of your conversations. Say thank you as much as you can, and you will see how positive things become.

RECOVERING FROM RELATIONSHIP STRAIN
Everyone in life will go through relationship conflicts. Everyone faces challenges in life, and often, some of the most difficult conflicts can be related to relationships. These might be with parents, siblings, friends, partners, or mission companions.

The best way to avoid relationship strain is by investing early and continuously. As Dr. Clayton Christensen said, "If you defer investing your time and energy until you see that you need to, chances are it will already be too late."[230] However,

---

[230] Clayton Christensen, "The Secret to Living the Life You Want," Next Avenue, July 25, 2012.

if you find yourself in a strained relationship, there is definitely still hope.

The following are examples from relationship experts on what you can do to improve your strained relationships.

COMMUNICATION
Almost all conflicts are a result of some level of miscommunication. Whether this is from assuming differences in needs or accidentally offending someone, the key is to understand how to improve the relationship. Follow conversational tips from Activity 4.5: Deepening Relationships through Conversations (Chapter 4c) to get discussions started. The next parts require a level of humility and vulnerability.

APOLOGIZING
In our relationships, in the same way that we should be quick to say thank you, we should be as quick as possible to say sorry. This can be uncomfortable if you aren't accustomed to saying it, but if you are in a relationship where you feel wronged and things aren't working well, sometimes the best thing to say is sorry. Even if the source of strain on the relationship was unintentional, having the humility to apologize first definitely smooths things over and will help the other person cool down and apologize.

Here's a story about how apologizing first helped me in a conflict with one of my college roommates:

There was a time when my roommates and I planned a large group date together, and I was the one who had to buy the tickets for the event beforehand. I asked all of my roommates if I should buy the tickets and if they were okay with paying for them, and they all confirmed, so I went ahead and bought all the tickets. Later, after I had already bought the tickets, my roommate told me that he could no longer attend. I asked him if he would pay for the tickets, and he told me that he didn't want to pay for them since he could no longer go. I was feeling upset at him since he originally told me that he was planning on going, so I sent him some passive aggressive texts. However, I had recently been reading on the importance of humility, so I decided that I needed to make amends to my situation and put what I had learned to the test. As we were lying down in our bunk beds, I told him that I was sorry for getting angry over text, and that I was happy to pay for the tickets he could no longer use. He ended up immediately apologizing as well, and then said he would pay for the tickets. We ended up deciding that as a compromise, we would both split the costs of the unused tickets. At that moment, I almost teared up after being touched about how my roommate suddenly had a change of heart after I was first to apologize, and we both left feeling much happier.

Okay, this might seem like a petty story, and you might be laughing about how I almost teared up about a stupid group date. All hate aside, I learned a pretty good lesson. Although I was very angry and felt like I was in the right, deciding to apologize for any emotional harm I had caused led my roommate's heart to soften. This opened him to react back with kindness toward me.

FORGIVENESS

In addition to apologizing, Dr. Daley mentions that he believes one of the most important activities in relationships is forgiveness. We have all learned in primary about the importance of forgiving others, and we hear many times in the scriptures about how we should forgive. Jesus told his disciples to forgive "seventy times seven," or in other words, to forgive a very large amount.

The research on forgiveness also shows how incredible forgiveness is at not only helping yourself and mending relationships, but also how it decreases health concerns like depression, anxiety, heart disease, and insomnia.[231] Whether this is someone you want to continue a relationship with, or if it is someone that is probably not healthy to have in your life in the future (a harmful ex, someone who was abusive in some way or someone who caused you trauma), some sort of a forgiveness exercise is essential to free the weight on your mind.

You can experience a burden lifting off of yourself with the following exercises that Dr. Andrew Brandt recommends:

ACTIVITY 4.8: FORGIVENESS EXERCISE

1. "Think about the incident that angered you and accept how it happened. Accept how you felt about it and how it made you react. In order to forgive, you need to acknowledge the reality of what occurred and how you were affected.

---

[231] Kirsten Weir, "Forgiveness Can Improve Mental and Physical Health," American Psychological Association, accessed November 21, 2020.

2. Acknowledge the growth you experienced as a result of what happened. What did it make you learn about yourself, or about your needs and boundaries? Not only did you survive the incident, perhaps you grew from it.
3. Now think about the other person. He or she is flawed because all human beings are flawed. He or she acted from limited beliefs and a skewed frame of reference because sometimes we all act from our limited beliefs and skewed frames of reference. When you were hurt, the other person was trying to have a need met. What do you think this need was and why did the person go about it in such a hurtful way?
4. Finally, decide whether or not you want to tell the other person that you have forgiven him or her. If you decide not to express forgiveness directly, then do it on your own. Say the words, 'I forgive you,' aloud and then add as much explanation as you feel is merited." [232]

THE LASAGNA PRINCIPLE

We have learned that happiness is highly influenced by the quality of our relationships. Tal Ben-Shahar stated that they may be the most important factor in our happiness, but also shared that there can be diminishing marginal returns to how we spend our time in something he calls the lasagna principle.[233] He states that his favorite food is lasagna; he loves it and can have it very frequently without getting tired of it. However, if he were to have it for every meal all the time, he would eventually not appreciate it as much. He says that

---

[232] Andrea Brandt, "How Do You Forgive Even When It Feels Impossible? (Part 1)," Psychology Today, accessed November 21, 2020.
[233] Tal Ben-Shahar, *Happier* (McGraw-Hill Education (India) Pvt Limited, 2007), chap. 3, Kindle.

in his life, his family is by far the most important thing and that he values his time with them more than anything else. [234]

However, he says, "Just because my family is the most meaningful thing in my life does not mean that spending eight hours a day with them is what would make me happiest; and not wanting to spend all my waking hours with them does not imply that I love them any less. I derive a great deal of pleasure and meaning from being with other people, but I also need my daily quota of solitude. Identifying the right activity, and the right quantity of activity, leads to the highest quality of life."[235]

Just because spending time with people that are important to you is the largest predictor of happiness, that doesn't mean that you have to optimize spending all of your time with other people. This principle also applies to any other activity that we have talked about. There is moderation in all things, and just know that it is important to derive pleasure and meaning from the things that you do.

---

[234] Ibid.
[235] Ibid.

TAKEAWAYS FROM CHAPTER 4C:

DEEPENING OUR RELATIONSHIPS

---

1. The way to get the most out of the relationships we have is to deepen them and make them more meaningful.
2. One way to deepen connection and intimacy with those in your relationships is through vulnerability. The exercises for vulnerability include activities that help you learn to ask for help and be more open about personal emotions and challenges.
3. Conversations are one the best ways to deepen relationships, as these are ways to communicate thoughts and emotions, connect, and provide connection.
4. Your relationships can be like a bank account—it is important that we balance the deposits and withdrawals we make.
5. Serving others and expressing gratitude are excellent ways to make deposits into and deepen our relationships.
6. If you have a relationship that is under strain, it is important to communicate clearly and forgive and apologize as necessary.
7. While we learned that relationships are the most important factor in our overall happiness, remember the lasagna principle: Just because lasagna is your favorite food,

that doesn't mean that eating it for every meal all the time is going to make you happier. It is healthy and important that we learn to balance our relationships and all aspects of our lives.

SECTION 5: EXERCISES WITHIN OUR COMMUNITIES

So far, we have learned the importance of investing time into improving our minds, our bodies, and our relationships. The last area we will work on is the community sphere. When I say community, I am referring to all the interactions outside of immediate relationships. This includes extended family, friends, and those in our churches, schools, missions, and all around the world. You can see in this diagram that we are in the final sphere.

We will start this section with Chapter 5a, which will discuss the multitude of benefits from being part of a community. Chapter 5b will then talk about challenges we can face in communities, and Chapter 5c will teach us how to thrive in our communities by focusing on having an outward mindset and an acceptance of common humanity.

Spheres of Influence

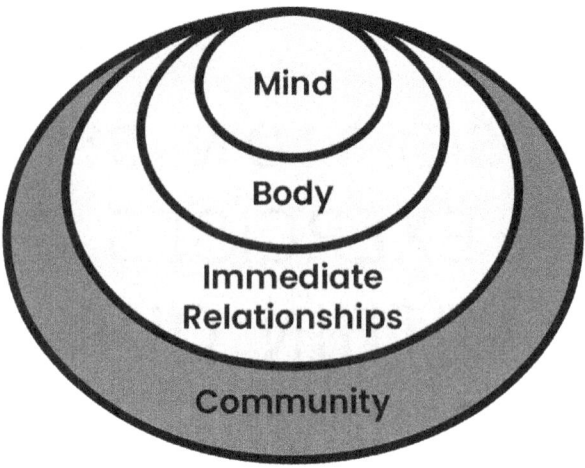

We will now discuss the "Community" sphere of influence.

Also, as this book is geared toward young church members like me, a big focus in this section is on having a happy and healthy relationship within the community of the Church of Jesus Christ of Latter-day Saints. If you aren't a member of the Church, feel free to apply any of the tips to the specific communities you are a part of.

CHAPTER 5A:

BENEFITS OF BEING ACTIVE IN OUR COMMUNITIES

Feeling like you are a part of a community and being actively involved in it is a key part of living a life of happiness and well-being. In the same way we learned in Section 4 about how both receiving support and supporting others in our immediate relationships can help our happiness and well-being, we can experience improvements in our well-being by receiving support from and providing support to our communities.

This chapter will talk about how membership and involvement in communities in general make us happier and will also cover the unique characteristics of our church community that contribute to our happiness.

COMMUNITIES MAKE US HAPPIER BY FULFILLING OUR NEED FOR CONNECTION

Remember the concept of self-determination theory? We learned how as humans, we have three basic needs to feel motivated and happy: autonomy, relatedness, and competence. We talked about the concept of competence in "Chapter 2c: Managing Challenges to the Happiness Balance," the concept of autonomy in "Chapter 2d: Spirituality and the Mind," and now, finally relatedness in this chapter.

Relatedness means that we feel a sense of belonging and attachment to others. It is an innate human need to feel like we fit in. Because of this, we naturally form communities with people like us, and being connected to others makes us happy. Especially in developed nations, investing in communities is probably the top method to improve widespread happiness. The United Nations World Happiness Report stated that in wealthy societies, cooperation and community may contribute more to happiness than income or other metrics.[236]

Communities also provide a high amount of interpersonal connection opportunities. Like I've said so many times, humans are social creatures that thrive off of connection. Studies have shown how the happiest people are those who have a variety of relationships in their communities and even make an effort to interact with community members like the grocery store clerk or mailman.[237] Research also shows

---

[236] United Nations, "World Happiness Report 2012," The World Happiness Report, accessed November 22, 2020.

[237] Gillian M. Sandstrom and Elizabeth W. Dunn, "Is Efficiency Overrated?: Minimal Social Interactions Lead to Belonging and Positive Affect," *Social Psychological and Personality Science* 5, no. 4 (May 1, 2014): 437–42.

how happy people are more connected to the neighborhoods they live in and also are active participants and volunteers in their communities.[238]

Communities can also help you be more resilient in the face of trials. While many people think that emotionally resilient people should tough things out on their own, resilience is more of a group characteristic. Like we learned in the last section on relationships, you can overcome trials much more easily with the help of others, especially those in your extended community relationships. Leaning on your community during hard times is an excellent way for individuals to increase their well-being.

Also, communities are a great way to cultivate happiness through the "upward spiral" effect. Barbara Fredrickson's Broaden-and-Build theory of positive emotion states that positive emotion begets more and more positive emotion.[239] When you have a positive interaction with someone, you are going to feel good, and you will make that person feel good. You will both head off in your separate directions, sending more positivity, until your positive wave gets magnified on a much larger, community-level scale.

We can experience this "upward spiral" experience in many communities that we are a part of. This includes our

---

[238] Allison Ross, "Happy People, Happy Neighborhood: Happiness and Sense of Community Among Florida Residents," Bureau of Economic Research, accessed November 21, 2020.

[239] Barbara L Fredrickson, "The Broaden-and-Build Theory of Positive Emotions.," *Philosophical Transactions of the Royal Society B: Biological Sciences* 359, no. 1449 (September 29, 2004): 1367–78.

relationships with our extended families, our schoolmates, sports teams, musical groups, extracurricular organizations, club members, and church members. This chapter and the next chapter, 5b, will focus on the example of the Latter-day Saint community, but we will find in Chapter 5c that the principles of an outward mindset and common humanity will benefit any organization that you are a part of.

FLOURISHING WITHIN THE CHURCH COMMUNITY

As with any community, religious communities and the Church of Jesus Christ of Latter-day Saints in particular provide many positive aspects that can increase our happiness levels. In Sonja Lyubomirsky's book, *The How of Happiness*, she mentions how religious people are generally happier than nonreligious people and cites a study stating how "Mormons" are healthier than many other groups due to their healthy diets and restrictions on premarital sex, alcohol, tobacco, and drug use.[240] She continues to say that those in religious communities have larger social networks, and religious people gain significant social support and sense of identity from their communities.[241] Members share basic beliefs inherent to their religions and also political and social values. The sense of community is deepened among members of a religious community in part because they share similar roles and values when they approach daily life.

Members of churches or religious institutions are also much more involved in volunteering and charitable giving, which are key factors in our happiness. Studies have shown how

---

[240] Sonja Lyubomirsky, *The How of Happiness*, 1st ed. (London, England: Piatkus Books, 2010), chap. 11, 229.
[241] Ibid.

service and volunteering improves many aspects of mental health and well-being. One study by BMC Public Health showed how volunteering increases self-confidence, provides a sense of purpose, decreases blood pressure and the risk of heart disease, encourages emotional connection through social interaction, combats depression, extends a sense of empathy where it may be lacking, enables a solid support system, provides valuable job skills and career experience, and improves social awareness.[242] Volunteering and supporting the community are huge for improving our happiness levels!

In a study by Harvard professor Robert Putnam and Notre Dame professor David Campbell, they discovered that the more frequently people attend religious services, the more generous and charitable they become across the board.[243] Religious people obviously give a lot to religious charities and spend lots of time serving their churches and synagogues, but they also give more to secular charities such as the American Cancer Society and spend more time serving in neighborhood and civic associations than secular people.[244] You would think that the more time and money people give to their religious groups, the less they would have left over for everything else, but the opposite turns out to be true.

Putnam and Campbell state that by many different measures, religiously observant Americans may be better neighbors

---

[242] Caroline E. Jenkinson et al., "Is Volunteering a Public Health Intervention? A Systematic Review and Meta-Analysis of the Health and Survival of Volunteers," *BMC Public Health* 13, no. 1 (August 23, 2013): 773.

[243] David Campbell and Robert Putnam, "Campbell and Putnam: Charity's Religious Edge – WSJ," Charity's Religious Edge, accessed November 22, 2020.

[244] Ibid.

and better citizens than secular Americans. They are more generous with their time and money and are more active in community life, and the main reason they found that religious people were better neighbors and citizens was their deep relationships with their religious group members. The friendships and activities within groups that share common values are what encourage selflessness and bring out the best in people, creating an upward spiral that can begin in a religious community and then spiral into the secular community as a whole.

Members of our church in particular take community involvement to another level, ensuring that members have social support through organizations such as the ministering program and even material support through fast offering and tithes. In line with what I mentioned earlier in this chapter about resilience being a group characteristic, Latter-day Saints do an excellent job of helping other church members overcome trials on a community level.

A study from the University of Pennsylvania also showed that Latter-day Saints are "the most 'prosocial' members of American society," showing how the average church member volunteers "as much as seven times more than that of the average American."[245] Church members donate an average of $1,821 a year to social and community causes, outside of donating 10 percent of their income to tithes and offerings in the church.[246]

---

[245] Jill DiSanto, "Penn Research Shows That Mormons Are Generous and Active in Helping Others," Penn Today, accessed November 22, 2020.
[246] Ibid.

"Regardless of where they live, they are very generous with their time and money," said Dr. Ram Cnaan, an expert in faith-based social services and the lead researcher of the study. "Through a theology of obedience and sacrifice and a strong commitment to tithing and service, Latter-day Saints are model citizens."[247] According the UPenn study, in addition to the living the greatest commandment of loving "God with all thy heart," members of our church seem to be doing a good job of living the second great commandment of loving "thy neighbour as thyself" in terms of donations and service.

In my personal experience, being a member of the Church has been foundational to my happiness and well-being. Having been born into the Church, most of my family, close friends, and mentors have been part of my church community. Nearly all of the community service I have been involved with has come through directly church-affiliated outlets like my two-year mission and Latter-day Saint Charities or through indirectly church-affiliated service groups such as BYU's Yserve, refugee organizations, international humanitarian groups, and the Boy Scouts of America. My fondest and most meaningful life memories come from growing up in my home ward in Sammamish, Washington, serving a two-year mission in New Jersey, and living my college and young adult years in Provo, Utah.

A 2014 article by *USA Today* listed Provo, Utah, as the happiest city in America, and stated that the fact that this community is built of like-minded souls (nearly 90 percent

---

[247] Ibid.

being members of the Church) likely factors into why Gallup-Healthways reported such high levels of well-being here.[248] I could see why it was ranked so highly on this poll—to this day, some of the happiest years of my life were spent living in Provo. Every day, I was constantly interacting with hundreds of my close friends, classmates, family members, professors, and community members that were genuinely invested in my happiness and well-being. On the street, policemen would greet me by name and ask me about my classes or about my motorcycle rebuild project. At the grocery store, the shopping cart guy would happily greet me and ask me about any good movies I've seen lately. On BYU campus, professors would stop me to ask about my family, and end our conversation with a hug or a sincere "I love you." Even in the bathroom, it was not uncommon for the guy using the urinal next to me to ask me how I was doing and wish me a cordial "Have a good day!"

In addition to day-to-day life, my experience within the church community was just as positive. In the ten different wards I was a member of in Provo, I always felt included and accepted, and almost always had a meaningful calling and responsibility. I was always greeted at church meetings and activities, and meetings with all of my bishops were encouraging and uplifting experiences.

The New York Post reported how British journalist Ruth Whippman, after getting "addicted to Mormon mommy blogs," decided to visit Provo to see if it truly was the "happiest

---

[248] Jayne Clark, "It's the USA's Happiest City, but Is It Worth Visiting?," USA TODAY, accessed November 22, 2020.

town in America."[249] Whippman felt like she hit the happiness jackpot when she first arrived, saying how she witnessed deep community involvement like neighbors dropping by unannounced with food and conversation. Whippman saw that church members in Provo were constantly interacting with their community members, going to potluck dinners, wedding showers, and neighborhood events.

Whippman said, "There's a lot of positive things to say about this community. If you have a problem, twenty neighbors will step in to help you. It's not fake, it's genuine and lovely. But at the same time, it's not as simple as that."[250]

While we learned in this chapter how religious communities—and the Latter-day Saint community in particular—report very high happiness levels, no organization is perfect. While the community of the Church has brought immense amount of support and happiness to both its members and surrounding community, we can some unique challenges face within it. As you read about my experience in the church community (and during my rant about living in Provo while attending BYU), many people definitely have positive experiences. But just because you or I have had positive experiences does not mean that everyone else has happy experiences in their communities. The next chapter, 5b, will discuss what some of these challenges might be, and the following chapter, 5c, will discuss what experts believe are some of the ways we can overcome these challenges.

---

[249] Mackenzie Dawson, "Are Mormons the Happiest People in America?," *New York Post* (blog), November 3, 2016.
[250] Ibid.

TAKEAWAYS FROM CHAPTER 5A:
BENEFITS OF BEING ACTIVE IN OUR COMMUNITIES

1. As humans are social creatures, being active members of our communities is critical for our well-being.
2. In the same way that immediate relationships help us feel connected, being part of communities is also very important in fulfilling our need to connect and belong. This is why being part of communities can help us overcome trials.
3. Kind of like how relationships are a two-way street, communities can be a perfect way to facilitate an "upward spiral," which is essentially a snowball effect of happiness in your communities.
4. An example of the benefits of communities is seen in the benefits of the Church of Jesus Christ of Latter-day Saints. Members of the Church report high levels of physical health and well-being due in part to the benefits of community involvement and service.
5. Communities with high numbers of church members report high levels of happiness and well-being. Provo, Utah, for example, was rated the happiest city in America in 2014.

6. Despite the many positives of being part of communities like the Church of Jesus Christ of Latter-day Saints, no organization is perfect, and there are still important actions to take to make sure that our communities flourish.

CHAPTER 5B:

CHALLENGES WITHIN OUR COMMUNITIES

In the last chapter, we learned how communities are an excellent vehicle in promoting deeper meaning, belonging, and happiness in our lives. However, there are certain things to be careful of in the groups and communities we are involved in, and in this chapter, we will learn about some of these challenges. We will go into some solutions to these challenges in the next chapter, 5c.

Continuing on the example of the Church's community, let's resume the discussion on Whippman's comment on how the Church community in Utah is "genuine and lovely," but at the same time might not be "as simple as that."[251] As you learned from my positive rant about living in Provo while attending BYU, many people like me definitely have positive experiences in their communities. But just because some people like me have had positive experiences does not mean that

---

[251] Ibid.

everyone else has positive experiences in their communities. In fact, it is very normal to face challenges and difficulties in the groups we belong to.

We learn from our church leaders like Elder David A. Bednar that at church, or in any community we are a part of, there are times that we can feel "insulted, mistreated, snubbed, or disrespected."[252] Sister Reyna I. Aburto of the Relief Society General Presidency stated how "women and men of all ages in all corners of the world" can face clouds of "depression, anxiety, and other forms of mental and emotional affliction."[253]

Whippman found in her interviews that while many church members were happy, they weren't without challenges of their own. For example, she found that some women in the Church that found difficulty balancing between careers and child rearing; she also met some members that struggled with depression while trying to put on a facade of happiness.[254] She also noted how "Mormon Utah has the highest rate of antidepressant use in the United States, twice the national average." Whether this increased usage in Utah is attributed to increased depression rates at higher altitudes, a higher level of proactivity in responding to mental illness from a pharmaceutical perspective, or challenges related the church

---

[252] David A. Bednar of the Quorum of the Twelve Apostles, "And Nothing Shall Offend Them," The Church of Jesus Christ of Latter-day Saints, accessed November 22, 2020.

[253] Reyna I. Aburto Second Counselor in the Relief Society General Presidency, "Thru Cloud and Sunshine, Lord, Abide with Me," The Church of Jesus Christ of Latter-day Saints, accessed November 22, 2020.

[254] Mackenzie Dawson, "Are Mormons the Happiest People in America," *New York Post* (blog), November 3, 2016.

community, the bottom line is that none of the communities we are part of are perfect.

Whether it's at church, school, in our relationships with our extended family, or in our hometowns, there will be times when the communities we are part of do not feel like the happy "upward spiral" that I described in the last chapter. Let's talk about some of these challenges we may face.

FEELING ALONE IN OUR COMMUNITIES
Danny Southwick, one of Angela Duckworth's PhD students in psychology at UPenn, who was also raised in Provo, Utah, described some of the difficulties facing happy communities. He stated how "one challenging aspect of living around a bunch of 'happy' people is that we can get hypnotized into the idea that bad things aren't supposed to happen." When you end up facing a trial in life (as we all do), being surrounded by happy people can make you feel very alone.

This is why one of the biggest challenges you can face while being part of a happy community is feeling alone. Even when you are surrounded by people at school, church, social events, family gatherings, or in clubs or sports teams, you can still feel very lonely. Despite today's high amount of digital connection, Americans today have fewer close friends than Americans did twenty-five years earlier.[255] Also, nearly half of all meals are eaten alone in America.[256] This is a

---

[255] Jeanna Bryner, "Close Friends Less Common Today, Study Finds," LiveScience.com, accessed November 22, 2020.
[256] Roberto Ferdman, "The Most American Thing There Is: Eating Alone," *The Washington Post*, accessed November 22, 2020.

significant issue, as loneliness has been found to be more dangerous for your health than smoking or being obese.[257]

And it's not just eating less meals together or having fewer close friends that make us feel lonely. If you remember from Chapter 2b, perceived loneliness is just as large of a culprit. How lonely you are is largely subjective; even if you're like Goob from *Meet the Robinsons* and surrounded by happy people, you can still feel very lonely.

One study titled "Dark Contrasts: The Paradox of High Rates of Suicide in Happy Places," published in the Journal of Economic Behavior and Organization, suggests how comparing our happiness to the happiness of others around us can make us feel lonelier and more unhappy. This study describes how being surrounded by people that are more content with their lives can make us feel isolated and alone and can put us at a higher risk of suicide.[258] This is why this study reports that states with the highest happiness levels can also have some of the highest suicide levels. An example it provides is "while Utah is ranked number one in life-satisfaction, it has the ninth highest suicide rate. Meanwhile, New York is ranked forty-fifth in life satisfaction, yet has the lowest suicide rate in the USA."[259]

This study suggests that the high suicide rate in the happy state of Utah may be attributed to the fact that some people

---

[257] Nick Tate, "Loneliness Rivals Obesity, Smoking as Health Risk," WebMD, accessed November 22, 2020.
[258] Mary C. Daly et al., "Dark Contrasts: The Paradox of High Rates of Suicide in Happy Places," *Journal of Economic Behavior & Organization* 80, no. 3 (December 2011): 435–42.
[259] Ibid.

within our communities may feel like they are alone and surrounded by many other people that are happier than them.

PERFECTIONISM IN OUR COMMUNITIES
Cultures of perfectionism can be a big factor into why we can feel alone in our communities. Dr. Daley mentions that today, both in and out of the church, there is a feeling that we have to be the best, improve, compare, get things right immediately, and not show failure.

There are many types of perfectionism, including physical, social, emotional, material, academic, professional, familial, and spiritual. The common thread of all these types of perfectionism is that perfectionism isn't real. No individual, family, job, friend group, or life is perfect. However, community members that hide their struggles behind closed doors are able to uphold the illusion of perfection by only sharing parts of their lives that are happy, beautiful, complete, painless, and flawless (thanks in part to the advent of social media). If we feel like almost everyone in our communities around us is perfect and not dealing with any sorts of challenges, it is no wonder that we can feel alone and depressed.

A pattern that the "Dark Contrasts" study suggests is that that when you are around a lot of happy and you don't feel happy, you feel very isolated. This study showed that Utah tends to rate higher happiness levels, possibly due in part to its homogeneity (many people are like each other). However, if you are a sad person in Utah, it can feel even more poignant if you are an environment of happy people. This can make you feel depressed more easily. This could be due to the fact that, humans have the tendency to compare, like we talked about in Section 2. A chief in a hunter gatherer society with more meat than others might feel rich in comparison to his tribe but might feel poor in America. While New York ranked low in life satisfaction, its suicide rate might be low because people might feel less lonely in New York because of the absence of an "in group."

Elder Dieter F. Uchtdorf states that the facade of perfectionism is a huge barrier to receiving the healing power of our church communities. He states, "The Church is not an automobile showroom—a place to put ourselves on display so that others can admire our spirituality, capacity, or prosperity. It is more like a service center, where vehicles in need of repair come for maintenance and rehabilitation. And are we not, all of us, in need of repair, maintenance, and rehabilitation? We come to church not to hide our problems but to heal them."[260]

As you know, I have loved and highly benefited from being a member of both the Church's community and the Provo, Utah, community while I lived there. But it wasn't perfect at all times, and it definitely did come with its own challenges. I can definitely see how Elder Uchtdorf's mention of an "automobile showroom" culture can apply to the community I lived in: Utah consistently ranks at the top in the nation for plastic surgery rates.[261] Utah also has some of the highest

---

[260] President Dieter F. Uchtdorf Second Counselor in the First Presidency, "On Being Genuine," The Church of Jesus Christ of Latter-day Saints, accessed November 22, 2020.

[261] Maren Jensen, "Web Exclusive: Utah Is One of the Top States for Plastic Surgery in the Nation," KUTV, July 8, 2018.

rates of antidepressant usage in the nation and ranks near the top of the nation for online pornography usage.[262]

Many church members in Utah who seek therapy express the difficulty of living with the pressure to "keep up with the Joneses." This means that some people feel a sense of comparison with their neighbors or community members, feeling pressure to keep up to the level of social class or accumulation of material goods around them. Feeling financial pressure to reach the level of materialistic perfectionism that surrounds us can also make us feel very alone.

A type of perfectionism that might be more exclusive to a church community is spiritual perfectionism. Many young men and women I have interviewed for this book have shared about feeling alone or shameful about their spiritual lives. One young woman shared that she felt alone in her level of spirituality during church meetings, when the majority of people that spoke shared deep spiritual convictions and experiences that she wished she could also share but did not feel like she was able to experience.

She and other young women and men I have interviewed also felt distressed because while they wanted to share some of their spiritual struggles, they were afraid to put themselves out there and show themselves as being one of the few "problem" people. Alice, a young member of the Church, stated how she felt considerable pressure to live up to a certain standard when she heard other church members say things like

---

[262] Deseret News, "Utah No. 1 in Online Porn Subscriptions, Report Says," Deseret News, March 3, 2009.

"The sisters would never do that!" or "Men, we need to be more like the sisters, they're such angels." She said, "I understand their intention is to be sweet, but for many women, especially those who are more prone to perfectionism and shameful emotions, they don't feel complimented. It just feels like more pressure to live up to an impossible standard."

Also, several young men and women I have spoken with shared how they felt a deep sense of embarrassment for either not serving a mission or from returning home early from their missionary service. They have told me that this has been a major source of mental struggle, as they felt alone or as if they were less valuable members of their church communities. In some instances, these experiences of feeling alone or unaccepted has driven them to choose to abandon their membership in the church. (If you are interested in resources for early returned missionaries, check out Appendix 4 for some great resources recommended by ERMs.)

As we have learned throughout this book, people have the deep desire and need to feel to they fit in and belong, and when you feel like you are alone and don't belong in your community, this is a strong cause for people to perceive themselves as being lonely. This next chapter, 5c, will teach us how to cultivate a feeling of belongingness in our communities. This will improve our happiness levels and contribute to the "upward spiral" in our communities through cultivating an outward mindset and a sense for common humanity.

TAKEAWAYS FROM CHAPTER 5B:

CHALLENGES WITHIN OUR COMMUNITIES

1. There are many challenges that members of a community can face, and the Church of Jesus Christ of Latter-day Saints is an example of a community where members may face unique challenges.
2. One large challenge that is present in almost every community is feeling alone. This can be exacerbated if you are in a community where others around you are very similar, appear to be happy, and appear to have little to no challenges in their lives.
3. Being surrounded by an illusion of perfection in our communities can drive us to perceive ourselves to be lonely, which can lead to a variety of mental health concerns like depression and even suicide.
4. It is important to learn ways to not feel alone in our communities and fight against an image of perfectionism and homogeneity.

CHAPTER 5C:

OUTWARD MINDSET AND COMMON HUMANITY

One time, while living in Utah, I was waiting at the train station in Salt Lake City to go home to Provo. As I sat waiting with a whole row of other commuters, a young man shuffled by. He was skinny, had tattered clothing, ragged hair, and scraggly beard. He was muttering to himself and was carrying a handful of colored markers in one hand and a beat-up skateboard in the other.

He walked up to the far end of our row of commuters and said, "Excuse me?" to a lady at the end of the bench. The lady averted her gaze and pretended not to hear him.

The young man continued down the row of commuters, talking to other people on the benches, trying to get their attention. But it was to no avail, as people either pretended to be asleep or to be occupied with other things.

I was curious as to what he was asking for, so by the time he came to me, I thought I would at least lend him a listening ear. I knew I didn't have any cash on me, but at the very least, I could treat him as a fellow community member and friend.

He came up to me and said, "Excuse me?"

"What's up?" I replied. I could tell that this young man had trouble speaking and may have been mentally handicapped.

The young man said, "I was wondering, it's my stepdad's birthday. Ever since he married my mom, he hasn't liked me. I rarely get to see him or my mom, but whenever I do, he is mean to me and doesn't let me spend time with them. It makes me sad. It's his birthday tomorrow, and I want to make his day. I don't have much money, so this card is all I have for him."

He proceeded to take a children's birthday card out of his pocket that was decorated with a cartoon dog and balloons. I was then expecting him to ask for a "donation" for his stepdad's birthday, and I thought to myself for a second, "Wow, this is a clever ploy to get money from people."

He then said, "I want to make his day and write him a nice note, but I'm not good at writing. I was wondering if you could write a note for me, telling him that I love him and hope he has a wonderful birthday."

At that moment, my heart sank. I realized that I had judged this young man and assumed the worst of him.

A wave of emotion washed over me. Here he was, a young man who was very different than me. He was from a different walk of life, a different background, and different physical appearance. However, at the very core, we had the same basic human need to love and be loved.

I thought to myself, "How many other times have I looked upon other people around me and focused on how we were different, as opposed to thinking about what makes us the same?"

Nearly moved to tears, I cleared my throat, and told him, "Of course I can do that! Give me some of those markers!"

As I began writing a note to his stepdad, wishing him the happiest of birthdays from his awesome stepson, suddenly, the row of people next to me awoke from their slumber. A man who previously hid behind his sunglasses lifted them up and asked, "Oh wait, sorry, what is it that you guys are doing here? Did you say a birthday note? I would love to write a birthday note!" The rest of the people sitting on the bench chimed in, also expressing that they wanted to add to the note. The young man, now overjoyed at his birthday card full of colorful messages, thanked us profusely, and then took off on his skateboard to give the card to his stepdad.

That young man made my day. Not only did he make me feel a sensation of warmth and love, but on my train ride home that day, I remember feeling a sense of connection to those around me. Instead of averting my eyes from the homeless man asleep on the corner of the train, I looked at him and saw him as someone that could be a friend or relative that I hadn't seen in a long time. As I sat by myself, I said a silent prayer of gratitude for the experience of being able to feel a sense of connection and oneness with my human family.

I learned a valuable lesson that day on the joy that an outward mindset can bring in our lives. Now, I'm not sharing this story to show off how nice of a person I am—I've done plenty of mean and terrible things in my life. I just wanted to share how impactful and meaningful that a sense of connection to others can provide.

It felt really good to be able to help someone by doing a small act, but I also learned that I can't make judgments about other people. Luckily, this young man went out of his way to reach out for help when he needed something. However, many people don't reach out when they need things. Often, you may not realize that people around you are feeling alone, truly struggling and in the need of love.

COMMON HUMANITY AND THE OUTWARD MINDSET
In the last chapter, we talked about how the biggest challenges in our communities can be from people that feel alone or excluded. You may or may not have felt the pain of feeling alone in your communities, but just remember from the last chapter that loneliness is a serious challenge that leads people to want to give up and even take their lives. One reason we found that people might feel lonely is due to feeling isolated in a sea of people that seem to live perfect lives.

In order to become forces for good in our communities—to create the "upward spiral" of happiness—the main thing we can do to help others and ourselves is to develop an outward mindset and embrace common humanity. By doing this, we can live happier lives in communities that denounce perfectionism, embrace differences and flaws, and even fight loneliness and suicide.

The key goal of this chapter is to foster a culture of relatedness in our communities. These can be people that feel rejected in our communities like your gay cousin, your drug addict teammate, your annoying classmate, your needy church friends, or yourself. Regardless of who we are, we all have the need to love and be loved.

If you are a person who hasn't struggled with feeling like you are alone or don't belong, you're lucky—many of your brothers and sisters on earth can't say this. Especially if you live in a homogenous community (a community where many people are similar), many people around you might be like you, and it might be easy for many of you to feel like you belong.

However, Danny Southwick (who grew up in Provo himself) says, "It is important to build social bridges with people that are different from you." While it might be easy for you to fit the mold, life can be harder for those that don't fit the mold. Realize that other people might be facing more difficulties than you are and try and connect with them. When you connect with others, Southwick says to "focus on the similarities instead of the differences. Identifying yourself as different is important, but it can be even more helpful to your community if you focus on similarities."

This is exactly what positive psychology says about emphasizing an outward mindset and common humanity, and this also goes along with the teachings of Jesus Christ.

The outward mindset describes a mindset of seeing other people as people, highlighting similarities, and seeing others' goals as part of a collective goal.[263] This is opposed an inward mindset, which highlights differences in others, and sees people as obstacles to achieving goals.[264]

Common humanity is a principle that we touched on when we talked about self-compassion in Chapter 2c. In any context, whether it is in your relationship with yourself or others, common humanity focuses on the similarities that we have between people, and how all people struggle and face trials in the same way that we do. Despite our own flaws and the flaws of others, we all have inherent worth. The concept of common humanity is healing to emotional pain and has been called the cure to isolation.[265]

Positive psychology teaches that embracing all others, regardless of differences, is critical for well-being. When I asked Tal Ben-Shahar about the balance between investing in relationships with those similar to us and investing in relationships with those who are different, he said, "While relationships and social support are important, so are inclusion and openness to others—both psychologically and of course morally." He suggested that my readers, including young members of the Church, can all benefit from developing inclusion and openness skills, citing studies on how these skills can improve cognitive performance, critical thinking, help us in

---

[263] The Arbinger Institute, "Mindset and the Basics of Arbinger's Work," The Arbinger Institute, accessed November 22, 2020.
[264] Ibid.
[265] Awareness in Action, "How to Benefit from the Power of Common Humanity," *Awareness in Action* (blog), July 16, 2018.

the transition to adulthood, increase our civic engagement, and promote our creativity.

Learning how to value and find commonalities with those who are different from us is a great skill to have in life because at many points in our lives—whether it's our extended family members, classmates, coworkers, or teammates—we will have to live life with people that are different from us. You can choose to despise their differences and suffer during all your interactions with them, or you can focus on your commonalities and even celebrate the benefits of their differences. I can tell you from my experience, doing the latter has been made my life much happier.

In addition to improving our mental well-being, the outward mindset and the principle of common humanity are also foundational parts of Jesus Christ's earthly ministry. Whether it was shown in His compassion toward all people—especially toward rejects of society like criminals, prostitutes, Gentiles, and the handicapped—or His universal atonement for all mankind, Christ personifies the belief that we should emphasize the commonalities between people and love people for their innate worth, regardless of their superficial differences. To truly follow Christ's example, we must not only accept others, but we must love and embrace all people.

HOW TO DEVELOP AN OUTWARD MINDSET AND COMMON HUMANITY IN OUR COMMUNITIES
Now that we have covered the importance of developing an outward mindset and common humanity, how do we begin developing it in our communities? Experts on the topic

suggest several things on promoting a culture of inclusion, including valuing differences, highlighting commonalities, being vulnerable, increasing proximity, and empathy.

Among all of these things, the key to making progress in a community begins at the individual level: you. If you decide to start making positive changes in your community, like Barbara Fredrickson describes in the concept of the "upward spiral," your actions will influence others positively, who will then take positive actions themselves, which will eventually snowball into a larger movement that brings happiness to your entire community.

VALUING DIFFERENCES

First, in order to promote a culture of inclusion, it is essential that you value differences of others in your community have. Sister Chieko N. Okazaki, a former member of the Relief Society General Presidency and one of the first minority General Officers of the Church, tells us how the community of the Church values and needs diversity. She says, "If you experience the pain of exclusion at church from someone who is frightened at your difference, please don't leave or become inactive. You may think you are voting with your feet, that you are making a statement by leaving. [Some may] see your diversity as a problem to be fixed, as a flaw to be corrected or erased. If you are gone, they don't have to deal with you anymore. I want you to know that your diversity is a more valuable statement."[266]

---

[266] Chieko Okazaki, "Your Diversity Is a More Valuable Statement" StayLDS. Com, accessed November 22, 2020.

In the same way that Sister Okazaki says that diversity is valuable in the Church, recognize and value diversity in others in your communities. To some extent, everyone has something special and interesting about them, and appreciating other peoples, unique attributes, skills, and interests will in turn encourage them to accept your unique qualities.

President Dallin H. Oaks tells us the importance of valuing differences in his General Conference talk *Loving Others and Living with Differences*, where he states that "the commandment to love one another surely includes love and respect across religious lines and also across racial, cultural, and economic lines."[267] He reminds young people to "avoid bullying, insults, or language and practices that deliberately inflict pain on others. All of these violate the Savior's command to love one another."[268]

Elder M. Russell Ballard also tells us in his General Conference talk *The Doctrine of Inclusion* how "good neighbors should put forth every effort to understand each other and to be kind to one another regardless of religion, nationality, race, or culture."[269] He also comments on church members who exclude others who don't fit into their communities, saying, "Occasionally I hear of members offending those of other faiths by overlooking them and leaving them out. This can occur especially in communities where our members

---

[267] Elder Dallin H. Oaks of the Quorum of the Twelve Apostles, "Loving Others and Living with Differences," The Church of Jesus Christ of Latter-day Saints, accessed November 22, 2020.

[268] Ibid.

[269] M. Russell Ballard of the Quorum of the Twelve Apostles, "Doctrine of Inclusion," The Church of Jesus Christ of Latter-day Saints, accessed November 22, 2020.

are the majority. I have heard about narrow-minded parents who tell children that they cannot play with a particular child in the neighborhood simply because his or her family does not belong to our Church. This kind of behavior is not in keeping with the teachings of the Lord Jesus Christ."[270]

At times that you feel like the attributes of others are so different that you have trouble finding a connection, highlight commonalities that you share. At all of our cores, we all value things like being understood and accepted and we all desire to love and be loved.

VULNERABILITY

An excellent step toward encouraging common humanity and inclusion in our communities is by being vulnerable with others. As we learned in Section 4, vulnerability leads to connection. Vulnerability can start a positive snowball effect, especially in communities that are plagued by a facade of perfection. Like Alice said in the last chapter, she felt lots of stress and pressure when she felt like she had to live up to an unrealistically high spiritual standard. However, when we are vulnerable by being open about our struggles and our flawed humanity, we can pave the road for others to open up about their own challenges as well. This is key to combating a culture of shame or secrecy of personal challenges, as overcoming challenges in a group setting is very effective.

Open communication is crucial in combating perceived loneliness in homogenous communities. When people realize that other people are going through a hard time and not

---

[270] Ibid.

fitting in the mold, they no longer feel isolated and alone. This opens up the curtain to show how what people are trying to hide is actually what is normal.

In terms of the community of the Church, being open about the unique circumstances we face is important toward fostering a sense of common humanity. Sister Okazaki uses the example of families to show that no matter how unique your family circumstances are, families do not stop being families. She said in her book *What a Friend We Have in Jesus* that real families face real challenges, stating, "A divorced family is not a broken family. It's a family with a particular set of circumstances that it needs to work with. A family with a gay child is not a failed family. It's a family with a member who needs special love and understanding and who has love and understanding to give back. A family with a pregnant teenager is not a dysfunctional family. It's a family with a complex set of decisions to make."[271] Like Sister Okazaki said, we can accept and be open about all circumstances such as family situations. Accepting differences of others is key to promoting acceptance and fighting loneliness.

INCREASING PROXIMITY

Increasing proximity with others is also an excellent way that we can foster connection within our communities. Bryan Stevenson, a law professor at NYU, founder of the Equal Justice Initiative, criminal justice lawyer, and bestselling author of *Just Mercy*, said in a BYU forum in 2018 that increasing proximity is very important in creating a healthy society. When we

---

[271] Chieko N. Okazaki, "What a Friend We Have in Jesus," Goodreads, accessed November 22, 2020,

are far from people in our communities that are different from us, it is very difficult to feel connected to them. He said that "there is power in proximity," and "when we get proximate, we can wrap our arms around those who are suffering."[272]

Remember that Jesus Christ was the ultimate example of proximity; instead of spending most of his time in temples with the elite, he was on the streets and walking through the countryside, interacting with all people from different walks of life in an intimate, face-to-face manner. We are able to learn much more from those that are different from us— whether it's the annoying person at school, the quiet neighbor down the street, or the hungry person downtown—by being proximate to their lives.

Also, embracing your own flaws is important to help other people. Stevenson says, "I do what I do because I'm broken too. It is the broken among us that can teach us the way that mercy works. We don't have to be whole and perfect to help others. We just have to have heart."[273]

After Stevenson's forum, I tried his advice on being proximate and signed up for several volunteer groups. Through one volunteer organization, I was able to become close to a refugee family in Utah that escaped a war-torn nation. We were different for sure, but after spending time in close proximity, we have become valuable friends today. Becoming friends with this family has definitely enriched the quality of my life, but I have also learned a lesson on how all people, no

---

[272] Media Contact: Natalie Ipson, "BYU Forum: Creating Justice," News, October 30, 2018.
[273] Ibid.

matter how different you think you are from the beginning, are very similar at our cores.

EXERCISING EMPATHY
One way to promote an outward mindset is through empathy. Dr. Daley explains how doing actions that show concern for other people's time can exercise your outward mindset. He says if we're sitting in traffic, let people merge in. Or when setting goals, think about how other people can benefit from them. This helps you practice thinking about others' needs and putting yourself in other peoples' shoes.

Sister Reyna L. Aburto also states how empathy can help to fight against isolation and stigma in our communities. She says, "Sadly, many who suffer from severe depression distance themselves from their fellow Saints because they feel they do not fit some imaginary mold. We can help them know and feel that they do indeed belong with us. It is important to recognize that depression is not the result of weakness, nor is it usually the result of sin. It 'thrives in secrecy but shrinks in empathy.' Together, we can break through the clouds of isolation and stigma so the burden of shame is lifted and miracles of healing can occur."[274] Empathy is a great step forward toward building an environment of healing our problems as opposed to an environment of hiding our problems.

---

[274] Reyna I. Aburto Second Counselor in the Relief Society General Presidency, "Thru Cloud and Sunshine, Lord, Abide with Me," The Church of Jesus Christ of Latter-day Saints, accessed November 22, 2020.

ACTIVITIES ON PROMOTING AN OUTWARD MINDSET AND COMMON HUMANITY

Now that we learned about the areas we can work on to develop outward mindsets and an appreciation for common humanity, here are some activities that can help us practice these:

ACTIVITY 5.1: COMMUNITY SERVICE

Like we mentioned earlier, service is strongly correlated with living a life of happiness and well-being. Service can help you get proximate to those different from you, which will pave the way to you valuing others' differences and developing empathy. Here are some ways to serve more; try scheduling these ideas into your lifestyle routines:

1. Find ways to help out in your community. The Church's service groups are an excellent way to do this. Every time there is a church event orchestrated by your ward, mission, or stake, jump on it! You will have a fun time bonding with others while working together, and you can do lots of positive things.
2. You can also do a lot of good through getting involved through organizations. JustServe is an excellent app to get service ideas in the community, and you can also sign up for notifications from community organizations that help refugees, the sick, the homeless, and the hungry. Many organizations outside of the church such as the American Red Cross (you can donate blood or help those in need) or Catholic Charities also do many amazing things.
3. If you see something you can do to help in your community, don't be afraid to hop in and help. Justin Su'a tells

us, "If you see a need, fill it. If you walk by trash, pick it up and throw it away. Be a go-getter. Do things without being told to. Others might think you're trying to suck up, but you know your motives. You're doing things to become better and to help others become better. You don't need others to notice your hard work because you're not doing it for them—you're doing it for you."[275]

4. You can always get small boosts of joy by doing acts of service to others. One thing I try and do is keep small snacks or treats in the car. When I see someone who is hungry on the side of the street, I like to give them a snack. I know that there's debate over whether this is prolonging the problem or encouraging panhandling, but the Savior instructed us to feed the hungry and to clothe the naked. One time, I saw a woman holding a sign in the middle of the winter without a coat. I rushed home, grabbed a warm coat, and handed it to her. Her gratitude for the coat warmed my heart, and later seeing her on the street wearing my coat made my day.

5. Sometimes the best way to serve others is by simply giving them attention. Try and give attention to those that are lonely and do not receive much attention; elderly people in particular can be lonely and will love spending time with you. Next time you visit elderly people in your ward, your grandparents, or a retirement home, take the time to have a conversation with them. Listen to their stories—you'll have fun hearing the crazy things they did when they were younger and all the amazing lessons that they've learned. Also, remember, many elderly people

---

[275] Justin Su'a, *Mentally Tough Teens: Developing a Winning Mindset*, First Edition (Springville, UT: Plain Sight Publishing, 2014), chap. 1, Kindle.

are in severe lack of physical touch beyond a handshake, especially elderly men. Go out of your way to give someone a hug or a pat on the shoulder—it can mean a lot!

ACTIVITY 5.2: PROMOTING VULNERABILITY IN OUR COMMUNITIES

Try out Activity 4.2: Vulnerability Practice (Chapter 4c) as a refresher on the key points of vulnerability. Also, remember that being vulnerable in your communities can pave the road for other people to open up about their challenges, which is key in overcoming perceived loneliness. Try the following things:

1. In a church or class setting, try to share your human flaws.
    a. In church settings, don't be afraid share the struggles you go through. It could be hard, but worth it. You'll be surprised to see how many people appreciate your vulnerability and are willing to share their challenges as well.
    b. In class, don't be afraid to share what you struggle with or don't understand. While it may make you feel dumb, you'll be surprised to see how many people have the same question but are just too scared to ask.

2. Promoting inclusion to encourage vulnerability
    a. Try and make your communities a safe place by openly talking about topics that traditionally are associated with stigma, such as mental health or personal challenges.
    b. Alice recommends us to try changing the language that we talk to others and ourselves from a judgmental tone to a compassionate tone. For example, she doesn't

use the word "should" anymore. You can really hear the difference between "I should pray more" and "I'd really like to pray more." One is judgment-focused and the other is action-focused.

c. If you notice judgmental comments or behavior, be assertive and respectfully help people understand why that behavior can be unhelpful.

ACTIVITY 5.3: EXERCISING AN OUTWARD MINDSET

1. The Monson Test: President Thomas S. Monson said, "Never let a problem to be solved become more important than a person to be loved."[276] From this quote, I like to try and do the Monson test in my life, which is to see if I prioritize unimportant tasks over people that need love.
2. Like Dr. Daley said, do little things that show concern for others' time. Let people merge in when you're caught in traffic or take time away from tasks at hand to be a listening ear to those going through tough times.
3. Metta meditation: In my positive psychology class at BYU, we learned about Metta, or Lovingkindness meditation. Try scheduling this type of meditation into your lifestyle routines, it is a great way to focus on your well-being and then the well-being of others in your relationships and community. The steps follow below. We can also similarly exercise an outward mindset by praying for others.
   a. Begin by sitting in a comfortable position and build awareness by focusing on your breath and sensations in your body.

---

[276] Thomas S. Monson, "Problem to Be Solved," The Church of Jesus Christ of Latter-day Saints, accessed November 23, 2020.

b. After taking time to do this, repeat the following:
   i. May I be filled with lovingkindness
   ii. May I be held in lovingkindness
   iii. May I feel connected and calm
   iv. May I accept myself just as I am
   v. May I be happy
   vi. May I know the natural joy of being alive
c. Now, shift the focus to others in your relationships and your community by repeating the following:
   i. May you be filled with lovingkindness
   ii. May you be held in lovingkindness
   iii. May you feel my love now
   iv. May you accept yourself just as you are
   v. May you be happy
   vi. May you know the natural joy of being alive

ACTIVITY 5.4: POSITIVE INTERACTIONS WITH OUR COMMUNITY MEMBERS

In your small interactions in your day-to-day, try to prioritize connecting over efficiency. This will bring positive boosts of emotion in your lives and will also help you exercise your outward mindset.

If you have a server at a restaurant or a customer service agent on the phone, instead of just keeping the interaction short and efficient, take an extra thirty seconds to give them a compliment or thank them for doing their job. You will notice that it makes you feel good to say something nice, and these people will make you feel even better when they respond with their gratitude. This is a great way to boost your mood throughout the day.

One time, I thanked a man who was giving me customer support for my cell phone plan and I told him that he did an excellent job helping me and he made my day. He was very pleased to hear that and responded by gifting me free equipment and further discounts, without even being asked! I'm not saying that you should be nice to get free stuff, but this is an example of the "upward spiral" in happiness. If you treat someone kindly, it will make them kinder to you and they will want to repay in kindness, which is always worth it, even without free stuff.

TAKEAWAYS FROM CHAPTER 5C:

OUTWARD MINDSET AND COMMON HUMANITY

---

1. The antidote to perceptions of loneliness and isolation is developing an outward mindset and a sense of common humanity in our communities.
2. Both research and Gospel teachings show us the importance of loving and including others. Not only does it decrease feelings of loneliness and isolation, but it also provides a variety of cognitive and mental benefits.
3. A key piece in having an outward mindset is to value differences of others and learning to see perspectives that are different from yours.
4. Vulnerability is an important step in developing a sense of common humanity, as sharing personal emotions and struggles not only strengthens your sense of connection with others, but also fights against shame and perfectionism that may be present in your community.
5. Increasing proximity to those that are different from us is an important piece in developing a sense of common humanity and connecting to those that are very different from us.

6. Exercising empathy is a great way to put an outward mindset into action. Putting our feet into others' shoes is the best way to connect with others and see their perspectives.
7. Activities such as service, being kind to others, and being honest about our feelings in public are great ways to promote an outward mindset, common humanity, and overall well-being in our communities.

MATERIALS LIST FOR CHAPTER 5C:

OUTWARD MINDSET AND COMMON HUMANITY

---

1. Small packaged food items to keep in your backpack or car to share with others
2. Extra clothing to keep in your backpack or car to share with others

CONCLUSION

If you have made it to the end this book, congratulations! You are now a much better caretaker of your mental well-being and are on track to having the "firmness of mind" we all strive toward. We have learned many things: what happiness truly is, how to balance pleasure with future meaning, how to develop a lifestyle routine, how to manage our thoughts and change our brains, how to take care of our bodies, spirits, relationships, and communities. I hope you use these skills for the rest of our lives.

To finish off this book, I have a couple things for you. After this conclusion, there are several appendices. Appendix 1 is a list of all the chapter takeaways in the book, so if you ever wanted a quick refresher without reading the whole book, you can just skim through those.

Appendix 2 is a repeat of the lifestyle routines worksheet in Section 1, but I included it again because now, with your knowledge of all the activities, you can now build a lifestyle routine using a lot more exercises to reference.

Appendix 3 is a list of all the activities in the entire book, paired with the chapter section they are found in. You can go through the list, pair them with a routine, and then you can go to the chapter they are listed in to see exactly what steps you need to take to do them.

Appendix 4 has some additional books to read and resources for early returned missionaries. After that is a detailed bibliography of all of the works that I cited in this book.

CLOSING THOUGHTS

I hope that reading this book has been as meaningful for you as it has been meaningful for me. Incorporating these activities in my life has truly made me a happier person: more positive in the day to day, more uplifting in my relationships, more productive and higher performing, and less anxious and stressed. I have also become more resilient to trials and difficulties.

I promise if you use these concepts in your daily life, you too will see a positive change in the same way I have seen this change in my life. If you give the things we learned about in this book an honest effort, you too can change your brain and develop "firmness of mind."

Happy reading and feel free to contact me for questions and feedback!

Ian Kahng

info@firmnessofmind.com

APPENDIX

APPENDIX 1:

CHAPTER TAKEAWAYS

TAKEAWAYS FROM THE INTRODUCTION
1. Like Maria, you can incorporate things in your life that will sustainably increase your happiness.
2. Happiness is our ultimate goal. Therefore, we should spend as much time as possible doing things that bring us closer to that goal.
3. We are poor predictors of what we think will make us happy. A lot of things that we think might make us happy (things like fame, beauty, material possessions, perfection, overachievement, or the "I will be happy when…" mentality) can be dead ends, and we should strive to be aware of when we think in these ways and try and keep these thoughts in check.
4. The true happiness we should be striving for is a sustained state, also known as well-being, that is a balance of present pleasure and future meaning. Our goal is to learn how to optimize the happiness balance in all the things we do.
5. In the next section, we will learn facts about how to unlock our brain's full potential so we can best achieve

this balance and set up a plan on how to implement regular happiness-boosting activities in our lives.

TAKEAWAYS FROM CHAPTER 1A: WHAT IS FIRMNESS OF MIND?

1. Both scripture and psychological science talk about a strong, healthy mental state (which I like to call "firmness of mind"). The new field of positive psychology focuses on the characteristics of a steadily happy brain as opposed to the defects of the brain.
2. Similar to a muscle, we can influence the physical structure of our brains through neuroplastic changes, and our happiness baseline levels can also be improved and strengthened.
3. Improving our happiness baselines has more to do with intentional activities than doing things like trying to control our circumstances. Regardless of things we have little or no control over, such as our genetic makeup, we can take action over our happiness through intentional activities we can control.
4. Many of these activities will exercise brain interactions between the higher reasoning part and the reactive impulsive parts of our brains to best achieve a balance of present pleasure and future meaning. Our youthful years are the best times to begin working on this.

TAKEAWAYS FROM CHAPTER 1B: INTRODUCTION TO LIFESTYLE ROUTINES

1. A lifestyle routine will be the groundwork to improving your well-being, and it is very important to learn to do this at a young age.

2. Research shows that people frequently do not do things that they know are good for them. Just knowing something is good for you isn't enough to get you to do it—you need to be ready for behavioral change and you need to build the proper routines to support it.
3. Beginning a new lifestyle routine depends on whether you are ready for behavioral change or not, and you are ready to change your behavior after you decide that the pros for changing your behavior outweigh the cons to your behavior. Chances are, if you've read this far in the book, you are at a spot in the change cycle (referred to earlier as the Transtheoretical Model of Change) that signifies that you are ready for change in your life.
4. Building a routine is critical to doing things that you know are good for you but aren't doing, and the process of building a routine and progressing toward a better life is rewarding in and of itself.
5. The behavior you do and the habits you perform are dependent on a process called the habit loop. The habit loop consists of a cue, craving, response, and reward, and changing your behavior depends on strengthening desirable habit loops and weakening undesirable habit loops.

TAKEAWAYS FROM CHAPTER 1C: SETTING UP LIFESTYLE ROUTINES

1. A lifestyle routine is founded upon goals, plans, and accountability.
2. There are two types of goals: higher level and lower level. Higher level goals are intangible and value-based, while lower level goals are more specific and achievable.

3. Overall, you should make sure that the goals you set for yourself give you present pleasure but are also attached to future meaning.
4. Your plans are designed to ensure that you achieve your goals. You will most likely achieve your goals if you plan them around parts of your habit loop. Plan obvious cues, attractive cravings, easy responses, and satisfying rewards to make achieving your goals a breeze.
5. Also, it is important to remember that things never go exactly as planned. That's why it is critical to incorporate If-Then plans (Plan Bs) in our routines, to be prepared for times when you fall off the wagon.
6. Accountability helps us change and refine our lifestyle routines to better fit our needs throughout our lives. The great way to incorporate accountability in our routines is to have a weekly accountability meeting with other accountability partners.
7. The key parts of accountability are to identify what success means to us, how to measure it, how to keep up success, and how to reassess when we aren't successful.
8. If you are keeping up your routine, it is pretty straightforward: keep doing what you are doing, and if something is working well, don't get complacent with your routine.
9. If you fall short of achieving your goals or sticking to your routine, with the help of your accountability partners, make sure that you reassess your routines, and incorporate more If-Then planning, self-compassion, and social support.

TAKEAWAYS FROM CHAPTER 1D: INTRODUCTION TO THE EXERCISES SECTION

1. The next sections, 2–5, will be where the rubber will meet the road where we can learn specific activities to do on a regular basis.
2. Section 2 is on activities for our minds, Section 3 is on activities for our bodies, Section 4 is on activities to do within our immediate relationships, and Section 5 is on activities to do within our communities.
3. It is critical that we do these activities, because this will help us change our brains in the same way that the London taxi drivers changed their brains.
4. You can pick and choose which activities you think will be the best for you, and you can plan simple versions of them into your lifestyle routines.

TAKEAWAYS FROM CHAPTER 2A: OUR BIASED BRAINS

1. Our brains can influence us to see things that are different from reality, often showing things in a more negative light than they really are.
2. Our brains are biased toward negativity in part because of evolutionary advantages to pay high attention to negative things in our environment, and also because the limbic system in our brains (that reacts to negative things) acts more quickly than the rational prefrontal cortex of our brains.
3. The amount that our brains are biased toward the negative can vary, but the important thing to realize is that no matter how negatively biased your brain is, you can begin rewiring your brain by incorporating positivity activities in your life.

4. A positive mindset can improve almost all aspects of life, increasing your ability to overcome challenges and even experience more luck in your life.
5. You can learn optimism through these activities in the next chapter.

TAKEAWAYS FROM CHAPTER 2B: REWIRING OUR BRAINS AGAINST BIAS

1. To positively rewire our brains, the main methods psychologists employ today are cognitive behavioral therapy (CBT) and acceptance and commitment therapy (ACT). Both teach us how to healthily manage our unhelpful thoughts by first being aware of them, but CBT focuses on disputing unhelpful thoughts, while ACT focuses on being mindful and accepting them.
2. Both approaches have their benefits and uses, and we will practice both of them. From there, you can decide which activities fit best with your needs.
3. As the goal of both approaches—and rewiring our biases—begins with awareness of our thoughts, we can begin by going over the major types, which are social comparison, catastrophizing, black-and-white thinking, personalization, mind reading, emotional reasoning, rumination, perceived loneliness, and stress/fear.
4. Journaling is a great way to recognize when you have any of the unhelpful thoughts listed above. After listing and identifying our unhelpful thoughts, we will learn ways to manage them.
5. The CBT method of managing your thoughts centers on you recognizing your ability to have control and influence over your thoughts, and to dispute unhelpful thoughts.

6. The ACT method helps us to be mindful and accept thoughts instead of arguing against them. Activity 2.4 teaches us a three-step process to the ACT method, which consists of defusion, expansion, and connection.
7. In addition to ACT and CBT, we can rewire our brains through gratitude, cultivating optimism, positively responding to stress/fear/rumination, and treating yourself with self-compassion. There are fifteen activities in each of these areas, so definitely go back in the chapters to see what kinds of things you can implement into your lifestyle routines.

TAKEAWAYS FROM CHAPTER 2C: MANAGING CHALLENGES TO THE HAPPINESS BALANCE

1. In addition to learning how to overcome biases to rewire our brains, it is also important that we balance pleasure and meaning.
2. To have a refresher on what this looks like, we will follow the hamburger model looking at the hedonism burger, the rat race burger, and the nihilism burger.
3. In order to overcome the hedonism burger, the main challenges are to attach purpose to our activities and also overcome hedonic adaptation.
4. The activities we have listed to overcome hedonism are overcoming shadow comforts and numbing behavior, anger, laziness, and navigating sexual feelings.
5. Overcoming the rat race burger lies in to learning to find pleasure in the journey as opposed to just focusing on the destination.
6. Activities to help us overcome the rat race burger include finding our character strengths, satisficing, and flow.

7. Overcoming the nihilism burger entails finding a sense of purpose and pleasure in life.
8. Overcoming nihilism is difficult, but when our dreams die, we can learn how to make new dreams.

TAKEAWAYS FROM CHAPTER 2D: SPIRITUALITY AND THE MIND
1. Spirituality is very important for our mental well-being, and much of what we've learned in Sunday school is actually backed by positive psychology.
2. The Gospel of Jesus Christ teaches many important principles for living a happy life including having a purpose and identity, the ability to choose, pursuing values over materials, and living a life of optimism.
3. The activities in this chapter will help you to improve your mental well-being through spirituality. Activities include ways to strengthen a sense of purpose, identity, and worth. They also help us to practice using our agency, focusing on the spiritual over the material, optimism, and developing spirituality in general.

TAKEAWAYS FROM CHAPTER 3A: PHYSICAL EXERCISE
1. Chemicals your body produces, called neurotransmitters, are largely responsible for the moods and emotions we feel.
2. People use drugs like antidepressants or stimulants to influence our neurotransmitter levels and subsequently, their thoughts and feelings, but taking care of your physical body through exercise, sleep, and proper nutrition can do just as good or sometimes a better job.
3. Even a moderate amount of exercise can be just as effective at decreasing depressive symptoms as antidepressants. Also, those who implement a regular exercise

routine are much less likely to return to being depressed than if they took an antidepressant.
4. Exercise can also help us perform better in school, improve our relationships, and decrease our rate of cognitive decline.
5. There are several reasons people don't exercise: not being sure how to exercise, not liking it, not able to make time for it, or unable to do it because of physical limitations.
6. If you don't know how to exercise, don't like physical exercise, or can't make time for physical exercise, or have limitations to physical exercise, this chapter has a variety of activities and resources to help you schedule these in.
7. There are other helpful physical "exercises" you can do that help your well-being, such as body scanning, yoga, spending time in nature, or having enough physical touch in your life. These are all proven ways to improve your happiness levels.

TAKEAWAYS FROM CHAPTER 3B: SLEEP
1. Sleep is critical because sleep produces the chemicals in your body necessary to stabilize your mood and have positive emotions. People who don't sleep well suffer on many levels including decreased mood, thinking, and physical health.
2. Not getting enough sleep can contribute to depression and suicide, and the early years are critical for getting enough sleep. Sleep provides emotional support and stability that will help you in perhaps the most pivotal time of your life.
3. Sleep helps you perform better at mental tasks including creativity and memory, and shirking on sleep before big events is a bad idea.

4. Adequate sleep is also critical for our interactions with others, as we are less able to think rationally and interact positively with others when we are sleep deprived.
5. Prioritize your sleep at the sake of overachievement. We learned about how overachievement is not a sustainable route to happiness in Section 2, and you will have a happier life overall if you have a healthy chemical balance and achieve less, than if you achieve more but have a worse chemical balance.
6. It is critical to sleep in a regular pattern the same amount every day, going to sleep at the same time and waking up at the same time every day. Disrupting this sleep pattern can be dangerous for your health.
7. This chapter provides activities and many ideas on how to get on a normal sleep schedule, improve your sleep quality, and get a healthy boost of energy without getting tired.

TAKEAWAYS FROM CHAPTER 3C: NUTRITION
1. Healthy nutrition is crucial in our mental well-being, as it provides the building blocks to make happy chemicals and our neural tissue.
2. The basic micronutrients we need for mental well-being are vitamins and minerals. The three basic macronutrients our bodies need are fats, protein, and carbohydrates.
3. Vitamins and minerals are very important to our mood and mental well-being. The most important vitamin that we should include for our mental well-being is vitamin D.

4. Fats are the main ingredient of our brains and nerve cells, and omega-3s are the most important types of fats for our mental well-being.
5. Proteins are a big ingredient of our neurotransmitters and are also great sources of low-glycemic energy. Try and get protein from a variety of sources and try and limit meat, especially in processed forms.
6. Carbohydrates are one of the main sources of energy for our brains, and slow-digesting carbohydrates are the healthiest way to go.
7. Be careful of eating too much sugar, as sugar is linked to a wide range of negative neurological effects.
8. Making sure you take enough food and water in your body will ensure that your brain will have what it needs to function.
9. The activity in this chapter suggests methods for building a brain nutrition plan.

TAKEAWAYS FROM CHAPTER 4A: BENEFITS FROM OUR RELATIONSHIPS
1. In the same way that living with my brothers and friend in college was foundational to my happiness, research shows that relationships are found to be the strongest factor in our happiness and longevity.
2. Relationships help us live longer, give us support, and give us a sense of purpose. One large indicator of how long you live is if you have a friend that you can call at 4am for help.
3. While culture may overemphasize romantic or parent-child relationships, we can get benefits from any type of close relationship.

4. Relationships are like a two-way street: They provide you social support and provide social support to others simultaneously.

TAKEAWAYS FROM CHAPTER 4B: PRIORITIZING OUR RELATIONSHIPS
1. If we want to get the full health and well-being benefits of relationships, we need to prioritize them.
2. We can do this by assessing how we spend our resources of time, money, and effort.
3. Make sure that you surround yourself with positive and supportive people in your relationships. Distance yourself from people who are toxic and abusive.
4. Remember that all relationships take work and beware of comparison in relationships and the "grass is greener mentality."
5. Activity 4.1: Personal Resource Allocation Inventory is a tool that can help us determine if we are properly prioritizing our relationships.

TAKEAWAYS FROM CHAPTER 4C: DEEPENING OUR RELATIONSHIPS
1. The way to get the most out of the relationships we have is to deepen them and make them more meaningful.
2. One way to deepen connection and intimacy with those in your relationships is through vulnerability. The exercises for vulnerability include activities that help you learn to ask for help and be more open about personal emotions and challenges.
3. Conversations are one the best ways to deepen relationships, as these are ways to communicate thoughts and emotions, connect, and provide connection.

4. Your relationships can be like a bank account—it is important that we balance the deposits and withdrawals we make.
5. Serving others and expressing gratitude are excellent ways to make deposits into and deepen our relationships.
6. If you have a relationship that is under strain, it is important to communicate clearly, and forgive and apologize as necessary.
7. While we learned that relationships are the most important factor in our overall happiness, remember the lasagna principle: Just because lasagna is your favorite food, that doesn't mean that eating it for every meal all the time is going to make you happier. It is healthy and important that we learn to balance our relationships and all aspects of our lives.

TAKEAWAYS FROM CHAPTER 5A: BENEFITS OF BEING ACTIVE IN OUR COMMUNITIES

1. As humans are social creatures, being active members of our communities is critical for our well-being.
2. In the same way that immediate relationships help us feel connected, being part of communities is also very important in fulfilling our need to connect and belong. This is why being part of communities can help us overcome trials.
3. Kind of like how relationships are a two-way street, communities can be a perfect way to facilitate an "upward spiral," which is essentially a snowball effect of happiness in your communities.
4. An example of the benefits of communities is seen in the benefits of the Church of Jesus Christ of Latter-day Saints. Members of the Church report high levels of

physical health and well-being due in part to the benefits of community involvement and service.
5. Communities with high numbers of church members report high levels of happiness and well-being: Provo, Utah, for example, was rated the happiest city in America in 2014.
6. Despite the many positives of being part of communities like the Church of Jesus Christ of Latter-day Saints, no organization is perfect, and there are still important actions to take to make sure that our communities flourish.

TAKEAWAYS FROM CHAPTER 5B: CHALLENGES WITHIN OUR COMMUNITIES

1. There are many challenges that members of a community can face, and the Church of Jesus Christ of Latter-day Saints is an example of a community where members may face unique challenges.
2. One large challenge that is present in almost every community is feeling alone. This can be exacerbated if you are in a community where others around you are very similar, appear to be happy, and appear to have little to no challenges in their lives.
3. Being surrounded by an illusion of perfection in our communities can drive us to perceive ourselves to be lonely, which can lead to a variety of mental health concerns like depression and even suicide.
4. It is important to learn ways to not feel alone in our communities and fight against an image of perfectionism and homogeneity.

TAKEAWAYS FROM CHAPTER 5C: OUTWARD MINDSET AND COMMON HUMANITY

1. The antidote to perceptions of loneliness and isolation is by developing an outward mindset and a sense of common humanity in our communities.
2. Both research and Gospel teachings show us the importance of loving and including others. Not only does it decrease feelings of loneliness and isolation, but it also provides a variety of cognitive and mental benefits.
3. A key piece in having an outward mindset is to value differences of others and learning to see perspectives that are different from yours.
4. Vulnerability is an important step in developing a sense of common humanity, as sharing personal emotions and struggles not only strengthens your sense of connection with others but also fights against shame and perfectionism that may be present in your community.
5. Increasing proximity to those that are different from us is an important piece in developing a sense of common humanity and connecting to those that are very different from us.
6. Exercising empathy is a great way to put an outward mindset into action. Putting our feet into others' shoes is the best way to connect with others and see their perspectives.
7. Activities such as service, being kind to others, and being honest about our feelings in public are great ways to promote an outward mindset, common humanity, and overall well-being in our communities.

APPENDIX 2:

LIFESTYLE ROUTINES WORKSHEET

ACTIVITY 5.5: LIFESTYLE ROUTINE WORKSHEET

We have already practiced making goals in Activities 1.2 (values), 1.3 (higher level goals), and 1.4 (lower level goals). Here, we can practice goals again, but in addition to goals, we can also design complete lifestyle routines, including plans and accountability.

Follow the guidelines below, and remember, building a lifestyle routine is a dynamic process, so you will be going through this sheet and making new versions over and over. Use this as a worksheet template to design your routines for the future, and if you want updated and easy-to-read printable versions of this worksheet, visit www.firmnessofmind.com to download them for free.

SETTING HIGHER LEVEL GOALS

Tips: Make sure these are tied to your values, they are vision based as opposed to outcome based, they are meaningful, they are pleasurable, they focus on your strengths, and they are approach-oriented as opposed to being avoidance-oriented.

MY HIGHER LEVEL GOALS:

SETTING LOWER LEVEL GOALS

Tips: Make sure these are very specific and very small. They should be easy and manageable. To start out, don't write too many. Also, make sure they are meaningful, pleasurable, and approach-oriented as opposed to being avoidance-oriented.

MY LOWER LEVEL GOALS:

SETTING PLANS TO ACHIEVE GOALS

Tips: Plan obvious cues, attractive cravings, easy responses, and satisfying rewards to make achieving your goals a breeze. Also, incorporate If-Then plans (Plan Bs) into our routines so you can prepare for times when things do not go exactly as planned

MAKE CUES OBVIOUS: ENVIRONMENTAL DESIGN

Make reminders in places that you frequently go by throughout the day. Put signs or reminders on places like your mirror, desk, or steering wheel. Display objects of good habits in the open; put out bowls of healthy snacks like fruits in the open, or put your water bottle out if you want to drink more water. Also, hide cues for unwanted habits; put away your TV remote or get rid of unhealthy foods. List the cues for your goals here:

MAKE CRAVINGS ATTRACTIVE: VISUALIZATION, SOCIAL SUPPORT

Imagine what it would feel like to achieve your goals through visualization and plan time to do this regularly. Also, plan ways to involve others in the completion of your goals, whether that is by finding buddies to do activities with, or by finding role models of people that exemplify your goals. List the ways to make your cravings more attractive through visualization and social support here:

MAKE RESPONSES EASY:

There are three ways to make your responses easier: slack, automaticity, and friction reduction. Give yourself plenty of slack when you plan your activities—try and keep them short, simple, and as effortless as possible. This is so you can build up momentum so you can develop automaticity. Try and plan your activities so they are automatic. If possible, plan them to occur at the same time and place, and use some sort visual aid to help you build momentum, like a calendar or a jar of paper clips. Also, reduce friction as much as possible, identify any potential barriers to your activities ahead of time, and plan friction reducers before you start your activities. List ways to make your responses easier here:

MAKE REWARDS SATISFYING:

Find ways to make your reward for completing a task or activity more satisfying. Create a list of things that you enjoy doing, or rewards you can incorporate in your routines, and plan as many of them as possible to be paired with the goals that you seek to accomplish. List the rewards for your goals here:

IF-THEN PLANNING (PLAN B)

Pair an If-Then plan, or Plan B, with every action or goal that you make. In the worst-case scenario that you don't end up doing something that you planned, have a second-best option. If you miss your daily jog, then plan to do fifty jumping jacks inside as an alternative. List the If-Then for your goals here:

ACCOUNTABILITY TO MEASURE AND ASSESS SUCCESS

The last piece to your plan is to use accountability. Use the space here to list things to make sure you cover during your accountability meetings with your accountability partners.

1. What does success look like?
   a. Balance of pleasure and purpose?
   b. Am I achieving my goals in the right way, for the right intention that they were set?

2. How do I measure it?
   a. Personal/spiritual interpretation
   b. Friends/family/leaders
   c. Professionals/counselors/resources

3. How do I keep it up?
   a. Name of Accountability partner 1:
      i. Did I contact them? Circle Y/N
      ii. Time/date of regular meeting:
   b. Name of Accountability partner 2:
      i. Did I contact them? Circle Y/N
      ii. Time/date of regular meeting:
   c. Name of Accountability partner 3:
      i. Did I contact them? Circle Y/N
      ii. Time/date of regular meeting:

4. What should I do if I fall short of my routines?
   a. Reassessment
   b. If-Then Planning
   c. Self-compassion
   d. Social Support

APPENDIX 3:

FULL ACTIVITIES LIST

Add any of the activities listed here as parts to your lifestyle routines. You can find the detailed instructions of each activity in the chapter that is listed with the activity.

1. Activity 1.1: Decide to Change
(Decisional Balance Sheet)   55
2. Activity 1.2: Values List   72
3. Activity 1.3: Lifestyle Routine Worksheet   94
4. Activity 2.1: Identifying Unhelpful Thoughts   134
5. Activity 2.2: Identifying with an
Internal Locus of Control   139
6. Activity 2.3: ABCDE Model for
Disputing Negative or Irrational Beliefs   141
7. Activity 2.4: ACT Mindfulness for
Managing Negative Thoughts and Feelings   145
8. Activity 2.5: Gratitude Letter   147
9. Activity 2.6: Gratitude Journal   147
10. Activity 2.7: Prayer of Gratitude   148
11. Activity 2.8: Affirmations   152
12. Activity 2.9: Positivity Box   158
13. Activity 2.10: Positive Visualizations   159

14. Activity 2.11: Best Possible Future Self 160
15. Activity 2.12: Savoring 161
16. Activity 2.13: Positive Reframing 161
17. Activity 2.14: Making Stress Your Friend 162
18. Activity 2.15: Take a Timeout 164
19. Activity 2.16: Distraction from Rumination 165
20. Activity 2.17: Treat Yourself like You Would Treat a Friend 170
21. Activity 2.18: Emphasize Common Humanity and Decrease Comparison 171
22. Activity 2.19: Compassionate Chair Activity 174
23. Activity 2.20: Mindfulness for Self-Compassion 176
24. Activity 2.21: Managing Shadow Comforts and Numbing Behaviors 186
25. Activity 2.22: Anger and Emotion Management 188
26. Activity 2.23: Navigating Sexual Feelings 191
27. Activity 2.24: Character Strengths 194
28. Activity 2.25: Satisficing 198
29. Activity 2.26: Flow 198
30. Activity 2.27: Creating a New Dream 200
31. Activity 2.28: Improving Mental Well-Being through Spirituality 209
32. Activity 3.1: Tips for If You Don't Know How to Exercise 224
33. Activity 3.2: Tips for If You Don't like Exercise 225
34. Activity 3.3: Ways to Schedule Exercise In 227
35. Activity 3.4: Other Physical "Exercises" to Improve Well-Being 229
36. Activity 3.5: Get on a Normal Sleep Cycle 242

37. Activity 3.6: Improving Your Sleep Quality 242
38. Activity 3.7: Getting an Energy Boost When Tired 245
39. Activity 3.8: Creating a Brain Nutrition Plan 263
40. Activity 4.1: Personal Resource Allocation Inventory 286
41. Activity 4.2: Vulnerability Practice 290
42. Activity 4.3: Asking for Needs from Others 291
43. Activity 4.4: Promote Connectedness and Intimacy 291
44. Activity 4.5: Deepening Relationships through Conversations 292
45. Activity 4.6: Service 296
46. Activity 4.7: Gratitude in Our Relationships 298
47. Activity 4.8: Forgiveness Exercise 301
48. Activity 5.1: Community Service 344
49. Activity 5.2: Promoting Vulnerability in Our Communities 346
50. Activity 5.3: Exercising an Outward Mindset 347
51. Activity 5.4: Positive Interactions with Our Community Members 348
52. Activity 5.5: Lifestyle Routine Worksheet 375

APPENDIX 4:

ADDITIONAL RESOURCES

FURTHER READING:
- *Positively Happy* by Sonja Lyubomirsky and Jaime Kurtz
- *Happier* by Tal Ben-Shahar
- *The Illustrated Happiness Trap* by Russ Harris
- *Grit* by Angela Duckworth
- *The Seven Habits of Highly Effective Teens* by Sean Covey
- *Hardwiring Happiness* by Rick Hanson
- *Authentic Happiness* by Martin Seligman
- *The Mental Health and Wellbeing Workout for Teens* by Paula Nagel
- *Mentally Tough Teens* by Justin Su'a
- *The How of Happiness* by Sonja Lyubomirsky
- *The Pursuit of Perfect* by Tal Ben-Shahar
- *Atomic Habits* by James Clear
- *How to Have a Good Day* by Caroline Webb
- *How Will You Measure Your Life* by Clayton M. Christensen
- *Daring Greatly* by Brené Brown

HELPFUL EARLY RETURNED MISSIONARY RESOURCES:
- Mission Fortify: a group that specifically helps ERMs. They have a Facebook page, website, blog, etc. of people who are going through the same things you are if you are an ERM.
- *Home Early, Now What?*: a great book for ERMs.
- *Early Homecoming*: another wonderful book for ERMs.
- LDS Family Services: they offer emotional tools like seven free counseling sessions to ERMs when they get home to help them transition.

ACKNOWLEDGEMENTS

In creating this book, I had the unique opportunity to have the help of a variety of supporters, especially from my professors, positive psychology experts, church leaders, beta readers, and my early sponsors. Thank you to these individuals who have helped support these charities and make this book a reality:

Aaron Beck
Abbey Chapple
Adam Sierra
Adam Weissmiller
Adrianna Silva
Alee Washburn
Alex Park
Alie Trinajstic
Alison Dodds
Allan Lozano
Alli Morley
Allison Bugno
Allison Roberts
Amanda Pugh
Amy Dolan
Andrea Soung
Angela Duckworth
Annabelle Clawson
Annabelle Finlayson
Ashley Kuchar
Aubree Lewis
Avery Barron
Belen Penaloza
Ben Sumsion
Ben Wasden
Benjamin Lim
Bonnie Jeppson
Brad Harris

Brett Merrill
Brian Martinez
Cameron Carbone
Carol Brown
Carol M. Peck
Casey and Barb Cluff
Cassandra Brown
Chahngoo Aaron Kahng
Charlie Bird
Chase Fowers
Chris Brown
Christopher Horner
Connor Bernal
Cooper Brown
Craig Manning
Craig Wilson
Curtis Lefrandt
Dan Daley
Dan Walton
Dane du Randt
Danny Southwick
Demetri Haddad
Derick Kim
Desiree Mitchell
Do Park
Don Hyun
Elena Castro
Elisabeth McClatchie
Emma Myers
Eric Koester
Erica Evans
Eunice Park

Frankie Breinholt
Gale Larsen
Gary Vatcher
Hahngoo Justin Kahng
Hana Dodd
Hunter Burbidge
Hyun Khang
Iraima Otteson
Isaac and Sarah Corcoran
Itza Miller
Jacob Selman
Jaesook Kwon
James McMurray
Jana Fuller
Jared Klundt
Jared Warren
Jazzi Zolman
Jennifer Stirling
Jocelyn Trask
Joey Merrill
John Farley
Jordan Lund
Julie Hougaard
Jungyeon Kim
Justin Su'a
Karyn Christensen
Kate Pingree
Katrina Hill
KC Sosa
Kelley Valentine
Kelly Morgan
Kelsey Eyre

Kenny Ahlstrom
Kensington Rhodes
Kim Josse
Kristine Millett
Kristy Yoo
Krystal Martinez
Kyle Dayton
Kyung Rhee
Kyung Un Rhee
Linda White
Lizzie Kearon
Luc Hansen
Madeleine Wallis
Margaret Kahng
Martha Knudson
Martin Seligman
Matthew Johnson
Max Alley
Max Fillmore
Megan Singer
Megan Warr
Melissa Gardner
Michael Nixon
Mingoo Ryan Kahng
Minhyun Kim
Mychal Chong
Natalie Bailey
Nick & Meli Kerr

Nick Anderson
Owen Allen
Paul Taggart
Rachel Finlayson
Rebekka Brimhall
Robert Kong
Rosy Bernal
Sam Hauber
Sam St. Clair
Shay Carl
Shioon Kim
Sonja Lyubomirsky
Soo Ryun Lee
Soo Y. Lee
Spencer Arnesen
Stephanie Balkman
Stephen Kahng
Stephen Q Spencer
Sue Murie
Tal Ben-Shahar
Ted Oh
Tell Hyer
Teresa Gottfredson
The Caldwell Family
The Cluff Girls
True DeMille
Tyson Horsley
Will Okazaki

WORKS CITED

INTRODUCTION

- Armenta, Christina, Katherine Bao, Sonja Lyubomirsky, and Kennon Sheldon. "Is Lasting Change Possible? Lessons from the Hedonic Adaptation Prevention Model." In *Stability of Happiness: Theories and Evidence on Whether Happiness Can Change*, 57–74, 2014. https://doi.org/10.1016/B978-0-12-411478-4.00004-7.

- Barragan-Jason, Gladys, Cristina M. Atance, Astrid Hopfensitz, Jonathan Stieglitz, and Maxime Cauchoix. "Commentary: Revisiting the Marshmallow Test: A Conceptual Replication Investigating Links Between Early Delay of Gratification and Later Outcomes." *Frontiers in Psychology* 9 (January 10, 2019). https://doi.org/10.3389/fpsyg.2018.02719.

- Ben-Shahar, Tal. *Happier*. McGraw-Hill Education (India) Pvt Limited, 2007.

- Chan, Melissa. "Here's How Winning the Lottery Makes You Miserable." *Time*, January 12, 2016. https://time.com/4176128/powerball-jackpot-lottery-winners/.

- Cox, James. "$3.5m Lotto Winner Spent Millions on Cocaine, Boob Jobs, Parties and Cars." *The Sun*, August 20, 2018.

https://www.news.com.au/lifestyle/real-life/true-stories/youngest-lotto-winner-callie-rogers-says-she-regrets-spending-her-millions-on-cocaine-cars-and-plastic-surgery/news-story/34ccd576569b34858678d941af7be8e5.

- Fredrickson, Barbara L. "The Role of Positive Emotions in Positive Psychology." *The American Psychologist* 56, no. 3 (March 2001): 218–26.
- Lyubomirsky, Sonja, and Jaime Kurtz. *Positively Happy: Routes to Sustainable Happiness*. 1st ed. United Kingdom: Positive Acorn, 2008.
- Romer, Daniel, Angela L. Duckworth, Sharon Sznitman, and Sunhee Park. "Can Adolescents Learn Self-Control? Delay of Gratification in the Development of Control over Risk Taking." *Prevention Science : The Official Journal of the Society for Prevention Research* 11, no. 3 (September 2010): 319–30. https://doi.org/10.1007/s11121-010-0171-8.
- Seligman, Martin. "What Is Well-Being? | Authentic Happiness." Accessed October 1, 2020. https://www.authentichappiness.sas.upenn.edu/learn/wellbeing.
- Sheldon, Kennon M., and Sonja Lyubomirsky. "The Challenge of Staying Happier: Testing the Hedonic Adaptation Prevention Model." *Personality and Social Psychology Bulletin* 38, no. 5 (May 1, 2012): 670–80. https://doi.org/10.1177/0146167212436400.
- Wong, Kapo, Alan H. S. Chan, and S. C. Ngan. "The Effect of Long Working Hours and Overtime on Occupational Health: A Meta-Analysis of Evidence from 1998 to 2018." *International Journal of Environmental Research and Public Health* 16, no. 12 (June 2019). https://doi.org/10.3390/ijerph16122102.

SECTION 1

- Arain, Mariam, Maliha Haque, Lina Johal, Puja Mathur, Wynand Nel, Afsha Rais, Ranbir Sandhu, and Sushil Sharma. "Maturation of the Adolescent Brain." *Neuropsychiatric Disease and Treatment* 9 (2013): 449–61. https://doi.org/10.2147/NDT.S39776.
- Armenta, Christina, Katherine Bao, Sonja Lyubomirsky, and Kennon Sheldon. "Is Lasting Change Possible? Lessons from the Hedonic Adaptation Prevention Model." In *Stability of Happiness: Theories and Evidence on Whether Happiness Can Change*, 57–74, 2014. https://doi.org/10.1016/B978-0-12-411478-4.00004-7.
- Ben-Shahar, Tal. "7 Lessons On Earning The Ultimate Currency: Happiness." *Positivity Daily* (blog), February 10, 2015. https://positivitydaily.com/7-lessons-on-earning-the-ultimate-currency-happiness-2/.
- ———. "Accepting Failure – The THEORY – The Pursuit of Perfect: How to Stop Chasing Perfection and Start Living a Richer, Happier Life – Tal Ben-Shahar." Publicism. Accessed October 12, 2020. https://publicism.info/psychology/perfect/3.html.
- Chachura, Rodion. "'Atomic Habits' by James Clear." Medium, September 10, 2020. https://medium.com/@geekrodion/atomic-habits-by-james-clear-dddd4dc762b9.
- Chen, Serena. "Give Yourself a Break: The Power of Self-Compassion." *Harvard Business Review*, September 1, 2018. https://hbr.org/2018/09/give-yourself-a-break-the-power-of-self-compassion.
- Clear, James. "The 3 R's of Habit Change: How To Start New Habits That Actually Stick." *James Clear* (blog), February 14, 2013. https://jamesclear.com/three-steps-habit-change.

- Cleveland Clinic. "80% of Americans Don't Get Enough Exercise — and Here's How Much You Actually Need." Health Essentials from Cleveland Clinic, November 20, 2018. https://health.clevelandclinic.org/80-of-americans-dont-get-enough-exercise-and-heres-how-much-you-actually-need/.
- Di Fabio, Annamaria, and Letizia Palazzeschi. "Hedonic and Eudaimonic Well-Being: The Role of Resilience beyond Fluid Intelligence and Personality Traits." *Frontiers in Psychology* 6 (2015). https://doi.org/10.3389/fpsyg.2015.01367.
- Fitzpatrick, Maria D., and Timothy J. Moore. "The Mortality Effects of Retirement: Evidence from Social Security Eligibility at Age 62." *Journal of Public Economics* 157 (January 1, 2018): 121–37. https://doi.org/10.1016/j.jpubeco.2017.12.001.
- Forbes, E. E., S. M. Brown, M. Kimak, R. E. Ferrell, S. B. Manuck, and A. R. Hariri. "Genetic Variation in Components of Dopamine Neurotransmission Impacts Ventral Striatal Reactivity Associated with Impulsivity." *Molecular Psychiatry* 14, no. 1 (January 2009): 60–70. https://doi.org/10.1038/sj.mp.4002086.
- Harris, Russ. *The Illustrated Happiness Trap*. 1st ed. United States of America: Shambhala Publications, Inc., 2013.
- Hines, Kevin. "After My Suicide Attempt, I Made This Plan to Stay Alive and Well | HuffPost Life." *The Huffington Post*, February 26, 2016. https://www.huffpost.com/entry/after-my-suicide-attempt-i-made-this-plan-to-stay-alive-and-well_b_9058776.
- KPBS Public Media. "HAPPY." KPBS Public Media. Accessed October 2, 2020. https://www.kpbs.org/news/2013/dec/12/happy/.
- LaMorte, Wayne. "The Transtheoretical Model (Stages of Change)." Behavior Change Models. Accessed October 7, 2020. https://sphweb.bumc.bu.edu/otlt/mph-modules/sb/behavioralchangetheories/behavioralchangetheories6.html.

- Lyubomirsky, Sonja, Rene Dickerhoof, Julia K. Boehm, and Kennon M. Sheldon. "Becoming Happier Takes Both a Will and a Proper Way: An Experimental Longitudinal Intervention to Boost Well-Being." *Emotion (Washington, D.C.)* 11, no. 2 (April 2011): 391–402. https://doi.org/10.1037/a0022575.
- Lyubomirsky, Sonja, and Jaime Kurtz. *Positively Happy: Routes to Sustainable Happiness*. 1st ed. United Kingdom: Positive Acorn, 2008.
- Maguire, Eleanor A., David G. Gadian, Ingrid S. Johnsrude, Catriona D. Good, John Ashburner, Richard S. J. Frackowiak, and Christopher D. Frith. "Navigation-Related Structural Change in the Hippocampi of Taxi Drivers." *Proceedings of the National Academy of Sciences of the United States of America* 97, no. 8 (April 11, 2000): 4398–4403.
- Mandela, Nelson. "Nelson Mandela Quotes (Author of Long Walk to Freedom)." Goodreads. Accessed November 25, 2020. https://www.goodreads.com/author/quotes/367338.Nelson_Mandela.
- Mental Health America. "Creating Healthy Routines." Mental Health America. Accessed November 25, 2020. https://www.mhanational.org/creating-healthy-routines.
- Miller, Jen. "How to Make (and Keep) a New Year's Resolution." *The New York Times*, December 18, 2017. https://www.nytimes.com/guides/smarterliving/resolution-ideas.
- Mind Tools Content Team. "SMART Goals: – How to Make Your Goals Achievable." SMART Goals. Accessed October 12, 2020. http://www.mindtools.com/pages/article/smart-goals.htm.
- Morecraft, Robert. "Prefrontal Cortex – an Overview." ScienceDirect Topics. Accessed October 3, 2020. https://www.sciencedirect.com/topics/medicine-and-dentistry/prefrontal-cortex.

- Munoz, Lisa. "From Conditioning Monkeys to Drug Addiction: Understanding Prediction and Reward." *Cognitive Neuroscience Society* (blog), June 5, 2013. https://www.cogneurosociety.org/series1predictionreward/.
- Oppong, Thomas. "The Arrival Fallacy: A Psychologist Explains Why Reaching Your Goals Won't Make You Happy." Medium, September 4, 2019. https://medium.com/better-marketing/the-arrival-fallacy-a-psychologist-explains-why-reaching-your-goals-wont-make-you-happy-b2cd359b07.
- Park, Denise C., and Gérard N. Bischof. "The Aging Mind: Neuroplasticity in Response to Cognitive Training." *Dialogues in Clinical Neuroscience* 15, no. 1 (March 2013): 109–19.
- Pychyl, Timothy. "Approaching Success, Avoiding the Undesired: Does Goal Type Matter?" Psychology Today. Accessed October 12, 2020. http://www.psychologytoday.com/blog/dont-delay/200902/approaching-success-avoiding-the-undesired-does-goal-type-matter.
- Rajmohan, V., and E. Mohandas. "The Limbic System." *Indian Journal of Psychiatry* 49, no. 2 (2007): 132–39. https://doi.org/10.4103/0019-5545.33264.
- Rivero, Lisa. "Shame and Motivation to Change." Psychology Today. Accessed October 22, 2020. https://www.psychologytoday.com/blog/creative-synthesis/201501/shame-and-motivation-change.
- Santos, Laurie. "What Is the G.I. Joe Fallacy? – Introduction." Coursera. Accessed October 4, 2020. https://www.coursera.org/lecture/the-science-of-well-being/what-is-the-g-i-joe-fallacy-3U4aX.
- ScienceDaily. "How We Form Habits, Change Existing Ones." ScienceDaily. Accessed October 5, 2020. https://www.sciencedaily.com/releases/2014/08/140808111931.htm.

- Sehmi, Sumita. "Give Yourself Permission to Be Human. An Interview with Harvard Professor and Happiness Expert Tal Ben-Shahar. | LinkedIn." Accessed October 12, 2020. https://www.linkedin.com/pulse/give-yourself-permission-human-interview-harvard-professor-sehmi/.
- Selig, Meg. "The LOVE Motivator." Psychology Today. Accessed October 22, 2020. http://www.psychologytoday.com/blog/changepower/201008/the-love-motivator.
- The Wellbeing Thesis. "Setting Meaningful Goals," September 4, 2019. https://thewellbeingthesis.org.uk/why-you-are-engaging-in-pgr-study/setting-meaningful-goals/.
- Sivers, Derek. "The Willpower Instinct – by Kelly McGonigal | Derek Sivers." Derek Sivers. Accessed October 25, 2020. https://sive.rs/book/WillpowerInstinct.
- The University of Pennsylvania. "PERMATM Theory of Well-Being and PERMATM Workshops." Positive Psychology Center. Accessed October 2, 2020. https://ppc.sas.upenn.edu/learn-more/perma-theory-well-being-and-perma-workshops.
- Voss, Patrice, Maryse E. Thomas, J. Miguel Cisneros-Franco, and Étienne de Villers-Sidani. "Dynamic Brains and the Changing Rules of Neuroplasticity: Implications for Learning and Recovery." *Frontiers in Psychology* 8 (October 4, 2017). https://doi.org/10.3389/fpsyg.2017.01657.
- Weinreb-Welch, Laurie. "Using Social Support to Help Our Healthy Behavior Goals." Penn State Extension. Accessed October 27, 2020. https://extension.psu.edu/using-social-support-to-help-our-healthy-behavior-goals.

SECTION 2

- Ackerman, Courtney. "16 Compassion Focused Therapy Training Exercises and Worksheets." PositivePsychology.com, December 1, 2017. https://positivepsychology.com/compassion-focused-therapy-training-exercises-worksheets/.
- ———. "Learned Helplessness: Seligman's Theory of Depression (+ Cure)." PositivePsychology.com, March 24, 2018. https://positivepsychology.com/learned-helplessness-seligman-theory-depression-cure/.
- Ben-Shahar, Tal. "7 Lessons On Earning The Ultimate Currency: Happiness." *Positivity Daily* (blog), February 10, 2015. https://positivitydaily.com/7-lessons-on-earning-the-ultimate-currency-happiness-2/.
- ———. *Happier*. McGraw-Hill Education (India) Pvt Limited, 2007.
- Desbordes, Gaëlle, Lobsang T. Negi, Thaddeus W. W. Pace, B. Alan Wallace, Charles L. Raison, and Eric L. Schwartz. "Effects of Mindful-Attention and Compassion Meditation Training on Amygdala Response to Emotional Stimuli in an Ordinary, Non-Meditative State." *Frontiers in Human Neuroscience* 6 (November 1, 2012). https://doi.org/10.3389/fnhum.2012.00292.
- Emamzadeh, Erash. "Materialism=Happiness?" Psychology Today. Accessed November 20, 2020. https://www.psychologytoday.com/blog/finding-new-home/201806/materialismhappiness.
- Epel, Elissa, Jennifer Daubenmier, Judith T. Moskowitz, Susan Folkman, and Elizabeth Blackburn. "Can Meditation Slow Rate of Cellular Aging? Cognitive Stress, Mindfulness, and Telomeres." *Annals of the New York Academy of Sciences* 1172 (August 2009): 34–53. https://doi.org/10.1111/j.1749-6632.2009.04414.x.

- Fabel, Austin. "The Research Backed Guide To Being Lucky." Medium, February 26, 2018. https://medium.com/@austinfabel/the-research-backed-guide-to-being-lucky-450d34f6f61b.
- Finlayson-Fife, Jennifer. "Ask a Mormon Sex Therapist Part 6 on Rational Faiths." Dr. Jennifer Finlayson-Fife. Accessed November 25, 2020. https://finlayson-fife.com/podcasts/post/ask-mormon-sex-therapist-part-6.
- Garfinkel, Sarah N., Emma Zorab, Nakulan Navaratnam, Miriam Engels, Núria Mallorquí-Bagué, Ludovico Minati, Nicholas G. Dowell, Jos F. Brosschot, Julian F. Thayer, and Hugo D. Critchley. "Anger in Brain and Body: The Neural and Physiological Perturbation of Decision-Making by Emotion." *Social Cognitive and Affective Neuroscience* 11, no. 1 (January 2016): 150–58. https://doi.org/10.1093/scan/nsv099.
- Habits for Wellbeing. "Learned Helplessness and the ABCDE Model." Accessed November 20, 2020. https://www.habitsforwellbeing.com/learned-helplessness-and-the-abcde-model/.
- Hanson, Rick. "Hardwiring Happiness FAQs." *Dr. Rick Hanson* (blog). Accessed November 25, 2020. https://www.rickhanson.net/hardwiring-happiness/faq/.
- Harris, Russ. *The Illustrated Happiness Trap*. 1st ed. United States of America: Shambhala Publications, Inc., 2013.
- Hawkley, Louise C., and John T. Cacioppo. "Loneliness Matters: A Theoretical and Empirical Review of Consequences and Mechanisms." *Annals of Behavioral Medicine : A Publication of the Society of Behavioral Medicine* 40, no. 2 (October 2010). https://doi.org/10.1007/s12160-010-9210-8.
- Healy, Melissa. "Suicide Rates for U.S. Teens and Young Adults Are the Highest on Record – Los Angeles Times." *The Los Angeles Times*. Accessed November 9, 2020. https://www.latimes.com/science/la-sci-suicide-rates-rising-teens-young-adults-20190618-story.html.

- "How Emotion Shapes Behavior: Feedback, Anticipation, and Reflection, Rather Than Direct Causation – Roy F. Baumeister, Kathleen D. Vohs, C. Nathan DeWall, Liqing Zhang, 2007." Accessed November 11, 2020. https://journals.sagepub.com/doi/abs/10.1177/1088868307301033.
- Komninos, Andreas. "Our Three Brains – The Emotional Brain." The Interaction Design Foundation. Accessed November 25, 2020. https://www.interaction-design.org/literature/article/our-three-brains-the-emotional-brain.
- Lemmon, Kristie. "Guidepost #2: Cultivating Self-Compassion through Common Humanity." *Kristie Lemmon* (blog), April 19, 2018. https://dbtnetworkofutah.net/guidepost-2-cultivating-self-compassion-through-common-humanity/.
- Lyubomirsky, Sonja, and Jaime Kurtz. *Positively Happy: Routes to Sustainable Happiness*. 1st ed. United Kingdom: Positive Acorn, 2008.
- Mastroianni, Brian. "Why Americans Are More Stressed Today Than They Were in the 1990s." Healthline. Accessed November 20, 2020. https://www.healthline.com/health-news/people-more-stressed-today-than-1990s#The-bottom-line.
- McGonigal, Kelly. "Kelly McGonigal: How to Make Stress Your Friend | TED Talk." Ted Conferences. Accessed November 20, 2020. https://www.ted.com/talks/kelly_mcgonigal_how_to_make_stress_your_friend?language=en.
- McKeown, Greg. "Today, Just Be Average." *Harvard Business Review*, October 30, 2013. https://hbr.org/2013/10/today-just-be-average.
- Mindset Works. "The Growth Mindset – What Is Growth Mindset – Mindset Works." Mindset Works. Accessed November 20, 2020. https://www.mindsetworks.com/science/.

- Morecraft, Robert. "Prefrontal Cortex – an Overview." ScienceDirect Topics. Accessed October 3, 2020. https://www.sciencedirect.com/topics/medicine-and-dentistry/prefrontal-cortex.
- Nagel, Paula. *The Mental Health and Wellbeing Workout for Teens : Skills and Exercises from ACT and CBT for Healthy Thinking*. First Edition. London, UK: Jessica Kingsley Publishers, 2019.
- Neff, Kristin. "Self-Compassion Videos by Kristin Neff." *Self-Compassion* (blog). Accessed November 20, 2020. https://self-compassion.org/videos/.
- ———. "The Physiology of Self-Compassion – Kristin Neff." *Self-Compassion* (blog), July 2, 2012. https://self-compassion.org/the-physiology-of-self-compassion/.
- Niebuhr, Karl. "Using the Path of Least Resistance to Build New Habits — Excerpt from The Happiness Advantage." Karlbooklover. Accessed November 21, 2020. https://www.karlbooklover.com/using-the-path-of-least-resistance-to-form-new-habits/.
- Niebuhr, Reinhold. "Serenity Prayer." Celebrate Recovery. Accessed November 23, 2020. https://www.celebraterecovery.com/resources/cr-tools/serenityprayer.
- Oppland, Mike. "8 Ways To Create Flow According to Mihaly Csikszentmihalyi [+TED Talk]." PositivePsychology.com, December 16, 2016. https://positivepsychology.com/mihaly-csikszentmihalyi-father-of-flow/.
- Publishing, Harvard Health. "Writing about Emotions May Ease Stress and Trauma." Harvard Health. Accessed November 20, 2020. https://www.health.harvard.edu/healthbeat/writing-about-emotions-may-ease-stress-and-trauma.
- Rapaport, Lisa. "Optimism Tied to Lower Rates of Heart Attacks, Death." *Reuters*. Accessed November 12, 2020. https://in.reuters.com/article/us-health-heart-optimism-idUKKBN1WI2BK.

- Roelofs, Jeffrey, Lea Rood, Cor Meesters, Valérie te Dorsthorst, Susan Bögels, Lauren B. Alloy, and Susan Nolen-Hoeksema. "The Influence of Rumination and Distraction on Depressed and Anxious Mood: A Prospective Examination of the Response Styles Theory in Children and Adolescents." *European Child & Adolescent Psychiatry* 18, no. 10 (October 2009): 635–42. https://doi.org/10.1007/s00787-009-0026-7.
- Schwartz, Barry, Andrew Ward, John Monterosso, Sonja Lyubomirsky, Katherine White, and Darrin R. Lehman. "Maximizing versus Satisficing: Happiness Is a Matter of Choice." *Journal of Personality and Social Psychology* 83, no. 5 (2002): 1178–97. https://doi.org/10.1037/0022-3514.83.5.1178.
- Scribner, Herb. "David Archuleta Opens up about 'PTSD,' Mental Health in New Yahoo Interview." Deseret News, November 28, 2018. https://www.deseret.com/2018/11/28/20659925/david-archuleta-opens-up-about-ptsd-mental-health-in-new-yahoo-interview.
- Shermer, Michael. "As Luck Would Have It." Scientific American. Accessed November 11, 2020. https://doi.org/10.1038/scientificamerican0406-35.
- Shilton, A. C. "You Accomplished Something Great. So Now What? (Published 2019)." *The New York Times*, May 28, 2019, sec. Smarter Living. https://www.nytimes.com/2019/05/28/smarter-living/you-accomplished-something-great-so-now-what.html.
- Shortsleeve, Cassie. "TIPS TO GET BETTER WITH DECISION MAKING PROCESS – Furthermore." Furthermore from Equinox. Accessed November 20, 2020. https://furthermore.equinox.com/articles/2018/10/make-better-decisions-maximizers-satisficers.

- Su'a, Justin. *Mentally Tough Teens: Developing a Winning Mindset*. First Edition. Springville, UT: Plain Sight Publishing, 2014.
- The First Presidency and Council of the Twelve Apostles of The Church of Jesus Christ of Latter-day Saints. "The Family Proclamation." The Church of Jesus Christ of Latter-day Saints. Accessed November 22, 2020. https://www.churchofjesuschrist.org/study/scriptures/the-family-a-proclamation-to-the-world/the-family-a-proclamation-to-the-world?lang=eng.
- The University of Pennsylvania. "PERMATM Theory of Well-Being and PERMATM Workshops." Positive Psychology Center. Accessed October 2, 2020. https://ppc.sas.upenn.edu/learn-more/perma-theory-well-being-and-perma-workshops.
- Vidal, Carol, Tenzin Lhaksampa, Leslie Miller, and Rheanna Platt. "Social Media Use and Depression in Adolescents: A Scoping Review." *International Review of Psychiatry (Abingdon, England)* 32, no. 3 (May 2020): 235–53. https://doi.org/10.1080/09540261.2020.1720623.
- Wang, C. K. John, Woon Chia Liu, Ying Hwa Kee, and Lit Khoon Chian. "Competence, Autonomy, and Relatedness in the Classroom: Understanding Students' Motivational Processes Using the Self-Determination Theory." *Heliyon* 5, no. 7 (July 1, 2019): e01983. https://doi.org/10.1016/j.heliyon.2019.e01983.
- Winch, Guy. "Guy Winch: How to Fix a Broken Heart | TED Talk." Ted Conferences. Accessed November 20, 2020. https://www.ted.com/talks/guy_winch_how_to_fix_a_broken_heart?language=en.
- Zenger, Jack. "The Ideal Praise-to-Criticism Ratio." Harvard Business Review. Accessed November 20, 2020. https://hbr.org/2013/03/the-ideal-praise-to-criticism.

SECTION 3

- Al-Abri, Mohammed A. "Sleep Deprivation and Depression." *Sultan Qaboos University Medical Journal* 15, no. 1 (February 2015): e4–6.

- Anjum, Ibrar, Syeda S Jaffery, Muniba Fayyaz, Zarak Samoo, and Sheraz Anjum. "The Role of Vitamin D in Brain Health: A Mini Literature Review." *Cureus* 10, no. 7. Accessed November 18, 2020. https://doi.org/10.7759/cureus.2960.

- Armstrong, Lawrence E., Evan C. Johnson, Colleen X. Munoz, Brittany Swokla, Laurent Le Bellego, Liliana Jimenez, Douglas J. Casa, and Carl M. Maresh. "Hydration Biomarkers and Dietary Fluid Consumption of Women." *Journal of the Academy of Nutrition and Dietetics* 112, no. 7 (July 2012): 1056–61. https://doi.org/10.1016/j.jand.2012.03.036.

- Ben-Shahar, Tal. "7 Lessons On Earning The Ultimate Currency: Happiness." *Positivity Daily* (blog), February 10, 2015. https://positivitydaily.com/7-lessons-on-earning-the-ultimate-currency-happiness-2/.

- Benton, David. "Dehydration Influences Mood and Cognition: A Plausible Hypothesis?" *Nutrients* 3, no. 5 (May 10, 2011): 555–73. https://doi.org/10.3390/nu3050555.

- Blumenthal, James A., Patrick J. Smith, and Benson M. Hoffman. "Is Exercise a Viable Treatment for Depression?" *ACSM's Health & Fitness Journal* 16, no. 4 (2012): 14–21. https://doi.org/10.1249/01.FIT.0000416000.09526.eb.

- Canadian Science Publishing. "Total Amount of Exercise Important, Not Frequency, Research Shows." ScienceDaily. Accessed November 17, 2020. https://www.sciencedaily.com/releases/2013/06/130620132406.htm.

- Clear, James. "The Productivity Guide: My Best Productivity and Time-Management Tips." *James Clear* (blog). Accessed October 4, 2020. https://jamesclear.com/productivity.
- Cummings, Sarah. "5 Sleep Tips That Can Help with Depression | NAMI: National Alliance on Mental Illness." National Alliance on Mental Illness. Accessed November 18, 2020. https://www.nami.org/Blogs/NAMI-Blog/January-2018/5-Sleep-Tips-that-Can-Help-with-Depression.
- Danziger, Shai, Jonathan Levav, and Liora Avnaim-Pesso. "Extraneous Factors in Judicial Decisions." *Proceedings of the National Academy of Sciences* 108, no. 17 (April 26, 2011): 6889–92. https://doi.org/10.1073/pnas.1018033108.
- Digitale, Erin. "Sleep Disturbances Predict Increased Risk for Suicidal Symptoms, Study Finds | News Center | Stanford Medicine." Stanford Medicine News Center. Accessed November 18, 2020. https://med.stanford.edu/news/all-news/2017/06/sleep-disturbances-predict-increased-risk-for-suicidal-symptoms.html.
- Dimitriu, Alex. "Sleep for Teenagers." Sleep Foundation, April 17, 2009. https://www.sleepfoundation.org/teens-and-sleep.
- Duckworth, Angela. "What Are Kids Really Learning from Their Extracurricular Activities? Practice and Character." *The Philadelphia Inquirer*, sec. News. Accessed November 18, 2020. https://www.inquirer.com/news/angela-duckworth-practice-repetition-teens-20191027.html.
- Goldberg, Carey. "Why To Exercise Today: It's Like Prozac Plus Ritalin." CommonHealth. Accessed November 16, 2020. https://www.wbur.org/commonhealth/2010/11/22/exercise-today.
- Haden, Jeff. "Exercise Scientists Say One 23-Minute Workout a Week Is Nearly as Effective as Three--but There Is One Catch." Inc.com, March 27, 2020. https://www.inc.com/jeff-haden/

exercise-scientists-say-one-23-minute-workout-a-week-is-nearly-as-effective-as-three-but-there-is-one-catch.html.

- Haiken, Melanie. "Lack Of Sleep Kills Brain Cells, New Study Shows." Forbes. Accessed November 18, 2020. https://www.forbes.com/sites/melaniehaiken/2014/03/20/lack-of-sleep-kills-brain-cells-new-study-suggests/.
- Hsu, Ted M., Vaibhav R. Konanur, Lilly Taing, Ryan Usui, Brandon D. Kayser, Michael I. Goran, and Scott E. Kanoski. "Effects of Sucrose and High Fructose Corn Syrup Consumption on Spatial Memory Function and Hippocampal Neuroinflammation in Adolescent Rats." *Hippocampus* 25, no. 2 (February 2015): 227–39. https://doi.org/10.1002/hipo.22368.
- Ikeuchi, Mayumi, Sachiko MORI, Hiromi JONO, and Tomoko Kutsuzawa. "Research on the Frontal Lobe Activation Effect of Music Therapy – Effect of Listening Music on Frontal Lobe Activation by Using Near-Infrared Spectroscopy –." *Japanese Journal of Complementary and Alternative Medicine* 15 (September 30, 2018): 91–101. https://doi.org/10.1625/jcam.15.91.
- Johns Hopkins Medicine. "Sleep/Wake Cycles." Johns Hopkins Medicine. Accessed November 18, 2020. https://www.hopkinsmedicine.org/health/conditions-and-diseases/sleepwake-cycles.
- Kay, Isa. "Is Your Mood Disorder a Symptom of Unstable Blood Sugar?" University of Michigan School of Public Health. Accessed November 18, 2020. https://sph.umich.edu/pursuit/2019posts/mood-blood-sugar-kujawski.html.
- Khalaf, David. "It's Okay to Go to Bed Angry." The Gottman Institute, August 30, 2018. https://www.gottman.com/blog/its-okay-to-go-to-bed-angry/.
- King, Barbara. "The Anthropology Of Walking." NPR.org. Accessed November 16, 2020. https://www.npr.org/sections/13.7/

2014/01/09/261054773/let-s-move-more-the-anthropology-of-walking.

- Knüppel, Anika, Martin J. Shipley, Clare H. Llewellyn, and Eric J. Brunner. "Sugar Intake from Sweet Food and Beverages, Common Mental Disorder and Depression: Prospective Findings from the Whitehall II Study." *Scientific Reports* 7, no. 1 (July 27, 2017): 6287. https://doi.org/10.1038/s41598-017-05649-7.
- Lee, Katherine. "Study Reveals Why All-Nighters May Be So Dangerous for Your Health." Everyday Health. Accessed November 18, 2020. https://www.everydayhealth.com/sleep/study-reveals-why-all-nighters-may-dangerous-your-health/.
- Lopez, Marangeli. "Study: A 10-Second Hug Can Make You Healthier, Happier." *NEWS10 ABC*, January 21, 2020. https://www.news10.com/news/national/study-a-10-second-hug-can-make-you-healthier-happier/.
- Louv, Richard. "No More 'Nature-Deficit Disorder.'" Psychology Today. Accessed November 23, 2020. http://www.psychologytoday.com/blog/people-in-nature/200901/no-more-nature-deficit-disorder.
- Lytle, Mary Ellen, Joni Vander Bilt, Rajesh S. Pandav, Hiroko H. Dodge, and Mary Ganguli. "Exercise Level and Cognitive Decline: The MoVIES Project." *Alzheimer Disease & Associated Disorders* 18, no. 2 (June 2004): 57–64. https://doi.org/10.1097/01.wad.0000126614.87955.79.
- Mischoulon, David. "Omega-3 Fatty Acids for Mood Disorders." Harvard Health Blog, August 3, 2018. https://www.health.harvard.edu/blog/omega-3-fatty-acids-for-mood-disorders-2018080314414.
- Nall, Rachel. "What Are the Benefits of Sunlight?" Healthline, May 25, 2018. https://www.healthline.com/health/depression/benefits-sunlight.

- Pase, Matthew P., Jayandra J. Himali, Paul F. Jacques, Charles DeCarli, Claudia L. Satizabal, Hugo Aparicio, Ramachandran S. Vasan, Alexa S. Beiser, and Sudha Seshadri. "Sugary Beverage Intake and Preclinical Alzheimer's Disease in the Community." *Alzheimer's & Dementia : The Journal of the Alzheimer's Association* 13, no. 9 (September 2017): 955–64. https://doi.org/10.1016/j.jalz.2017.01.024.
- Publishing, Harvard Health. "Should You Get Your Nutrients from Food or from Supplements?" Harvard Health. Accessed November 18, 2020. https://www.health.harvard.edu/staying-healthy/should-you-get-your-nutrients-from-food-or-from-supplements.
- Raman, Ryan. "How to Safely Get Vitamin D From The Sun." Healthline, April 28, 2018. https://www.healthline.com/nutrition/vitamin-d-from-sun.
- Reiner, Andrew. "The Power of Touch, Especially for Men (Published 2017)." *The New York Times*, December 5, 2017, sec. Well. https://www.nytimes.com/2017/12/05/well/family/gender-men-touch.html.
- Relojo-Howell, Dennis. "Vitamin Deficiency Can Affect Your Mental Health – Here Are 5 Supplements for Mental Health." *Psychreg* (blog), May 28, 2020. https://www.psychreg.org/vitamin-deficiency-mental-health/.
- Shevchuk, Nikolai. "Adapted Cold Shower as a Potential Treatment for Depression." *Medical Hypotheses* 70 (February 1, 2008): 995–1001. https://doi.org/10.1016/j.mehy.2007.04.052.
- Shokri-Kojori, Ehsan, Gene-Jack Wang, Corinde E. Wiers, Sukru B. Demiral, Min Guo, Sung Won Kim, Elsa Lindgren, et al. "β-Amyloid Accumulation in the Human Brain after One Night of Sleep Deprivation." *Proceedings of the National*

Academy of Sciences of the United States of America 115, no. 17 (24 2018): 4483–88. https://doi.org/10.1073/pnas.1721694115.

- Sio, Ut Na, Padraic Monaghan, and Tom Ormerod. "Sleep on It, but Only If It Is Difficult: Effects of Sleep on Problem Solving." *Memory & Cognition* 41, no. 2 (February 2013): 159–66. https://doi.org/10.3758/s13421-012-0256-7.
- Smith, Brendan. "Inappropriate Prescribing." https://www.apa.org. Accessed November 16, 2020. https://www.apa.org/monitor/2012/06/prescribing.
- Su'a, Justin. *Mentally Tough Teens: Developing a Winning Mindset*. First Edition. Springville, UT: Plain Sight Publishing, 2014.
- Tanaka, Hideki, and Shuichiro Shirakawa. "Sleep Health, Lifestyle and Mental Health in the Japanese Elderly: Ensuring Sleep to Promote a Healthy Brain and Mind." *Journal of Psychosomatic Research* 56, no. 5 (May 1, 2004): 465–77. https://doi.org/10.1016/j.jpsychores.2004.03.002.
- Turagabeci, Amelia R., Keiko Nakamura, and Takehito Takano. "Healthy Lifestyle Behaviour Decreasing Risks of Being Bullied, Violence and Injury." *PLOS ONE* 3, no. 2 (February 20, 2008): e1585. https://doi.org/10.1371/journal.pone.0001585.
- University Hospitals Case Medical Center. "Sleep Deprivation Linked to Aging Skin, Study Suggests." ScienceDaily. Accessed November 25, 2020. https://www.sciencedaily.com/releases/2013/07/130723155002.htm.
- Uvnäs-Moberg, Kerstin, Linda Handlin, and Maria Petersson. "Self-Soothing Behaviors with Particular Reference to Oxytocin Release Induced by Non-Noxious Sensory Stimulation." *Frontiers in Psychology* 5 (January 12, 2015). https://doi.org/10.3389/fpsyg.2014.01529.

- Willson, Cyril. "The Clinical Toxicology of Caffeine: A Review and Case Study." *Toxicology Reports* 5 (November 3, 2018): 1140–52. https://doi.org/10.1016/j.toxrep.2018.11.002.
- Wilson, Debra Rose. "Serotonin: Facts, Uses, SSRIs, and Sources." Medical News Today. Accessed November 18, 2020. https://www.medicalnewstoday.com/articles/232248.
- World Cancer Research Fund. "Meat, Fish & Dairy." World Cancer Research Fund, April 24, 2018. https://www.wcrf.org/dietandcancer/exposures/meat-fish-dairy.
- Worrall, Simon. "Eating a Burger or Driving a Car: Which Harms Planet More?" National Geographic News, March 11, 2015. https://www.nationalgeographic.com/news/2015/03/150311-cow-agriculture-cattle-dairy-beef-health-food-ng-booktalk/.
- Yoo, Seung-Schik, Ninad Gujar, Peter Hu, Ferenc A. Jolesz, and Matthew P. Walker. "The Human Emotional Brain without Sleep--a Prefrontal Amygdala Disconnect." *Current Biology: CB* 17, no. 20 (October 23, 2007): R877-878. https://doi.org/10.1016/j.cub.2007.08.007.
- Young, M. Rita I., and Ying Xiong. "Influence of Vitamin D on Cancer Risk and Treatment: Why the Variability?" *Trends in Cancer Research* 13 (2018): 43–53.

SECTION 4

- Ben-Shahar, Tal. "7 Lessons On Earning The Ultimate Currency: Happiness." *Positivity Daily* (blog), February 10, 2015. https://positivitydaily.com/7-lessons-on-earning-the-ultimate-currency-happiness-2/.
- ———. *Happier*. McGraw-Hill Education (India) Pvt Limited, 2007.

- Benson, Kyle. "The Grass Is Greener Where You Water It." The Gottman Institute, August 17, 2017. https://www.gottman.com/blog/the-grass-is-greener-where-you-water-it/.
- Brandt, Andrea. "How Do You Forgive Even When It Feels Impossible? (Part 1)." Psychology Today. Accessed November 21, 2020. http://www.psychologytoday.com/blog/mindful-anger/201409/how-do-you-forgive-even-when-it-feels-impossible-part-1.
- Brent, Lauren J.N., Steve W.C. Chang, Jean-François Gariépy, and Michael L. Platt. "The Neuroethology of Friendship." *Annals of the New York Academy of Sciences* 1316, no. 1 (May 2014): 1–17. https://doi.org/10.1111/nyas.12315.
- Christensen, Clayton. "Clayton M. Christensen Quotes (Author of The Innovator's Dilemma)." Goodreads. Accessed November 21, 2020. https://www.goodreads.com/author/quotes/1792.Clayton_M_Christensen.
- ———. "The Secret to Living the Life You Want." Next Avenue, July 25, 2012. https://www.nextavenue.org/secret-living-life-you-want.
- Davis, Todd. "Take Stock Of Your Emotional Bank Accounts." FranklinCovey. Accessed November 26, 2020. https://resources.franklincovey.com/mkt-gbv1/getbetter-take-stock-of-your-emotional-bank-accounts.
- Designed to Thrive. "Fostering 4AM Friends." Designed to Thrive. Accessed November 25, 2020. https://designed2thrive.org/2020/04/fostering-4am-friends.html.
- Dunn, Elizabeth W., Lara B. Aknin, and Michael I. Norton. "Spending Money on Others Promotes Happiness." *Science* 319, no. 5870 (March 21, 2008): 1687–88. https://doi.org/10.1126/science.1150952.

- Emerson, Ralph Waldo. "A Quote by Ralph Waldo Emerson." Goodreads. Accessed November 25, 2020. https://www.goodreads.com/quotes/29365-it-is-one-of-the-beautiful-compensations-of-life-that.
- FranklinCovey. "Habit 5: Seek First to Understand, Then to Be Understood®." FranklinCovey. Accessed November 25, 2020. https://www.franklincovey.com/the-7-habits/habit-5/.
- Galván, Veronica V., Rosa S. Vessal, and Matthew T. Golley. "The Effects of Cell Phone Conversations on the Attention and Memory of Bystanders." *PLOS ONE* 8, no. 3 (March 13, 2013): e58579. https://doi.org/10.1371/journal.pone.0058579.
- Gottman, John. "Frequently Asked Questions – Research." The Gottman Institute. Accessed November 23, 2020. https://www.gottman.com/about/research/faq/.
- Hanks, Julie. "How Idealizing Motherhood Hurts Mormon Women." *Dr. Julie Hanks* (blog). Accessed November 21, 2020. http://www.drjuliehanks.com/2016/01/02/how-idealizing-motherhood-hurts-mormon-women/.
- McKenzie, Sarah K., Sunny Collings, Gabrielle Jenkin, and Jo River. "Masculinity, Social Connectedness, and Mental Health: Men's Diverse Patterns of Practice." *American Journal of Men's Health* 12, no. 5 (September 2018): 1247–61. https://doi.org/10.1177/1557988318772732.
- Mineo, Liz. "Over Nearly 80 Years, Harvard Study Has Been Showing How to Live a Healthy and Happy Life." *Harvard Gazette* (blog), April 11, 2017. https://news.harvard.edu/gazette/story/2017/04/over-nearly-80-years-harvard-study-has-been-showing-how-to-live-a-healthy-and-happy-life/.
- Post, Stephen G. "Altruism, Happiness, and Health: It's Good to Be Good." *International Journal of Behavioral*

Medicine 12, no. 2 (June 1, 2005): 66–77. https://doi.org/10.1207/s15327558ijbm1202_4.
- Productions, Moody, Grooters. "5 Love Languages." The 5 Love Languages®. Accessed November 25, 2020. https://www.5lovelanguages.com/5-love-languages/.
- Su'a, Justin. *Mentally Tough Teens: Developing a Winning Mindset.* First Edition. Springville, UT: Plain Sight Publishing, 2014.
- Taking Charge of Your Health & Wellbeing. "Daring to Be Vulnerable with Brené Brown." Taking Charge of Your Health & Wellbeing. Accessed November 21, 2020. https://www.takingcharge.csh.umn.edu/daring-be-vulnerable-brene-brown.
- The Arbinger Institute. "Free Supporting Resources | The Outward Mindset Book." The Arbinger Institute. Accessed November 25, 2020. https://arbingerinstitute.com/Landing/TheOutwardMindset.html.
- The First Presidency and Council of the Twelve Apostles of The Church of Jesus Christ of Latter-day Saints. "Standards for Youth." The Church of Jesus Christ of Latter-day Saints. Accessed November 23, 2020. https://www.churchofjesuschrist.org/study/manual/for-the-strength-of-youth/_manifest?lang=eng.
- Unknown, Author. "Make New Friends (but Keep the Old)." Kids Environment Kids Health – National Institute of Environmental Health Sciences. Accessed November 25, 2020. https://kids.niehs.nih.gov/games/songs/childrens/make-new-friends/index.htm.
- Weir, Kirsten. "Forgiveness Can Improve Mental and Physical Health." American Psychological Association. Accessed November 21, 2020. https://www.apa.org/monitor/2017/01/ce-corner.

SECTION 5

- Apostles, David A. Bednar of the Quorum of the Twelve. "And Nothing Shall Offend Them." The Church of Jesus Christ of Latter-day Saints. Accessed November 22, 2020. https://www.churchofjesuschrist.org/study/general-conference/2006/10/and-nothing-shall-offend-them?lang=eng.
- Apostles, Elder Dallin H. Oaks of the Quorum of the Twelve. "Loving Others and Living with Differences." The Church of Jesus Christ of Latter-day Saints. Accessed November 22, 2020. https://www.churchofjesuschrist.org/study/general-conference/2014/10/loving-others-and-living-with-differences?lang=eng.
- Apostles, M. Russell Ballard of the Quorum of the Twelve. "Doctrine of Inclusion." The Church of Jesus Christ of Latter-day Saints. Accessed November 22, 2020. https://www.churchofjesuschrist.org/study/general-conference/2001/10/doctrine-of-inclusion?lang=eng.
- Awareness in Action. "How to Benefit from the Power of Common Humanity." *Awareness in Action* (blog), July 16, 2018. https://www.awarenessinaction.org/how-to-benefit-from-the-power-of-common-humanity/.
- Campbell, David, and Robert Putnam. "Campbell and Putnam: Charity's Religious Edge – WSJ." Charity's Religious Edge. Accessed November 22, 2020. https://www.wsj.com/articles/SB10001424052748703766704576009361375685394.
- Clark, Jayne. "It's the USA's Happiest City, but Is It Worth Visiting?" USA TODAY. Accessed November 22, 2020. https://www.usatoday.com/story/travel/destinations/2014/04/24/what-makes-provo-the-happiest-town-in-the-usa/8093283/.

- Daly, Mary C., Andrew J. Oswald, Daniel Wilson, and Stephen Wu. "Dark Contrasts: The Paradox of High Rates of Suicide in Happy Places." *Journal of Economic Behavior & Organization* 80, no. 3 (December 2011): 435–42. https://doi.org/10.1016/j.jebo.2011.04.007.
- Dawson, Mackenzie. "Are Mormons the Happiest People in America?" *New York Post* (blog), November 3, 2016. https://nypost.com/2016/11/03/are-mormons-the-happiest-people-in-america/.
- DiSanto, Jill. "Penn Research Shows That Mormons Are Generous and Active in Helping Others." Penn Today. Accessed November 22, 2020. https://penntoday.upenn.edu/news/penn-research-shows-mormons-are-generous-and-active-helping-others.
- Ferdman, Roberto. "The Most American Thing There Is: Eating Alone." *The Washington Post*. Accessed November 22, 2020. https://www.washingtonpost.com/news/wonk/wp/2015/08/18/eating-alone-is-a-fact-of-modern-american-life/.
- Fredrickson, Barbara L. "The Role of Positive Emotions in Positive Psychology." *The American Psychologist* 56, no. 3 (March 2001): 218–26.
- Institute, The Arbinger. "Mindset and the Basics of Arbinger's Work." The Arbinger Institute. Accessed November 22, 2020. http://arbingerinstitute.com/BlogDetail?id=48.
- Ipson, Media Contact: Natalie. "BYU Forum: Creating Justice." News, October 30, 2018. https://news.byu.edu/news/byu-forum-creating-justice.
- Jenkinson, Caroline E., Andy P. Dickens, Kerry Jones, Jo Thompson-Coon, Rod S. Taylor, Morwenna Rogers, Clare L. Bambra, Iain Lang, and Suzanne H. Richards. "Is Volunteering a Public Health Intervention? A Systematic Review

and Meta-Analysis of the Health and Survival of Volunteers." *BMC Public Health* 13, no. 1 (August 23, 2013): 773. https://doi.org/10.1186/1471-2458-13-773.

- Jensen, Maren. "Web Exclusive: Utah Is One of the Top States for Plastic Surgery in the Nation." KUTV, July 8, 2018. http://kutv.com/features/person-2-person/web-exclusive-renato-saltz-surgery.
- Lyubomirsky, Sonja. *The How of Happiness*. 1st ed. London, England: Piatkus Books, 2010.
- Monson, Thomas S. "Problem to Be Solved." The Church of Jesus Christ of Latter-day Saints. Accessed November 23, 2020. https://www.churchofjesuschrist.org/media/image/quote-monson-8cab44f?lang=eng.
- Nations, United. "World Happiness Report 2012." The World Happiness Report. Accessed November 22, 2020. http://worldhappiness.report/.
- News, Deseret. "Utah No. 1 in Online Porn Subscriptions, Report Says." Deseret News, March 3, 2009. https://www.deseret.com/2009/3/3/20304992/utah-no-1-in-online-porn-subscriptions-report-says.
- November 04, Jeanna Bryner, and 2011. "Close Friends Less Common Today, Study Finds." livescience.com. Accessed November 22, 2020. https://www.livescience.com/16879-close-friends-decrease-today.html.
- Okazaki, Chieko N. "What a Friend We Have in Jesus." Goodreads. Accessed November 22, 2020. https://www.goodreads.com/work/best_book/2879259-what-a-friend-we-have-in-jesus.
- "Your Diversity Is a More Valuable Statement. - StayLDS.Com." Accessed November 22, 2020. http://forum.staylds.com/viewtopic.php?t=5587.

- Presidency, President Dieter F. Uchtdorf Second Counselor in the First. "On Being Genuine." The Church of Jesus Christ of Latter-day Saints. Accessed November 22, 2020. https://www.churchofjesuschrist.org/study/general-conference/2015/04/on-being-genuine?lang=eng.
- Presidency, Reyna I. Aburto Second Counselor in the Relief Society General. "Thru Cloud and Sunshine, Lord, Abide with Me!" The Church of Jesus Christ of Latter-day Saints. Accessed November 22, 2020. https://www.churchofjesuschrist.org/study/general-conference/2019/10/31aburto?lang=eng.
- Ross, Allison. "Happy People, Happy Neighborhood: Happiness and Sense of Community Among Florida Residents." Bureau of Economic Research. Accessed November 21, 2020. https://www.bebr.ufl.edu/survey/website-article/happy-people-happy-neighborhood-happiness-and-sense-community-among-florida.
- Sandstrom, Gillian M., and Elizabeth W. Dunn. "Is Efficiency Overrated?: Minimal Social Interactions Lead to Belonging and Positive Affect." *Social Psychological and Personality Science* 5, no. 4 (May 1, 2014): 437–42. https://doi.org/10.1177/1948550613502990.
- Su'a, Justin. *Mentally Tough Teens: Developing a Winning Mindset*. First Edition. Springville, UT: Plain Sight Publishing, 2014.
- Tate, Nick. "Loneliness Rivals Obesity, Smoking as Health Risk." WebMD. Accessed November 22, 2020. https://www.webmd.com/balance/news/20180504/loneliness-rivals-obesity-smoking-as-health-risk.

Made in the USA
Monee, IL
13 June 2021